Without
Overcoming Adversity

By*: Mario Arnauz Bonds*
Personal Touch Press

M B

Without Sight but Full of Vision:
Overcoming Adversity

ISBN 9780615702933

Ordering Information:
Special discounts are available on quantity purchases by corporations, associations, and others. For details, contact the author at info@mabspeaks.com. For order by U.S. trade bookstores and wholesalers, please contact Ingram Book Company:
Tel (800) 234-6737; Fax: (800) 876-0186 or visit www.ingrambook.com.

COVER PHOTOGRAPHY BY: David A. Blass

GRAPHICS DESIGN BY: Stephen F. Wilkes

Some names and locations have been changed. Some details from others are included.

DEDICATION

I dedicate this work to one of my biggest best friends, Antoine William Banks, who departed this life on November 17, 2013. Antoine was 28-years-old, and the greatest friend a friend could ask for. From insecurity-to-success, Antoine walked with me. Having been there through much of my troubles, Antoine couldn't wait to get his hands on a copy of this memoir, and as he departed before reading it, I offer this finished work to his honor, spirit and memory. Thank you Antoine for the irreplaceable friendship, love and joy you brought into my life. I love you, and I'm comforted knowing that you knew I loved you.

I also dedicate this work to Janet Streets Dupree, a selfless woman who became a Mother to me in my teenage years and beyond.

I dedicate this book to my Grandma, who despite insurmountable difficulty, still lifted me up.

I thank Johnnie Mae Bonds, Marilyn Bagel, Vinson Flounroy-Young, Lemar Jenkins, Kindred Bryant Bonds, Michele Weil and Chuck Fax, Karen and Basil Petrou, Chatora Johnson, Karen and David Blass, Donnie Simpson, Antoine Johnson, Karen and Keith Champion, Blythe Champion, Keenan Dupree, Beverly Betz-Zachery, Cathryn Krebs, Adam Treadwell, Catheryn Perry-Thibault, Jane and Brian Smith, Pastor Sharon Ruff, Pastor Brian K. Fleet, Tedrick Mecos, Peter Nguamsanith, Allison Kirsch, and everyone God has given me. All of you mean the world to me.

A huge thanks to my Glee Project family— Blake Jenner, Aylin Bayramoglu, Nellie Veitenheimer, Lily Mae Harrington, Ali Stroker, Abraham Si Lim, Dani Shay, Tyler Ford, Maxfield Camp, Shanna Henderson, Charlie Lubeck and Michael Weisman for inspiring me to finish this book. A huge appreciation and thank you to Robert J. Ulrich, a mentor, and Casting Director who changed my life. Many thanks to Ryan Murphy, Zack Woodlee, Nikki Anders, NBC Universal, 20th Century Fox and the Oxygen Network.

NOTE TO READER

A multitude of adverse experiences had me trapped in a prison, with each painful memory being a bar in my cell. I have broken those bars, and with this childhood memoir, I wish to show you how I did it. I am living proof that even bad cards can result in a winning hand. Will you join me in being a winner?

This is for anyone who has given up on their dreams, anyone who is suffering because of their past, and anyone who has lost hope. No matter your adversity, you can still stand too. Through all of my troubles, I kept courage, and held on to my love for education and the performing arts, to ultimately reach my ultimate dreams through NBC Universal. Walk with me, and see that nothing can hold you back.

PROLOGUE

Seven-year-old Adonis, one of Mario Bonds' older brothers, sulked as he sat alone in the basement. His mother, Marchell, had just spanked and sent him to time out. Adonis was sulking because his other brothers and sisters, not including the little triplets, were upstairs watching *Mary Poppins*, and he wanted to join them. Eventually, Marchell relented and told him to come back upstairs to watch TV with the others. Before the film ended, the four boys and two girls, already in their designated living room sleeping spots, had fallen asleep.

Adonis came in and out of consciousness before a sound from the TV fully awakened him. The TV station's programming for the night was over, and there was a continuous beeping to signal that fact. Turning off the television, Adonis reassumed his spot on the living room floor and listened to his baby triplet siblings crying somewhere upstairs. He figured they were obviously hungry and that Mother would handle them in time. Just then, at about 3:00 a.m., the front door open and in walked his father Nathan, back from another late night out. Adonis, harboring a dislike for his father, immediately pretended to be sleeping.

Nathan walked into the kitchen, fixed himself something to eat, and then walked past the living room that contained his sleeping children. He paused at the bottom of the stairs, confused. He could hear the youngest children, the triplets, Maria, Marian and Mario crying; it was their feeding time. He knew that Marchell should have been up preparing the five-month-old children for the babysitter. What was she doing?

"Marchell. *Marchell.*" Nathan yelled, his voice booming. When Marchell didn't respond, Nathan sprinted up the stairs. He first stopped in the triplets' room, pushing the door fully open. He saw their pitiful, hungry faces as their cries grew louder with his entrance.

"Marchell, get up and get in here and feed these kids." he hollered, leaving the triplets' room. Quickly, he walked to the room where he and Marchell slept. He noticed something strange: Marchell had closed the bedroom door that was broken off its hinges. She had never done this before. Nathan pushed the door open, and then placed it against the wall where it had always been. Turning on the light, he saw Marchell lying in the bed.

"Marchell, get *up*," he said, his voice urgent.

Downstairs, Adonis began to shake his siblings, trying to wake them. He shook his eldest brother Marcus first, whispering: "Get up. Marcus. He 'bout to hit Momma again."

"Chell, get up. Do you hear me?" Upstairs, Nathan continued yelling, his voice full of mounting desperation. *Smack.*

"Don't hit our Momma." the six children screamed, now standing at the foot of the stairs. To their astonishment, the next sound they heard was deep, adult sobs. It was Nathan. Unbelievably, their father was crying. Something was wrong.

With Marcus, age 12, in the lead, the children raced upstairs and into the room where their parents slept. They saw their mother lying there motionless, and Nathan, bent and pitiful, kneeling at the side of the bed.

"Go get me a spoon." Nathan yelled. "Somebody go get me a spoon." Adonis charged from the room, down the stairs and to the kitchen. He frantically searched for one, but to no avail. Throwing caution to the wind, he grabbed a fork instead and raced upstairs. Perceptive even at age seven, Adonis cursed the odds that when he really needed a spoon, one wasn't around, but when he made his PB & J sandwiches, there were always plenty of them for the grabbing.

Nathan took the fork from his son and screamed, "A *fork*? This is all you can find?" He then tried to use the end of the fork to do the job he thought a spoon would have done. He tried in vain to force Marchell's mouth to stay open, but it wouldn't. Her teeth were shut, her mouth sealed tight. Nathan sobbed again, disbelief and grief overwhelming him. Oh, all the wrong he had done to Marchell. His wife was dead; he knew it.

Nathan left the room to call the paramedics and Marchell's kin, while his children crowded around their mother, crying, begging "Mommy, get up. Mommy, get up." But Mommy wouldn't get up. The impossible reality that something horrible had happened to their mother gripped each child. Was it their father's fault that Momma wouldn't get up? Was Momma pretending to be asleep? Somehow, somewhere, the young children knew that Momma wouldn't speak again.

After calling the authorities, Nathan left the house, unable to handle his grief. All nine children were watched by the neighbors next door until family members arrived.

Meanwhile, Grandma Pearl rejoiced that her shift at the nursing home where she worked was almost over. She would be leaving for home at 7:00 a.m. As she busied herself with work, her supervisor summoned her, his voice urgent.

"Ms. Bonds, your son Rick is here." Pearl wondered why Rick had showed up an hour early. It was only 6:00. She gathered her things and went to speak with her boss, who wrung his hands and said, "Your son says your daughter-in-law has died."

Pearl's heart seemed to stop. Her throat tightened and an overwhelming grief threatened to overtake her. She had to stand strong. Once in the car with Rick, she prayed as hard as she could, needing to understand the horrible news she just received.

"I don't understand this." she told God, "Nathan and Marchell were having problems and got away from you, but I prayed to you. You told me you were gonna restore them. You said you were gonna bring them back to you. Why would you take this young mother, Lord, and she got *nine kids*? Three triplet babies and six other kids and the oldest ain't even twelve yet. God, you gotta satisfy my spirit with this."

"What's gonna happen now, Ma?" Rick asked as he drove.

"I'm gonna take care of those kids. I got to. I don't know how I'm gonna do it, but I got to."

"Ma, you're 48. You don't need—"

"This I know I got to do. Marchell would want me to."

CHAPTER 1— Half Light

I am Mario Arnauz Bonds, a guy who looks nothing like what I've been through. My parents had two sets of twins, two single born children and a set of triplets. I have the honor of being one of the triplets. After my mother died of a brain aneurysm in February of 1988, my father abandoned my siblings and me, leaving us to be raised by his mother, Grandma Pearl. As a small child, I was goofy, witty, said to be too smart for my own good, excessively analytical—my family called me a nerd—and could easily entertain myself. I was revered a weird kid, famous for making random noises, constantly imitating people, and always finding something in the house to bang on as a drum. I enjoyed the pleasures of playing hide and seek with my siblings and dangerous adventures outside, but my greatest pleasure was to listen to the news and adult radio/television with Grandma. By "adult," I mean the news, seminars and religious programs that five-year-olds don't typically find entertaining. Whenever I slept too long during an afternoon nap, my grandmother allowed me to stay up late with her.

I was born with a rare eye disease called Morning Glory Syndrome, a degenerative condition that deteriorates the optic nerve and detaches the retina. Unfortunately, I have the rarest form of this rare disease. Typically, people with Morning Glory only have it in one eye, but I have it in both, and as a child, I experienced its full wrath. At age five, I had full sight in both eyes.

We were living in Howarits, Maryland when early one cold autumn morning in 1993, I was awakened by Grandma. We were picked up by a deacon from our church. I was very grumpy, wondering why on earth Grandma and I were alone with this old man who looked as if his scalp needed mopping. It was 4:30 in the morning and I wanted nothing more than to go back to sleep. During the ride, Grandma told me that I was going to the hospital to get my right eye fixed. Her words went in one ear and out the other. I didn't think or notice that anything was wrong with my eyes.

Once at the children's hospital in Washington, DC, I was taken to the "Play Room," and this cheered a five-year-old up right away. It was full of little people just like me. PBS Kids' television was on and the room was full of toys and games. Just as I was settling in to have loads of fun, a tall man shuffled over to me, accompanied by Grandma.

"Mario," he said, his voice academic, "it's time for your surgery. We're going to make sure you can still see everybody from your eyes." To five-year-old me, this man was out of his mind if he thought I was going to happily leave all of the toys to go into surgery. I didn't know what "surgery" was. True, he made it sound like a happy, fanciful place that would magic me into magic Mario, but still I protested, bursting into tears, begging to be left alone.

"Mario," came Grandma's tough, but soothing voice, "Shh, Mario. They're trying to make sure you can still see. You need to stop crying and come on." My crying wouldn't cease, but I did reluctantly follow Grandma and the doctor to go have a meeting with this "surgery."

A few things struck my attention in the room where they took me. There was a bed covered with plastic and loud crinkly medical paper, two other men and a large, tubular-shaped object lying on the bed. I was helped onto the bed as Grandma stood next to it.

"Now Mario, you like the smell of bubblegum?" asked the doctor, his voice ritualistically polite.

"Yeah," I said my voice thick with the ghost of sobs.

"I'm going to put something over you that smells like bubblegum. It's going to be OK. It's a mask, like a superhero." I thought, *Superheroes wear masks that smell like bubble gum?* I would have rather smelled McDonalds.

Without further preamble, the mask was placed over my face. Before it was fully in place, I became delirious. I struggled violently, desperate to get off the bed and bolt for the door. I could hear Grandma calling my name, but it didn't matter. She was on *their* side. I caught the scent of the mask and it smelled nothing like bubblegum. It smelled gassy, scary and threatening. Dr. Sanders removed the mask from my face, and I trembled, my sobs returning. I hoped it was over. Were they backing down? Did they finally understand I was horrified? No chance. Whether they understood my fright or not, they weren't backing down. Within moments, my world shattered as Grandma and two other pairs of hands held my five-year-old frame down on the medical bed as I watched the doctor place the scary superhero mask over my face once again.

A deep disbelief gripped me as I yelled for Grandma to help me, but instead, she was helping the men hold me down. I strained, spat, tried to kick and punch, but it was no use. The human hands acting as restraints had my arms plastered on the bed at my sides, and my frail ankles and wrists stood no chance against the manpower holding them in place. I had no choice but to breathe into that horrible mask, then the horror mounted. I inhaled the reek of the so-called bubblegum. A ferocious dizziness came and my mind began to cloud. Although I could still feel their hands, it sounded as if the voices of the people holding me in place were fading away. I floating into unconsciousness.

What seemed like seconds, but was actually hours later, I woke up, safe and sound with Grandma and a squat nurse at my side. First, I noticed that my right eye was covered with what seemed to be a huge amount of tape. I was later told that the eye surgery had been only meant for my right eye. The doctor's hope had been to salvage the remaining vision and try to prevent its possible loss in future. But the surgery wasn't successful, and instead it took all of the remaining vision in my right eye. My grandmother knew the odds before permitting Dr. Sanders to perform the surgery, and she had to make a tough decision. As Morning Glory is a merciless condition, whether I had gotten the surgery or not, it was inevitable that I would eventually go blind in the right eye. From that day, only my left eye had vision, however minimal it was.

When I returned from the hospital on the following morning, as if they couldn't wait for this moment, my also five-year-old cousin Sefra and my sisters Marian and Maria hounded me with questions. In amazement and with desperate curiosity, they waved their hands over my face, trying to understand at what instant my field of vision for the left eye ended. They moved from the left side of my face, to the right side asking, "Does it hurt?" or "Can you see this?" and the often-unnecessary "How many fingers am I holding up?" I was lying on the floor in Grandma's room on a pile of blankets, where I'd slept for the night, and Grandma was prepping in the bathroom as we were due for another follow-up eye appointment. She feared that my cousin and sisters were hurting my feelings and screamed, "Get out of here and leave him alone." Without delay, they dispersed.

Once the hospital days were behind me, I wasn't at all bothered by having one working eye. It didn't seem any different. I didn't really get the idea that only one eye was working. Sure, I was operating in half light, but I could still see, play, run and watch my favorite TV programs. Dr. Sanders told Grandma that I would have to wear an eye patch over my right eye for a few weeks, and immediately, I needed to get glasses to protect the remaining vision in my left eye. Dr. Sanders theorized that the glasses would prevent the left eye from experiencing the same breakdown the right eye had undergone. As Morning Glory was and still is immensely rare, Dr. Sanders and his team didn't have a clear clue as to how to properly treat it or about its typical progression. And now that I had glasses, I would soon be introduced to the world of being teased.

To family, friends and bullies, I became four-eyes, and Steve Urkel, the nerd. Five-year-olds don't understand the irony of something positive been used as an insult. Therefore, I hated being called a nerd. As a result of all the teasing and bullying, losing and breaking my glasses became routine. I didn't want to be a four-eyed, Steve Urkeley nerd. I wanted to be smooth and cool like all of the other people around me. My older brothers Markis, Nathan Junior, Adonis and Kevin weren't going around wearing glasses. In addition, why weren't my cousins Sefra, Shawn, Hasan, O'Mon and J.R. wearing extended eyes? I hated that image and broke those accursed glasses every chance I could. It was later suggested that hardly ever wearing my glasses may have increased the probability of my total blindness. But before that happened, my left eye would be my only source of vision for the three years that followed.

CHAPTER 2— PREMATURE CHALLENGES

My introduction to female romance came when I was only five-years-old. Naturally, with games, coloring, Disney movies, field trips, candy, contests and opportunities to get praise, kindergarten was one of the most fun periods in my life. Boy, do I miss some of those elementary joys. I was surprised to find that despite my new four-eyed appearance, girls in kindergarten liked me, particularly the white ones. I was a chocolate child, baby-faced with a soft-hearted demeanor. Maria, Marian and I were in the same kindergarten class. My sister Maria, being the mischievous one, set a white girl named Katie up for her first heartbreak. Timid when it came to girls, I wasn't sure how to handle the situation.

One day during class reading time, a point at which the teacher read to us, Maria overheard Katie talking about how I was her boyfriend and how sweet and cute she thought I was. Katie was merely joking, although she did long for me to be her boyfriend. As Maria had just finished a blue-flavored ring pop, she thought that it would be nice to give the remaining plastic ring to Katie, as a token of my recognition and esteem. I knew nothing about this until after it happened. Meanwhile, the teacher was almost done with the book. I looked and saw that Katie, seated in front of me, was crying, her sobs audible over the teacher's reading. Stunned, I looked at my sister seated next to me and she laughed. Katie's sobs were getting really noticeable now. Completely nonplussed, I smiled, but my smile vanished when I saw what Katie was holding. I knew that the empty plastic ring had belonged to my sister, and must have been just given to Katie. My confusion didn't last very long. I laughed along with Maria, still wondering why Katie was crying about the plastic ring. Heaven knows, I would soon find out in an embarrassing way.

My sister's laughing, interspersed with Katie's sobs grew louder. Maria whispered to me what she had done. The humor left me at once. I began to panic, my heart beating quickly. I didn't know whether Katie's crying had increased due to my laughing at her. I wanted to kick my sister and disappear all at once. Of course, our amateur soap opera got the teacher's attention.

"Katie, what's wrong?" asked Ms. Kent. The room fell silent. If I were light-skinned, I would have been redder than ripe tomatoes. My little heart beat fiercely and I thought of making a run for the door. All of the side conversations and jokes from the other students, once immersed in their own entertainment, had ceased. Everyone was waiting to find out why Katie was crying. During an agonizing pause I thought would never end, Katie sniffed repeatedly, hiccupping as she tried to gather herself so she could answer.

"Sweetie, are you alright?" came Ms. Kent's soft question.

Katie held up her hand with the plastic ring and proudly proclaimed, her voiced still thick with emotion and satisfaction: "Mario gave this to me." Then, her sobs overtook her again. If a disappearing act were truly possible, I would have performed one.

I yelled, "No I didn't." That was the wrong thing to say. Katie's sobs increased, if that was possible. Utterly embarrassed as the other kids laughed, I shot my sister a revolting look. I was ordered to stand outside the classroom to think about what I had done until Ms. Kent could speak with me.

Needless to say, the embarrassment in front of all of my peers was far more effective than the talk that followed with Ms. Kent.

"You don't make fun of people and play tricks with someone's feelings," Ms. Kent lectured. "You also disrupted class."

I pleaded with Ms. Kent to understand that I *hadn't* given the ring to Katie, and that it was a joke pulled by my sister, but Maria denied my accusations. Even when I hoped to get her in trouble at home with Grandma, no one would hear that I didn't do it. They wouldn't believe me in this case, nor would they in my sister's next set-up with Katie and me two weeks later.

That time, Ms. Kent was in front of the classroom, reading again, and I had to use the restroom. After being granted permission to do so, I got up and stood behind my sister, who was incidentally next in line for the restroom. As if fate had put comedy in cue for this moment, the bathroom door opened and out stepped little Katie, her eyes brightening when she saw me. My sister whispered to Katie something that I couldn't hear, and Katie's face lit up with anticipatory surprise. My sister stepped back and said: "You can go first." Then she whispered to me: "Katie wants to kiss you." I was amused and shocked by this revelation, but could I trust my sister?

I wanted to be out of there. Kissing Katie was out of the question. She would announce it to the whole world and I would be laughed at again. I walked towards the bathroom door and Katie grabbed me. "Aren't you gonna kiss me?" she asked. As I hurried into the bathroom, relieved that I would escape her, to my utter horror, Katie rushed in behind me and closed the door. She turned to me, an expectant look on her face. I didn't make a sound about it because I was stunned into silence and hoping to God I could end this ordeal before Ms. Kent turned around. Thankfully, none of the other students were paying attention. Inside the bathroom, Katie started crying. I desperately tried to shush her, but it wasn't working. In between sobs, she squealed: "Kiss me." As she advanced on me, I softly pushed her back, still trying to silence her. Finally, I threw caution to the wind and smooched a girl for the first time. It was repulsive. Her lips were cracked and her breath smelled of the egg and tuna sandwiches we had eaten earlier for lunch. She hugged me as satisfied sobs overtook her.

Abandoning my more-than-full bladder, I extricated myself from her hug, bolted for the bathroom door and tried to quietly leave. I figured if Katie stayed behind, it would be OK if Ms. Kent was watching the door now. Ms. Kent would look away and then Katie could come out later. Not a chance.

Ms. Kent was looking at the bathroom after all, and of course, Katie didn't wait. Ecstatic, but still crying, she trudged along behind me and the world stopped. The entire class was staring as Ms. Kent shouted at us to leave the classroom and wait for her outside. Once again, I was in a Katie-centered embarrassment, orchestrated by my sister. This time, I didn't fight it or plead with Ms. Kent to understand that it wasn't my fault. I did explain to her that Katie came in after me because she likes me and blah, blah, blah. Ms. Kent wasn't hearing it. Much to my delight, Katie and I were separated. Katie was transferred to another class the next day. My saying that it was all her idea, and that she was nuts broke Katie's heart. Little did I know that hers was the first of many hearts I would break.

Back at home, Grandma had her hands full, raising twelve grandchildren and caring for her daughter Renee, who was under psychiatric treatment. The two-story subsidized house we lived in was rather accommodating for all of its occupants. With four bedrooms, an attached apartment, a spacious living room, dining room and family room, and a rather large basement, we had struck gold in our poverty. The house belonged to a church, which had allowed my grandmother to rent it after hearing her story of having to give up her job to assume custody of so many grandchildren after the death of her daughter-in-law. Renee was expected to be living with us indefinitely. Whenever Renee's problem was at its worse, we children would hide from her as she looked for us throughout the house.

On one such unconventional hide-and-seek occasion, a few of my older siblings hid in the kitchen while the rest of us hid in closets. Renee walked into the kitchen, determined to find one of us. Sensing movement, Renee peaked under the kitchen table and goofily sung "Who behind the table?" We all burst into laughter, giving all of our hiding spaces away. Renee's "Who behind the table?" became a frequent family joke for years.

After my mother's death, Grandma had initially only assumed responsibility for my brothers and sisters and me. There was Marcus (the eldest), Nathan Junior and Nancy (male and female twins), Adonis and Asia (male and female twins), Kevin, and lastly, Maria, Marian and Mario (triplets). After Mother died, my dad turned to drugs, a life of crime, and sex to cope. He gave exclusive custody of us to his mother.

My Aunt Haily, Grandma's eldest daughter, had been jailed, and the state of Maryland agreed to pay Grandma Pearl to keep Haily's three children—my cousins Hasan, Shawn and Sefra. The result was that Grandma was now taking care of twelve grandchildren, all with the use of social security survivor's benefits and welfare assistance. Between my eye appointments, managing my Aunt Renee, dragging us all to church and trying to raise twelve children, Grandma—in her early fifties—had her work cut out for her. Grandma was a fearless warrior, and I love her for that. And she told me that she wouldn't have been able to manage without the help of Sister Pat George.

Pat George was a social worker Grandma met when she first came to Maryland decades prior. When Pat George heard of my grandmother's plight, she stepped in and for years, offered her help and resources. She brought toiletries, presents on Christmas, food and frequently surprised my grandmother with extra money for us.

"Finally, I asked her why she was doing so much for us. Then, I thanked her so much for everything she was doing," Grandma told me one day. "She ain't even getting paid for the extra stuff she doing for us. I couldn't understand it, but I thank her and thank God so much. A lot of it comes from her own pocket. I couldn't do this without Pat George." Pat George was also an attendee of our church. I am thankful she was Grandma's lifeline during some of our periods of hardships.

Sister George's help was critical but, unfortunately, Grandma's management worries increased when my Uncle George, his girlfriend Lisa, and their two children, my cousins O'Mon and J.R. came to stay with us. With all of us in one house, I had a harsh introduction to my family's detrimental dysfunction. On many occasions, I wanted to disappear, but where could a five-year-old go for refuge? Why was a five-year-old seeking refuge anyway?

The question of whether boys should like girls, or whether boys should never like boys is a sexual identity notion no five-year-old should ever be forced to contemplate. I cannot, however, deny the early, confusing introductions I had to homosexuality at the tender ages of five and six. The first introduction came one morning when my male cousin O,Mon, who was four, and me were taking a bath that was being supervised by one of my older sisters. At that age, we children were sometimes made to bathe together. My sister, age 12, made O'Mon and I do strange things to one another. At first, I was nonplussed, and thus unresponsive to her instructions, but after being egged on by her for several minutes, I finally caved and did as I was told. At five years old, during a bath, I was forced to fellate my little cousin with my big sister playing audience. At some point, she made four-year-old O'Mon do the same to me. I knew O'Mon was a boy and I didn't understand why she was making us do these things. Although at first it was strange, eventually my five-year-old mind found what O'Mon was doing amusing. Stimulus had nothing to do with it. It was a new game that we could play, and my sister had introduced us to it. Just children, O'Mon and I repeated these acts several times over the next two years.

As an adult, it took some time to destroy the prison bar this memory had built for so long. Accepting and understanding that my sister was a misguided child has helped me deal with this. In truth, forgiveness set me free.

My cousin Shawn (Aunt Haily's son) and I were joined at the hip as children and teenagers, but he soon became another introduction to homosexuality. This occurrence took place in 1994, when at age six, I was still being made to bathe with my male cousins. Shawn was eight. As Shawn and I bathed and played Batman and Robin in the tub, he lay down in the tub and began splashing the water with his member. He forced me to touch his member. With a child's innocence, I did so, laughing at how Shawn's member grew and reminded me of a hot dog. He then grabbed mine and each of us splashed what we were holding in the bath water. I was surprise that mine grew just like Sean's. Suddenly, the door opened and our "splash" game was interrupted by none other than my grandmother.

"What are y'all doin'?" Grandma asked, her voice muffled as she chewed the last bite of a sandwich. Many thoughts went through my head at once. Was what we were doing wrong? Instantly, all of the spankings I could remember receiving flooded my mind. The time I ripped wall paper off the wall at one of Grandma's friends' houses, and received a butt-naked spanking for it. I wondered whether Grandma would skin us alive. Grandma loved us, but she was a strict disciplinaria

"Nothin'," I said innocently. Shawn and I stood up in the bath water.

"Were y'all playing a nasty game?"

"What? No," Sean fired back.

"We're playing Batman and Robin," I offered.

"Well ... What's wrong with y'all's ding dings?"

"I don't know," we said in unison. Grandma left and didn't return to spank us, and Shawn and I didn't return to what we had been doing. For years, these two memories, coupled with the countless times my older siblings forced me to watch pornography at age six and seven, had me quite trapped in a dizzying emotional prison. I was just a child, and these experiences had an immense, adverse impact on my development. As an adult, yes, having compassion for the fact that the persons who did these things to me were older kids

who perhaps, should have known better, has
helped me make peace with these experiences,
although they did birth sexual identity confusion.

CHAPTER 3– MOVE, MOVE AND DADDY NATHAN

In early 1995, my family moved to Springdale, Maryland. By now, Aunt Haily had been released from jail, and she and her children were living on their own again. For now, Uncle George, Lisa and their kids had their own place as well. Grandma was only responsible for my father's nine children again. My father was also now out of jail.

Maria, Marian and I were seven and in the second grade at Grossman elementary. The countless jokes students made with the school's name were crude and shamefully funny. It was at Grossman that I really came to terms with the fact that I was different. All of my class materials were in large print. In addition, the paper I used had bigger lines and wider line-spacing than that of the lined paper my peers used. I was embarrassed whenever the teacher gave us class work and I was handed the obviously strange paper. I would hover over my desk, thinking I was blocking others from seeing that my paper was different. Of course they noticed, and of course the teasing followed.

"The lines on his paper big as shit. Ay, Mario, you can't see or something?"

Sometimes, I would sneak the regular paper for use, only to be scolded for it later; my letters always overlapped the lines.

It was at this school where I met Beverly Betz-Zachery, a woman with whom I struggled and fought against when it came to learning things about being blind. Little did I know that she would later become one of the most important figures in my life.

I have many memories from my time living in Springdale as a child. I'll try to recount them here. I remember meeting my first childhood best friend, Michael, who lived across the street from us and was the first white friend I ever had. I remember the countless times my brother Kevin was forced by Grandma to cut my hair late at night when he would have rather been asleep, the countless times Grandma forced him to let me play Super Mario Brothers on his Nintendo.

I remember very clearly that *Power Rangers* was my favorite show. I thought I was the Green Ranger and was so emphatic about it that Grandma banned me from watching the show. Still, I would sneak and watch anyway, and my sisters could definitely be counted on to tell on me. I remember opening all of the doors to the mirrors in the bathroom and standing on the edge of the tub, staring at them, amused by how it looked as if it were thousands of Marios all around the room. I would attend the Lighthouse for the Blind camps during the summers. I used to play sports at the rec center and eat bag after bag of Skittles until my tummy hurt. The Cartoon Network was my comfort during scary moments, like when Grandma had her first heart attack, which scared the daylights out of me.

My father popped up for the first time after being released from jail, and would playfully smother my sisters and me with pillows and pummel us with punches. We begged him to stop, but he wouldn't until he was ready to. He thought he was playing with us, but we felt differently.

Once the water was cut off for weeks on end and we survived from jugged water brought over by uncles and aunts. Grandma would heat up a few of the jugs of water for us to use for washing up. In the toughest times, Grandma always knew what to do. We didn't stay in Springdale long, and we briefly moved into Haily's house in Clarkson, Maryland. It was a trying, nightmare of a time.

After leaving Springdale to stay with Haily in Clarkson in the fall of 1995, things became stranger. All of our older siblings had been sent to stay with our grandmother on our mother's side, whom we called Ma. Ma lived in Hilson, Maryland. As he had done so many times before, my father disappeared, leaving his mother and us triplets to stay with Haily and her kids in their two-story house. Grandma and Haily argued constantly. During their arguments, my aunt would scream at Grandma as if she were scum. She would bang on things and use every curse word imaginable. She called Grandma so many disrespectful names without remorse or the slightest regard that she was cursing her own mother. It was as if she were talking to a dog, not her mother. I hated my aunt when she did this and I wanted to rip her to shreds every time she made Grandma cry. Grandma was good to me and hearing her cry made me feel gutted and miserable.

Feeling helpless and trapped because she thought Haily's was the only help she would find, Grandma maintained her composure most of the time, and would seldom yell, but quickly resume a solemn calmness that she credited Jesus for giving her. Every confrontation I witnessed between Haily and Grandma planted a seed of anger in me. For years, I was quick to yell, scream, rage and more because I was given the OK for such responses at a time when I was very impressionable. When we left Haily's house, we moved into an apartment in Daloons, Maryland before the calendar year changed. We moved into a small development called Side Pawn that would be our home for nearly two and a half years. I had an emotional rollercoaster of a time there. The experiences in Side Pawn brought me heartbreak, sadness, disappointment and gave me painful memories that held me prisoner for years. My siblings and I endured several types of abuse that no child should ever have to experience. My father made appearances now and then, but he disappointed and hurt us every time he did. There were a few joys while living in Side Pawn, but I still grew to resent the years that I spent there.

It was then 1996. After moving to Side Pawn, my twin sisters and I were transferred from Grossman to Jastice Elementary, which was a seven-minute walk from our apartment complex. When our older siblings came to live with us, they were transferred to Daloons High. By now, the vision in my left eye was fading quickly. I was eight years old and since our stay in Springdale, I had already had two surgeries on the left eye. The retina had detached and Dr. Sanders attempted to reconnect it with temporary success. Now, the retina was detaching again and my optic nerve was deteriorating rapidly. For now, I still had vision, but paper with massive letters, closed-circuit televisions with enlargement capability and an Orientation and Mobility instructor for teaching me how to get around with limited vision was my norm.

My vision teacher, Ms. Betz-Zachery, was a pain in a blind kid's ass. She made me learn Braille when I didn't want to. However, Mrs. Barns, my mobility instructor, was awesome. Mrs. Barns was a large white woman with a strong Boston accent and an angelic heart. I was always taken with new and animated accents. It was the way to my heart. She frequently visited my home and took me out for McDonald's, ice cream and other fun things, all as a guise. Naturally, my special outings with Mrs. Barns were lessons meant to teach me independent travel as a blind person, and sweets were the incentive. I thought Mrs. Barns to be an absolute fool. Was she crazy? I wasn't blind. I could see clear as day. I loved the funny hair she had, and thought our outings were a lot of fun.

She wasn't anything like Ms. Betz-Zachery and her horrible Braille. I didn't know that the doctors knew total blindness was eminent for me. I hated the large letters I had to read, but I was satisfied. Ignorantly, I found Braille to be an unnecessary nuisance. Everyday, Ms. Betz-Zachery and I fought over my Braille work. She introduced me to a Braille writer, a metallic manual contraption with nine buttons and a cursor. In the center of the Braille writer is a spacebar. On either side of the space bar are four buttons. The first three buttons on either side of the spacebar are used to make the various Braille signs. To the left of the spacebar are dots one, two and three. To the right, four, five and six. These dots/buttons are pushed in various combinations to make different Braille letters and words. For example, dot one alone stands for the letter A. Dots one, four and three create the letter M and so on. Ms. Betz-Zachery had to teach me how to read and write Braille quickly, and I hated her for it. To me, my vision wasn't going anywhere and I was being forced to do something stupid. I didn't want to learn the blind man's language.

As time progressed, I realized that my school work was becoming more in Braille, and less in large print. I continued to fight Ms. Betz-Zachery tooth and nail. I didn't think it strange at all that I was gradually sitting closer to the TV to better see *The Simpsons* and *Power Rangers*. To me, it was normal; it was what I had to do.

My favorite pastime was to draw cartoons and portraits of people. I was quite skilled. I could draw or paint a replica of my favorite cartoons and people with unbelievable exactness. I thought everyone was nuts for thinking that my sight was leaving. They saw the things I drew, didn't they? I rationalized that my vision couldn't be going because I was still able to draw. Why didn't they see this as proof that the doctors might be wrong? In the spring, Ms. Betz-Zachery—bless her—or someone in her department entered one of my drawings in a nationwide contest at the National Playhouse in Maryland. The prize was a fifty dollar check, made out to the student. To my amazement, I won. Grandma and I attended the ceremony and everything. We were told that I wouldn't receive the check for a month or two. This was a joyous period in my young life that my father soon ruined.

Thinking that my slow vision loss was tormenting me, Jastice Elementary and the Vision Department saw to it that I developed a relationship with the school's guidance counselor. I liked her. Ms. Nina was a short, fat, sweet and funny white woman. I spent a lot of time in her office, not crying or being upset, just being a kid. As she also had been responsible for my Playhouse entry, on one of my visits, I asked her when I would receive my check.

She laughed and said: "We can call them right now." She dialed the number and handed me the phone. I listened intently, my body tensed with excitement and nerves as I prepared to be professional. The answering machine picked up and when the beep came, rather confused, I spoke: "Hi, my name is Mario Bonds. I was callin' to check on my check for the Sonic drawing. They told me I won. Thank you." The counselor didn't inform me how I could have been more polite or use proper telephone skills; I didn't know any. Instead, she laughed her heart out; overcome by the daringness and maturity my high little voice had attempted. Surprisingly, a response came in the mail a week later.

It was Saturday, and the mail came after noon. My sister Nancy retrieved the mail and quizzically exclaimed, "For Mr. Mario Bonds?" her voice was thick with ghetto influence. "It say it's from the National Playhouse."

"Be quiet," came Asia's voice. "That's Mario's check for that drawing contest. Hide it until Grandma gets home. He here." It didn't dawn on me that they were talking about our father, nor did I wonder why they had reason to hide things from him. After he disappeared when we left Springdale, I was glad whenever he was here. Moreover, wouldn't he be proud of me? Finally, I was in competition with my cousins. I now had someone to call Daddy, just like they did. Although he had never really shown me fatherly love, I took pride in knowing that my dad was here in Side Pawn and wasn't in jail. As my siblings discussed where to put the check, my father appeared. We all were in the living room, and unknown to us, he had been sleeping—or pretending to sleep—in the den, directly behind the living room.

With vicious intent, he walked over to my sister Nancy and said, "Gimme the check." He had heard. I could sense the mood in the room had changed. My siblings didn't want this to happen. I didn't know why they didn't want our father to know about the check. He would help me do something fun with it, right? I soon found out why my sisters wanted to hide my check.

My father took my check and immediately left the house. He returned two minutes later, told me to put on some shoes and to come with him. I obeyed. I felt great, thinking here we go, he's going to help me do something fun with my money. He and I walked to the convenience store in our neighborhood, which also processed checks. My father cashed my check, and ecstatic that he was probably going to buy me something, I was relieved that he had taken the check after all. But of course, I was wrong for being relieved.

He took me to the back of the convenience store, purchased three large ice creams and gave them to me. Then, he took me home, and I didn't see him for weeks. I later learn that my father took my money and purchased drugs with it. It broke my heart that he bought me ice cream for $2 and used the rest of my winnings for drugs. The playhouse win meant a lot to me. More importantly, my father and his support meant a lot to me. How could he use me like this? Didn't he love me? How could he not care about what won me the $50 in the first place? How could he not care about what I wanted to do with my money?

"I'm sorry, Mario," Grandma said to me one afternoon after she found me crying about my father taking my winnings.

"I was going to buy you some trucks with that money. I'm sorry." Grandma wasn't as sorry as I felt. The character I had been so pleased to call "Daddy," even after all his abuse, had struck again. I carried an eight-year-old's broken heart with me for years. Grandma, in an attempt to make me feel better, and true to her kind spirit and love for me, surprised me one day. She called me in from playing outside and took me to her bedroom. She closed the door and told me to sit on the bed. Needless to say, I was horrified. I wondered what on earth I had done to get in trouble this time. Had she heard me cursing outside moments earlier?

"What you been doing?" she asked. Usually, I could judge her emotion by her voice, but not this time.

"I was playin' with Samantha," I said weakly, fidgeting.

"You know why I brought you in here, Mario?"

"No."

"Here," she said, placing a box in my hand. Amazed, I opened the box on Grandma's bed and desperately felt inside.

"A tape recorder radio." I screamed goofily. I thoroughly inspected the machine inside and I knew exactly what it was. Grandma had gone to the store and purchased a small radio with two cassette players in it just for me. It was equipped for making cassette copies and recording voices. Thanks to Grandma, I was as happy as a kid on Christmas for a while.

"Go on now," she said. I left, quite contented.

Despite my father's previous downfalls, I was a desperate eight-year-old and longed for the continued opportunity to have a father, someone to call Daddy. Although I hugely resented him for stealing my money and never being there for us, I still wished for him to be around. I had already spent years not understanding why my Dad wasn't around. When he did pop up, I hoped that the rumor he would marry a woman from our church was true. I wanted a Mom, a Dad, and a family that wasn't dysfunctional. I wanted him to love us. I wanted him to cease taking our food stamp-procured food and belongings and selling them for drugs. Weren't we already on welfare? Didn't he know this? That food was bought with food stamps, not meant for drug exchanges. Despite my father's ugliness, I needed him, I wanted him. I cried, I hurt for him after him abandoning us the first few times. I didn't care. I just needed someone to call Daddy.

Although I nearly hurled the first time he made me drink eggs, I forced myself to believe in his rule to drink them for muscle building. I had to be strong like him. I needed him to call me son and love me. To my surprise, my father with all his failures, mistakes and "try to do good but couldn't" mentality were taken away from me again, just when I started to get used to knowing my father was free and could visit any day.

The night I watched my father get arrested and taken to jail for the last time was far too much for me to handle. Until my early twenties, my mind was imprisoned by this memory. On a clear sky night in late spring of 1996, the entire occupancy of our Side Pawn apartment was gathered outside. The police were after my father who was already on probation. This time, he was going away for a long time for robbery. I sat on the curb of the long parking lot that spanned the entire length of the apartment complex and wept in disbelief. I glanced at the end of the parking lot where the dumpsters sat, and watched as the police restrained my father. Soon my eight-year-old mind couldn't watch anymore. For a moment, I no longer cared that I was going to be blind. I now welcomed it. I intently and unblinkingly stared into the headlights of a car, willing the bright lights to instantly and permanently blind my left eye so I wouldn't have to see the horror story unfolding in front of me. Closing my eyelids wouldn't be enough.

My father yelled and fought against his captors. Grandma cried, telling all of us to go back into the apartment. From there, as if scripted for a movie, my memory fades to black. That was the last time I saw my father until sixteen years later. I wasn't able to confront him until I broke free from the prison bar this memory created, which didn't happen until age twenty-two.

CHAPTER 4– A DIFFERENT LIGHT AND FELIS

My favorite outdoor pastime was to ride a bike. I loved riding down hills, doing Pop-a-Wheelies and racing my friends. My left eye was my best friend, with or without those extended glass eyes. With the glasses, things would have been safer. Nevertheless, I was a half-blind daredevil, on my bike and on the move. As I had my cousins to play with, my days with partial vision were somewhat filled with a few childhood joys. By now, Aunt Haily and her kids, her fiancé Robert, my Aunt Renee, Uncle George, his wife and their children were all living with my siblings, Grandma and me in our small Side Pawn apartment. The head count of occupants was twenty.

How many nights certain adults stayed would vary from night to night, but it was clear that this was their place to stay. I lived through heart-wrenching family fights, both physical and verbal, that would serve to torment me in my later teen and early adult years, until I broke free from the mental prison bars these memories created. I hated all of it.

I know Grandma did her best, but at times, I had disappointment in her that, despite her accepted election to raise us, she continually allowed her grown-up children to come into our lives and run things to our detriment. They caused countless problems and offered us much abuse. Her children were the cause of a lot of my insecurities, heartache and would later be responsible for causing us to be put out of several homes. Grandma suffered from what I call "Mother's Syndrome" which at the time, didn't seem to have fully bled over to my siblings and me. Women who have Mother's Syndrome unknowingly act as if their adult children can do no wrong, and they do anything to stop consequence from finding their children. Their adult child can be 100-percent guilty, but the mother will never hear of deserved harsh punishment for them. Grandma's children did whatever, whenever they wanted to us. They all were around to watch my transformation from a partially sighted child, to a totally blind one; what a spectacle, no pun intended. The vision in my left eye started to rapidly deteriorate in late spring.

I still had usable vision, but the eye test results weren't looking good. Moreover, I was sitting nearly nose to the screen in order to watch my favorite television shows. During this time, Grandma had an important decision to make. Hunsville County public schools tried countless times to get Grandma to permanently send me to the residential Maryland School for the Blind in Baltimore, Maryland.

"It would just be for the rest of his public school years. He'll be around kids just like him and they'll teach him all he needs to know," they would tell her desperately on many occasions.

Never wavering, Grandma said no. "Ain't nothing wrong with Mario," she told them again and again, "He's just going blind. That boy got a good brain. That boy ain't dumb. Y'all just need to teach him. Ain't nothing wrong with him. I don't want him ending up like them other kids that be snottin' and unaware. Ain't nothing wrong with him; he need to be around regular kids. The Individualized Education Plan classes he in is good enough." This was the best thing Grandma ever did for me. She fought to keep me in public school so that I could have a mainstream educational experience. She felt this would guarantee proper social skills as well. If it wasn't absolutely necessary and another alternative wasn't possible, Grandma didn't believe in segregating the disabled. As long as the school system gave me the materials I needed as Grandma had requested, she believed I'd be just fine in public school. As I was a major rebel, Hunsville County still pushed. They had me labeled malfunctioning and a troublemaker.

My regard and respect for Mrs. Barns changed briefly when I blamed her for trying to make me blind. One afternoon, she came to Jastice and pulled me out of my third grade class. She took me to Ms. Nina's office and told me to sit; she had something exciting to give me. I wondered where Ms. Nina was.

"Mario," began Mrs. Barns, "I have a surprise for you."

"Yeah?" I said quizzically.

"It's a special instrument." She was rummaging in her bag now. I stared at her and the mess on Ms. Nina's desk as she used the desk to hold her bag as she searched. With the words "special instrument," I assumed that Mrs. Barns—because she was so nice and kind—had purchased a musical instrument for me. I loved the piano, recorder, drums, guitar, sax, organ, you name it, and thought she had literally brought me an instrument. I was beyond astonished when she brought out something that looked nothing like a musical instrument. She handed the object to me and it took several moments before I realized what it was.

"This is the instrument," she said ecstatically. I took it from her and examined it closely. I was holding three white metal tubes, with a fourth tube that was covered with black rubber. All four tubes were being tightly held in place by a rubber string that was attached to the end of the rubber tube. There was a rubber string that ran in between the metal tubes as well. I noticed that it had a few bits of red tape on it. My eyes widened as I fully understood what she had given me. A fury filled me and without warning, I threw the object as hard as I could at Mrs. Barns. It struck her hard between the left side of her neck and her shoulder. She yelled my name and hurried over to me. I became inconsolable, my rage out of bounds. I screamed at her and tried to leave.

"Oh, Mario," said Mrs. Barns, concerned, my physical assault ignored.

"It's not an *instrument*. That's not an instrument," I screamed, pulling against her grip on my upper arms. She desperately tried to calm me, grabbing my arm and trying to sit me down.

"Mario, it's going to help you get around when you can't see with your eyes anymore. Oh, Mario. Settle down. Oh honey, I'm sorry."

Mrs. Barns hadn't handed me a musical instrument. Instead, she had given me my first cane. I had seen those things before. In that instant, my young mind went back to the countless times I saw what I thought to be "blind weirdos" on the street, walking with those "sticks," as I called them. I was sure that Mrs. Barns was trying to make me blind. She didn't care about me. Again, she and everyone else were forcing me to be blind. Why didn't they understand that I could still see? I didn't need help walking around. For Christ's sakes, didn't she know I was still drawing pictures and riding bikes? Eventually, I had to cave. It took weeks, but I finally relented and started learning how to use my new "instrument," the cane.

The doctors and educational instructors all agreed that teaching me how to live and operate as a blind person before going totally blind was the best plan of action. Ms. Barns and Ms. Betz-Zachery scheduled me to meet Mr. Jones, a blind guidance counselor at another Elementary school.

He was to be my example that things would be OK once I went blind.

"Now Mario, Mr. Jones is blind and he's a guidance counselor," Ms. Barns informed me on the day we were to meet him. As I was highly disinterested in meeting a blind man, my throat was tight with anger. I was disgusted to meet someone my instructors wanted me to turn into after going blind.

"I'm tellin' you, you gonna be just fine," Mr. Jones had told me in a voice akin to Elvis's as we talked in his office at Gladisnoon Spellmen elementary. He presented me with a Braille watch and promised to check on me as I grew up. However, I didn't hear from Mr. Jones again until the eighth grade, nearly seven years later. I was thankful for that. As I sat in his office and listened to him talk, I imagined him grabbing me and screaming: "I'm blind … Join the club, young man."

In the fall, Dr. Sanders was preparing to perform a final surgery on my left eye. He hoped for the small possibility that I wouldn't lose all vision in the left eye, but he couldn't be sure. We had already been through this probability gamble with the right eye, and again, the odds supported total blindness over having a little vision after the surgery. As a result, everyone was on the "prepare Mario for total blindness" mission and needless to say, it still wasn't going well.

Despite the demands of Mrs. Barns and other mobility instructors, I refused to use my cane around friends and family, and would only use it during a mobility lesson. Frequently, I ran into many walls and sustained a bloodied nose and a large, noticeable knot on my forehead. In denial, I tried to ignore how seeing was becoming quite difficult. As using the cane would have meant accepting that I was going blind, and I refused to do that, I was too embarrassed to use it around friends, especially Felis, my first crush.

Felis was a pretty, light-skinned girl with dazzling eyes, and remarkable hair. She found me cute as well. So within three days of knowing one another in third grade, she became my first girlfriend. Our puppy love relationship lasted throughout third grade, through the summer—she lived in the apartments behind us—and into the fourth grade.

Fourth grade came, bringing September 25th with it, and my life was changing fast. I was now nine years old and I was "going together" with Felis, who eventually played a vital role in my accepting that my vision was leaving, and being relieved to realize that I actually did like girls. However, at the start of fourth grade, despite slamming into things, Felis was the reason why I continually denied my vision loss.

In front of Felis, I felt like I should be as normal as possible. I continued to break my glasses, and I habitually left my cane in the Special Ed room with the Special Ed instructor, Mrs. Ogg. When Felis was around, I walked quickly as if my vision were as clear as ever. I made sure that I learned the cool man's swagger that my brother Markis used when he walked.

Every morning when I entered our fourth grade classroom, I would tell myself: "Mario, you can see. Walk straight across the front of the room." I willed myself to see my desk, which was next to the window. Although my vision was very blurry, I refused to accept that to be true. I forced my brain and eyes to communicate, making myself believe that I was right on track. "You can see it," my mind would say. "Almost there. Oh my God, Felis is behind me." BANG. I would slam into the projector in the middle of the room, or oftentimes, right into the very same desk I so desperately willed myself to see, and they always fell over and hit the floor with an attention-grabbing bang.

The class would laugh and taunt me: "Nigga can't you see?" and, "Ha-ha, that four-eyed 'bama keep runnin' into shit."

To my delight, as the first female that ever gave me butterflies, Felis never turned her back on me. With my attraction to Felis, I thought perhaps I was normal after all. Because of the homosexual things my sister Asia made me do at five, the curiosity Shawn had given me, and the shameful, confusing private-part games I played with my cousins, up until then, I had found myself eyeing other boys. I didn't understand why I found them to be cute and a few times, I came close to urging some of my male friends to play the private-part games my cousins and I played at home. I was relieved when I realized that a girl could catch my nine-year-old eye as well. My interest in the shameful games and thinking guys were cute ceased when Felis came into my life.

Felis was a very sweet girl. I taught her how to properly guide a blind person and I would happily cling to her arm as if it were my saving grace. We had a true puppy love boyfriend and girlfriend swagger. Felis actually made me believe that going blind would be OK, as long as I had girls and their arms to which I could cling. This was my newfound vision. Was I really going blind? With Felis, I didn't feel like it, but her scary and bulbous mother soon brought an end to our charade. When her mom found out about her hanging out with boys, Felis was forbidden to play outside after school. After her mom's demand, I only saw her in class. She was a truly obedient daughter; she heeded her mom's words and stayed clear of all boys, including the harmless half-blind boy Mario.

For the rest of my time at Jastice, it was hard to breathe whenever I was around her. The fall of 1996 brought the loss of my first girlfriend due to a parent's demand and I have never forgotten that heartbreak. As it felt as if my rescuer had been taken from me, I resented Felis's mother. The time spent with Felis was important, as it helped me realize that I would one day still marry a woman, and that I didn't have to be trapped by my secret of what I had done with my cousins, and almost had done with other boys. I no longer wanted to do those things; I wanted girls. All of this is a lot for a child to go through. Having sexual confusion at age nine, on top of all the other struggles, was far too painful, and there was no one to help me sort things out. With the loss of Felis, I felt worthless and blind all over again. I quickly went back to the practice of trying to seem normal, while at the same time trying to get people to notice me. I wanted my father more than ever when I lost Felis, and the concern for losing my vision returned. By December of 1996, I would really know the full emptiness of being fatherless.

On December 16, 1996, my life changed significantly. Just like the day I had the not-so-successful surgery on my right eye, this day began with Grandma and me going to the children's hospital at the crack of dawn. A different deacon from the church drove us this time. His name was Deacon Brown, husband to Addie Brown, Grandma's best friend.

At the children's hospital, the usual occurred: a visit to the playroom to wait to have another meeting with "surgery." This time, I didn't play with any of the toys, nor did I care for the children's programming on the large television. I knew why I was here. I felt scared, disappointed in Grandma and ready to go back to sleep. Why was she taking me through this again? I pouted and kept my arms folded. I also wasn't too happy that she hadn't given me anything to eat either. Why couldn't I eat until after the surgery? After an agonizing wait, a nurse came to collect us.

"Hi Mario," she said, her New York accent amusing.

"I'm Elaine."

"Elaine?" I asked animatedly. I remembered the character named Elaine on Seinfeld so I thought it was awesome to meet someone named Elaine.

"Yes, it is, sweetie."

"He like *Seinfeld*," Grandma told Elaine, gathering her purse around her.

"Come on, Mario." Grandma and I followed Elaine to the examination room where I knew I would receive more eye drops. I hated those drops. They burned and made my face scrunch up. Once the awful drops were applied to my eyes, Elaine told me to lie down on a bed covered with more awfully loud medical paper. I liked her name, so I complied without quarrel. I remembered that type of bed. I didn't even become agitated when Elaine began to roll the bed out of the room. I thought of the episode of *The Simpsons* in which Homer sat in a wheelchair and said: "There are chairs with wheels, and here I was using my legs like a sucker." I laughed to myself. I was in Elaine's care. Grandma traveled along beside us and I felt mildly entertained, watching the doors and people fly past as I lay comfortably in my hospital gown and sheets.

"Grandma," I began, "They ain't gonna use that gum mask is they?"

"I don't know," was Grandma's response.

"No sweetie, we won't. This time, we're gonna give you a shot." Elaine's words were friendly, but the word "shot" should never be spoken around Mario Bonds.

"A shot?" I questioned nervously.

"He scared of shots," Grandma giggled.

We entered a large hospital room that had a lot of strange machines in it. I glanced around the room to do a bubblegum-gas-mask check. Once I was sure the place was completely devoid of any masks, my little heart relaxed. The nurse wasted no time getting to business. She was gentle, but her movements were urgent and precise. She first took my right arm and rubbed alcohol into the fold of it. I knew what this meant and I tensed. Grandma started talking to Jesus about me.

"I'm gonna die, Grandma," I said, tears forming. Within seconds, the room filled with my sobs, interspersed with Grandma's talk with Jesus. She wanted me to hear her talk to Him. I felt a bee sting-like pain in my arm where the alcohol had been. I started loudly repeating the Jesus things Grandma was saying. I became lightheaded and befuddled. All of a sudden, the room turned blue and Elaine and Grandma faded away as the anesthesia carried me into unconsciousness. When I awoke several hours later, I would see the world in a very different light.

CHAPTER 5– THE OTHER SIDE

When I awoke, I couldn't see anything, which I thought was strange. I reached up to my left eye and felt relieved to find that it was covered by a large patch. Of course, the patch would block all light. Anxiously, I ripped the patch from my eye and instantly lost control. I still couldn't see. I just removed the eye patch and still couldn't see anything. What was going on? I was in disbelief, my breath frantic and arms flailing. The room would be momentarily black, and then full of bursts of light and weird colors and moving shapes, and then things would go black again. My eye was confused. Blindly, I thrashed about the bed, desperate to see something. I screamed, trying to get up from the hospital bed.

"I can't see. Grandma, I can't see. Help me."

Grandma, anxious but in control of herself, was still saying words to Lord Jesus. Just as soon as my tirade began, I blacked out again. I was told later that Elaine had quickly returned and sedated me again.

When I awoke for the second time a few hours later, I was much calmer than before. I was even given two popsicles. Not being able to see, I found them hard to eat. Grandma explained to me that I could have thrown up or died going crazy right when I woke up from surgery.

"The nurse made you go back to sleep because of how upset you were." As I finished my sweet treat, Dr. Sanders's voice started up. In my head, his voice was now associated with evil. I knew that it was he who was responsible for the thing covering my eye. For the minutes that followed, Grandma was briefed on the probabilities and possibilities of my new life as a blind child.

"I reattached his retina with a recently introduced medical band. He won't be able to see right away, but if this has been successful, his vision will return, although it won't be much if it does. The band, we hope, will hold the retina in place but, we will have to wait and see how his eye responds to it. He may even see double vision for a while. That patch must stay on him at all times. You need to put these eye drops in his eyes in the morning and before bed at night." I hadn't the slightest idea what he was talking about. What did he mean about seeing double vision and some vision returning? I guessed he didn't know I'd snuck a peek under the patch upon first waking. I couldn't see a thing. I was helped out of bed, clothed and guided out of the hospital, to a cab and then home. I cried the entire time, clinging to Grandma who tried her best comforting me. She Jesus-talked all the way home.

Back at home in Side Pawn, I trailed the walls to orient myself. Surprisingly, I still remembered the layout of the apartment. Naturally apprehensive about my new state of darkness, for the first few months, I clung to a wall everywhere I went in the apartment. But right now, just home from the hospital, my only intent was to be alone in the bathroom so I can take the accursed patch off for a second without Grandma knowing.

Once in the bathroom, I felt for the light switch and flicked it up for on. Quickly, I lifted the eye patch. Desperately, I waved my right hand over my left eye, as my left hand held the eye patch away from my face. I couldn't see a thing. The bathroom was black, then gray, and would go back to black again. Sure, I had been told to not take the eye patch off, but I didn't care. They said the eye should remain covered, but again, I didn't care. I wept, falling to my knees. I positioned my back against the bathroom door as I sat, legs folded, still willing my left eye to see my waving hand as my tears poured. Nothing changed. My eyes were useless. What would become of me? I felt like my life was over. I didn't want to be like Stevie Wonder and Ray Charles. How would I ride a bike again? How could I ever draw again? Would a girl want a blind boy? Now that I was on the other side of seeing, I was full of fear of what would become of me in my new blind life. I dwelled in a child's misery until I heard Grandma calling me. Quickly, I put the eye patch back in place, made sure it was secure and then felt for the door handle.

"Yes?" I said once the door was open and my face was clear of tears.

"Come on out here," she said affectionately.

Grandma had already made everyone aware of my new condition, informing them that I was most likely permanently blind. Grandma told everyone that Dr. Sanders said that my vision would most likely not return, and that if it did, it would be very little. I wanted to cry when my cousins and sisters came in from playing outside, and for the first time, I couldn't see them. I didn't cry though; I pretended as if my new condition meant nothing. They sounded genuinely concerned this time; they weren't pesky nosy five-year-olds anymore. I was miserable.

Later that night, as I slept on the sofa in the living room, listening to Asia and Adonis talk of how they enjoyed their fifteenth birthday today, I felt very sorry for myself. They briefly discussed me, thinking I was asleep. They talked about how it was "effed up" that I wouldn't be able to see anymore and how sorry they were for me. They were fifteen-year-old twins showing genuine compassion for their little blind brother. I felt special in that instant. My brother Adonis was responsible for trying to instill relentless strength in me. He worked out constantly and exuded might, remarkable strength, and a "don't mess with me or mine" attitude. As I lay there, my mind drifted back to my first real fight, during which Adonis had egged me on.

On a warm spring day a year earlier, I was at the playground with my cousins, sisters and neighborhood friends. A rather large boy had been teasing me about my glasses, and my jeans that Grandma had made into shorts for me by cutting them at the knee. He was also making fun of my dark skin. The boy's teasing wouldn't stop. He followed me around, taunting me, annoying me. He took his bullying to the next level when he decided to push me. I swung a punch that missed him, and he laughed. Within seconds, we had an audience. All of the kids gathered around us. I was afraid. I wasn't a fighter and my vision wasn't the best. The boy began yelling insults again. Just as I was going to back down and run home, I heard a deep and booming voice say: "Mario, you better not be a punk."

I looked up. My brother Adonis—the tough teenager—was there. I knew I was stuck. I couldn't have Adonis dismiss me as a coward, a softy. I had to uphold the macho Bonds-men's name. I pounced, my advances ferocious. I pummeled the boy with punches to his face. To my utter astonishment, he started crying, begging me to stop. I paused, my hand poised for another blow as his pink tongue flopped around in his gaping mouth. I hit him hard. In this instant, I felt inexplicably sorry for him and I knew I should turn away, but I didn't. I was still pumped up from Adonis being there and seeing me in action. I wasn't a punk. Half blind, sure, but not a punk. I punched the boy one last time, square in the nose. I felt like a bad person as the crowd of kids yelled and praised me as I ran home. I felt sorry for the fat kid.

My memory was interrupted by Asia talking more about my condition. She wondered what it was like for me to no longer be able to see anything. My mind briefly went back to the countless occasions my cousin Sefra, sisters Marian and Maria and I would act as background singers for Asia when she recorded herself singing Monica's "For You I Will" from the movie *Space Jam*'s sound track. She would put two radios side-by-side, one set to record and the other set to play the instrumental of Monica's single. Then, we would record the song again and again until she was pleased with it. Her voice was pure, beautiful and infectious. Coming out of this sweet memory, I felt miserable and wished I could live permanently in happier times, when I still had sight. I wanted my father so badly, but of course, he couldn't be there.

After going totally blind, I spent nearly two months out of school. The two-month period was spent with me being a prisoner of the apartment and at countless eye doctor appointments. Grandma and I would head off to the eye doctor two to three times a week. As we had to use public transportation, and it was the heart of winter, she would get me dressed up in multiple layers of clothing, a large winter coat that nearly swallowed me, and she would have my head and face completely covered. I was really rather snug and well-protected. Grandma, however, wasn't as snug and comfortable. She wore what she could afford. My eyes still flood with tears when I recall how she developed walking pneumonia on account of our frequent visits to the eye doctor in the freezing winter cold. As we were inseparable, I panicked when anything was wrong with Grandma, sickness or otherwise. The night before being diagnosed with pneumonia, she complained of her body hurting when she hugged me good night.

"Grandma, what's wrong?" I asked, settling back down on the sofa where I was to sleep (still a full house).

"I don't know," she said, hugging me. "I'm hurting all over."

"Ma, you need to go to the hospital?" asked Haily from the den.

"No. I'll be alright." No matter what Grandma said, I panicked. I knew something serious was wrong, and that she had probably gotten whatever it was because of her dedication to me and my eyes. Nevertheless, she was a soldier and beat the walking pneumonia in no time.

My instructors, teachers, friends and family all deluged me with get well cards, sweet treats and prayers during my recovery. I felt cut off from the world. I entertained myself by listening to Michael Jackson, books on tape, *The Lion King* and television. When I finally returned to school, I wasn't ready for what was waiting for me. I was the source of so much laughter and ridicule. Kids can be cruel and my peers at Jastice were clear evidence of this fact. I was jeered and nagged at, teased for my cane, and I wanted nothing more than to disappear. There were a few kids and teachers that missed me, but for the most part, I was a new thing to make more fun of. I became disrespectful and I resented everyone, adults and students alike. Ms. Betz-Zachery's job became more intense; I was now blind so my Braille skills needed to improve as soon as possible. Again I fought, refusing to continue learning to read and write Braille. Her technique for persuading me to use Braille during our lessons was always the same.

"I'm not Brailling," I would say with defiance.

"OK. No Braille, no lunch. Lunch has already started and it's gonna be over. You can forget about recess, too." I resented her every time she tried to make me Braille, or even more when she threatened to take my lunch and fun time because I wouldn't obey. I thought her to be the meanest woman in the world. She would say these things, and then go right back to chewing her gum or flipping pages. Then, she would make her move. She would open the classroom door so that I could smell the lunch food fumes and hear the hubbub of my peers talking and laughing in their anticipation of recess. Slowly, but surely, my little fingers would find their way to the Braille writer keys, and I would sulkily give in to her horrid demands to Braille. Today, I'm glad she was devoted and hard on me; I needed that. I was nine years old, blind and feeling as if I was in a world where I didn't belong. I know Ms. Betz-Zachery understood this, but in my mind, my blindness was partly her fault, too.

Hunsville County again pressured Grandma into sending me to The Maryland School for the Blind. Not only had they labeled me a troublemaker, I was also being called an impaired learner. My grades were barely more than mediocre and I was always far behind my sighted peers. Not budging an inch, Grandma flatly refused. They passed her off as a selfish, confused and neglectful guardian, but Grandma knew exactly what she was doing. She maintained, "Ain't nothing wrong with that boy. They just need to teach him and give him the things he need to do his school work, and he'll be fine. That boy got a good brain."

Grandma knew the side of me that was nerdy, into everything and overly analytical. My vocabulary was quite enhanced because of the television programs and adult radio stations with which I would entertain myself. Grandma wouldn't see me sent away from home for just anything. She wanted them to continue to work with me because she had faith that my intelligence would shine. She didn't care that I was rebelling and fighting the school system; she understood that I had just gone blind, and my adjustment to my new life wouldn't be a piece of cake.

For the remainder of my fourth grade year, my work habits didn't change. As I knew things were getting worse with my left eye, I remained a hard shell to crack. In the end, my left eye did reject Dr. Sanders' new retina band. I had a major allergic reaction which produced a fluid-filled, fleshy bag in the front of my eye. The bag hung from the inside of my eyelid and was so large that the eye couldn't close. Blinking was impossible. Eventually, Dr. Sanders had to remove the allergy bag, and the medical band he had so desperately hoped would work. It was official. Mario Bonds was totally blind, and there was nothing anyone could do about it.

Coupled with the stress of going blind was the constant drama and dysfunction in my family. I understand now more than ever that the countless family fights I witnessed made me act out even more. I hurt for Grandma every time her adult children hurt her feelings, broke her heart and nearly emotionally destroyed her. Of particular consequence on my young mind were the fights Grandma had with Haily.

"Haily, I'm trynna do my best in here, taking care of these kids and everything else," Grandma said during one of their fights.

"Yeah, we all doin' our best, Ma. You ain't got to worry about shit. Me and Robert and my kids will be gone. I'm moving to Georgia and I ain't coming back to Maryland."

"For what, Haily? I'm sorry you feel that way. I ain't got no money and Lord knows I'm doin' all I can."

"Like I said, Ma, you ain't gotta worry about my kids and me anymore. I ain't coming back to Maryland." Haily's voice rose with every sentence she spoke until she was out of control. "I ain't stepping a foot back in Maryland." She was screaming and my sisters and I cringed at her words that followed: "Fuck that, I ain't even coming back for your Goddamn funeral. Matter fact, I will spit on your grave. You ain't got to worry about me, Ma." I knew these words crushed Grandma. I felt terrible and wanted to comfort her, but I was afraid of getting involved, and being told to stay in a child's place. I hated my Aunt Haily for saying these things to Grandma.

At Haily's words, Grandma retreated to her bedroom and wept. Haily gathered her kids, reclaimed all of the gifts she had given Grandma, my siblings and me, and within hours, was gone. This hurt because she took my cousins Sefra, Hasan and Shawn with her. By now, we all were very close. I wouldn't see my Aunt Haily and my cousins for two years. Haily wasn't the only out-of-control adult child of Grandma's who broke her heart and gave me terrible childhood memories, though.

"No. No, Grandma," I cried desperately, clinging to the living room wall. One rainy night, my siblings and I were huddled in the living room of the apartment, witnessing a horror. My Uncle

George was stoned and delirious. He was a 26-year-old, stuck in a child's mind. He had ongoing resentment for Grandma. He was angry with her, and believed that she had turned her back on him when she took custody of his brother's kids (my siblings and me). He had Grandma pushed up against what sounded to be the front door; my hearing was really good. For some odd reason, he had a knife.

"Why this 'bama got a knife," Nancy said.

He was serious. "You did this to me Ma, you did this," George yelled, completely crazed. He hadn't heard a word Nancy said.

"You wanna kill me, George? Huh? You wanna kill me George?" Grandma said calmly. She had no fear in her voice.

"No. Noooo." I cried, wishing I could disappear.

"You wanna kill me, George?" Grandma continued. "Do it then. Do it."

"This nigga crazy," said Nancy, "Where's Marcus?" Marcus, the eldest of us all was a street-smart thug and we all knew that George feared him. Marcus had no tolerance for offenses against his siblings or his Grandma, no matter who the offender. I tried to bury the memory of this night after it happened, but to no avail. In the end, George didn't kill Grandma, but his and Grandma's cries and screams from that night would haunt me for years. As a consequence, I became more of a headache at school, even getting into physical fights despite having lost my vision.

My acting out at school increased when I realize how poor we were. After Haily and her kids left, Grandma still had to deal with my Uncle George popping up and leaving his kids. We had very little food, and George's kids didn't help our plight. I am filled with gratitude when I think of how Grandma starved herself so that we could eat. One week, we survived on bread and jelly. The following week, Grandma gathered all the pennies she could find and sent my brother Marcus to buy the cheapest spaghetti ingredients. She then made the largest pot of spaghetti imaginable, and we would eat this for breakfast, lunch and dinner for nearly two weeks. After the spaghetti was gone, Grandma used everything left in the kitchen to make a stew. I knew we had a serious problem, and it broke my nine-year-old heart to know that Grandma refused to eat sometimes so that we could. I offered her my food instead, but she declined it.

Overcome by the family dysfunction and my blindness, I returned to what I considered to be a game that Asia had showed me at age five. On countless occasions, I would do non-stimulating, playful oral things to my little cousin JR, and he would do the same to me. We sincerely treated it like a game. It was a prison punishment if caught during cops and robbers. I did discover another, more appropriate, but more forbidden pastime during all of the familial turmoil. My brother Kevin was quite a skilled drummer and pianist. He was so talented that at age 16, he was playing for several church choirs. Whenever he left the apartment, I would sneak out his drum snare and high-hat, and I would bang on them for hours on end. Needless to say, he was quite livid when he discovered his equipment had been touched. His keyboard became a toy to me as well. As I couldn't draw pictures anymore, my mind turn to the supreme auditory art, music. My quest to be just like my big brother would ultimately become the driving force behind my becoming a skilled musician in later years. Within three years, I was playing the drums at church and was becoming quite a talented pianist. Kevin is truly my biggest inspiration. Nevertheless, abusing his instruments as a way to act out because of life's pressures wasn't something he could understand, nor tolerate. As if I needed anything else to give me an excuse to act out, life would throw my whole family yet another emotional curveball: my brother Marcus committed murder.

Late one night, in the summer of 1997, as was our ritual each night, my sisters and I were watching *The Simpsons* and laughing our heads off. Grandma and George were the only ones home with us. Adonis, Kevin, Marcus, Nancy, Nathan Junior and Asia were out in the neighborhood. As we laughed at Homer Simpson's stupidity, a series of gunshots met our ears. They were distant, but it was clear that the shots were definitely in our neighborhood. Grandma came out of her room, and George ran onto the balcony to see if he could see anything. Just then, the front door opened. Unknown to Grandma, Marcus rushed into the bedroom that he, Adonis and Kevin shared and hurriedly changed outfits. Then, he was out the front door again.

"I bet those gun shots had something to do with Marcus," said George in his scratchy smoker's voice.

Having told Grandma about Marcus switching his clothes and rushing out of the apartment again, George helped feed more fear and suspicion. She always had a sixth sense about things that involved her loved ones anyway. She panicked that this may have something to do with my brothers. She had been out twice that night, looking for them to tell them to come inside, but to no avail. George burst into conversation about what sort of shots they were, what kind of gun he guessed it was and how he knew it had to have something to do with Marcus, Adonis, Kevin and Nathan. He felt certain that someone had just met their demise. My sisters and I were speechless, the TV now long forgotten. We stayed up late that night, along with Grandma, waiting for my older siblings to return home. My grandma had a bad feeling about what had happened, and she prayed, hoping to get to the bottom of it. Unable to take the waiting, Grandma left the apartment to find my older brothers.

She found instead the crime scene, still packed with onlookers and police vehicles. There was another vehicle riddled with bullet holes, and a few body bags lying on the street. Once she had clearly seen the faces of the bodies pulled from the car, she was relieved. None of the dead boys were her grandchildren. She saw Kevin and told him to go home; he wouldn't obey. The knowledge that my brother Marcus had committed murder wouldn't come that night; it would come in a more terrifying, shocking way in the fall.

I was ten years old and in the fifth grade as the hot summer of 1997 was finally over. Although the school was merely a three-minute walk from the apartment, Hunsville County insisted that I ride a special ed bus to school to guarantee my safety. On this particular morning, my brother Marcus took me out to the bus.

"I'ma have ten dollars for you after school, Mario," he told me as we rounded the front of the bus.

"OK," I said weakly, my voice full of fear. Marcus then gave me a dollar. My mind repeatedly said "murderer, murderer." I hated my brother Marcus for what he had done. I didn't know any of the details about why he had killed someone, I just knew the rumors. I'd overheard my brother Adonis and Kevin talking about the summertime shooting, and how Marcus had killed a few guys. So there I was, an analytical ten year old, feeling frightened and disgusted that my older brother, whom I had once respected, was a murderer. I didn't want his dollar, nor did I care for him taking me to the bus.

"Today is your half day, right? What time the bus bring you back?" he asked.

"12:30." I replied. Again, I thought "murderer, murderer." And then I thought, "I don't want your dollar. Please don't pick me up." It was a fantastic thing that my brother couldn't read minds. He helped me on the bus, and that would be the last time I would see him for many years. At the time of the writing of this chapter, I still hadn't seen him.

After school, my two sisters and I returned to find the apartment in ruins. Marcus hadn't been there to get me from the bus anyway. Everything from my cassette tapes to Grandma's purses and church hats had been disturbed. The couch pillows and bed covers and sheets were thrown all over the floors throughout the apartment. Grandma and my older siblings were not home. My sisters and I were worried sick.

"What the hell?" my sister Maria said. She was always the most bold of the three of us; cursing was routine for her.

"What happened to my tapes?"

"The whole apartment is messed up. Oh my God," said Marian as she walked through the apartment. The front door opened and in walked Grandma and my older sisters Nancy and Asia.

Within minutes of their arrival, the front door opened again and in walked Nathan Junior and Adonis.

"What happened?" I asked loudly.

"The police got Marcus," answered Asia.

Grandma said nothing. She headed straight for her bedroom to start cleaning it. My brother Adonis proved to be a flood of information. He began explaining the situation, more to Asia and Nancy than to us kids. His voice was deep and booming with his increasing adolescence.

"Someone snitched," he began in his street tongue. "The police came here first asking for Nathan Junior Bonds 'cause they thought Marcus was Nathan Junior. They jacked Nathan Junior up until we got them to listen. Then, once they realized they was lookin' for the wrong person, they started interrogating, asking 'Where's Marcus Bonds, where's Marcus Bonds.' All we said was we didn't know. Then they started jacking the apartment up lookin' through shit. But 'cause whoever snitched snitched, they found Marcus and now he down at the station with no bond."

My sisters blew out their breath exasperatedly, disbelieving this bad news about our older brother. My throat was tight. I'd heard all I needed to hear. My brain was twisted with confusion, fright and horror. I was emotionally arrested for years by the knowledge of having a brother in jail for murder. Following Marcus's arrest for murder, later labeled self-defense,

Grandma was desperate to move us out of Side Pawn. She had spent too many nights over the years looking for my brothers outside, praying that they wouldn't be dead, and that they would stay out of trouble. Marcus's arrest was evidence to her that she was raising us in the wrong place. Fearing neighborhood retaliation, she made moving her top priority. We were living in the heart of the ghetto and with Marcus' lock-up for alleged murder, she knew that our lives depended on her getting us far away from the hellish ghetto. Marcus was being charged with manslaughter and second-degree murder and he was facing the death penalty or life in prison. The December night this news came was the saddest night for all of us.

It was nearly 12:00 a.m. the night this news came, and my brothers, older sisters and Grandma cried bitterly about Marcus's plight. I heard my brother Adonis walk in and out of the apartment onto the balcony and back again. No one cared to explain anything to Marian, Maria and me; we overheard what was happening. All night, I worried, wondering what would become of all of us and Marcus. I would soon find out.

Grandma's push to get us away from Maryland was successful in the days that followed, and Virginia became our new home.

CHAPTER 6– AVE, VIRGINIA

Uncle Rick, Grandma's second oldest son, came to our rescue. He had left Virginia nearly a decade earlier and had started his own church in Delaware. Because of this, we hardly ever saw him. Uncle Rick had three children, his two sons, Rick Junior and David, and one daughter, Dinia. He and his wife Marsha still owned a townhouse in Martins, Virginia. They had rented to tenants several times, and were considering selling until they heard of Grandma's problem. Uncle Rick persuaded Grandma to move into his home. He promised to only charge her $800.00 a month. Hadn't he considered that Grandma's income depended on Social Security and didn't even scratch $1500.00? Nevertheless, a week before Christmas in 1997, we left Side Pawn and moved to Martins, and my older siblings were livid. My sister Nancy and her twin Nathan Junior were turning eighteen soon, so they managed to persuade Grandma to allow them to live with our other Grandma in Hilson, Maryland. This left Asia, Adonis, Kevin, Marian, Maria and me left to move with Grandma. Adonis, Asia and Kevin hated having to leave behind their friends and the life they had built in Side Pawn and in other neighborhoods in Maryland. They complained and talked about how much they couldn't stand Grandma and how they couldn't wait until they were eighteen and able to break away. I always felt bad when they talked like this, but I pushed it away. I especially ignored it when Kevin talked like this. I truly admired him and wanted to be just like him, music and all. To me, he could do no wrong and I believed him to be better than that. I understand now that they were just being pouty teenagers, unhappy because they couldn't get their way.

The townhome in Martins was a three-story house with four bedrooms and two and a half baths. Grandma, of course, occupied the master bedroom; Asia had her own bedroom while Marian and Maria shared one. Kevin and Adonis shared the fourth bedroom in the basement while I slept in the rec area. Our new home took some getting used to. The local schools were already on Christmas holiday break, which left us with nothing to do. Things became a bit more fun when Grandma and Haily reconciled and she allowed cousins Hasan, Shawn and Sefra to spend the night during the holiday.

Maria, Marian and me thought Christmas was a pitiful ordeal, just like all the others. I walked to and fro on the first level of the townhouse, thinking how at ten years old, how it sucked not to get a thing on Christmas. I vowed that my future kids would never experience a present-less Christmas. As an adult, I regret feeling this way. Although we were poor, on welfare and had familial woes to boot, my grandma was doing her best. I was elated when on the day after Christmas, Grandma sent us over to my Aunt Dianne's house to spend the rest of our holiday. Dianne was sister to my deceased mother. I got presents over there. Nancy had purchased a set of walkie-talkies for me and I truly felt like a kid at Christmas now. I felt like my vacation would never end.

For the time, I didn't have to worry about a new school or learning Braille again and I had already forgotten that I was supposed to be missing my friends and teachers back at Jastice. On the contrary, losing friends had become so common with our frequent moving that I was now numb to the effect. I didn't think much about Ms. Betz-Zachery or Mrs. Barns. All I knew was that we were living in a house, and for the first time, we had a phone and cable TV. I was living on top of the world until the holiday ended, and school became a requirement again.

In early January, 1998, Grandma registered us triplets in AcSteven Elementary. My sister Marian and I were placed in Mrs. Smith's fifth-grade class, while my sister Maria was placed with a different teacher. I guess they thought three in the same class was overkill. After a week there, I was introduced to my vision instructor and orientation and mobility instructor. They were my replacements for Ms. Betz-Zachery and Mrs. Barns.

Ms. Harx, the orientation and mobility instructor, was no Mrs. Barns. She was without a cool accent, and seemed rather mute. She was a hard-to-read, subdued woman who hardly did anything substantive with me. We merely walked around the school on Fridays, going over the same routes week after week. There were no outings for getting used to being blind in the public and no challenging missions for mobility independence. I guess Ms. Harx thought it too premature. I did, however, think she was the "best instructor in the world" when she bought the Robins Five compilation cassette tape for me. I was so excited and I played it to death until the tape inside somehow ended up on the inside of the cassette where it was unreachable. I fell in love with "Ben," "Rockin' Robin," "A.B.C," "I Want You Back" and so many more. The Jackson Five and Michael Jackson's *Dangerous* album were my medicine during the tumultuous times I had in Martins. That is, until Grandma found the *Dangerous* CD, passed it off as demon music and destroyed it. I was heartbroken. Michael Jackson had been, and still is my escape from turmoil and hard times.

Ms. Kelly was introduced as my vision/Braille instructor. I have never forgotten her soft, singsong animated voice. She is also easily remembered because of her foul breath. Each day she worked with me, I willed myself not to laugh or give off anything that revealed my thoughts about her breath smelling akin to rotten milk. Nevertheless, I always gave into fits of giggles, and Ms. Kelly never knew why. It irritated her, though. I knew my older siblings were quite skilled at letting adults know what they thought. At ten, I still wouldn't dare divulge my rude but honest thoughts. Ms. Kelly was astonished that I had been totally blind for a while, but still couldn't read and write Braille proficiently. She set to business quickly.

She pulled me out of Mrs. Smith's class on Monday, Wednesdays and Thursdays for about three hours. We worked hard on reviewing the Braille alphabet I did know, and learning the rest I didn't. She felt that at this stage, I should have been a grade-two Braille reader and writer. She was disappointed in Hunsville County. The truth was simple. Hunsville County only had me working on grade-one Braille, and because of my fighting and refusing to study, I never grasped it. Ms. Kelly—despite the vile breath and goofy voice—did have an awesome personality. Her mere presence made me want to learn.

In grade-one Braille, every word is spelled out, letter by letter. For example, every letter in the word "understand" would be spelled letter by letter, with a Braille symbol representing each letter. In grade-two Braille, there are contractions used to decrease the amount of Braille signs used when writing, and to increase finger-reading speed. For example, there is a contraction to combine letters that frequently appear together such as S-T, S-H, T-H, W-H, C-H, C-O-M, C-O-N, C-C, G-G, O-U-T and so on. There are special symbols when combined that make up the short version of entire words that would be much longer in grade-one. For example, the S-H sign, followed by the O-U-T sign, and then the letter T writes out the word "shout" with only three signs, instead of the original five Braille letters of the word "S, H, O, U and T." A contraction written by itself represents an entire word. For example, the contraction S-T standalone represents the word "still," and the S-H stand alone contraction represents "shall." During my short time in Martins, Ms. Kelly taught me all of the Braille I needed to know, including the numbers. The Braille number sequence follows the letter A through J, with A being the number one, and J being zero. There is a number-sign symbol placed in front of the letter to differentiate between the use of an A verses the number one. For example, the Braille number-sign followed by the dots for letters "B," "C" and "I" would read as the number 239. "B" is the second number of the alphabet, while "C" is the third and "I" is the ninth. When Ms. Kelly finished with me, by the time I left Martins at the close of the school year, I was reading and writing grade-two Braille. I was even a little better in Braille math. I was so excited about my new reading language, I went home and began teaching my sister Marian and my cousin Sefra how to read and write it.

Since Grandma and Haily had reconciled, things turned back to business as usual and within a month of us being in Uncle Rick's home, Haily, her fiancée and my cousins moved in with us, much to the dismay of my older siblings. Sefra was registered in our school, and Hasan and Shawn were registered in a local middle school. At the start, things were quite blissful. It still felt like living on ice at times; I hadn't forgotten the hateful things my Aunt had said about spitting on her own Mother's grave. To add insult to injury, George came to stay with us as well. His wife and kids had stayed behind in their house in Riverdale, MD. Once again, we had a full house that was just as dysfunctional as it had been in Maryland.

My sisters and I made friends quickly. We became hugely popular in no time. No one made fun of me for being blind and I wasn't afraid to use my cane like I had been in Maryland. Looking back, I realize that I was comfortable using my cane in Martins because the kids would *only* know me as the blind kid, not the sighted kid who all of a sudden went strange. The student body got to know me because of my piano playing and cartoon imitations.

I'll never forget my first piano performance, during the spring concert when much of my family was there, and in front of the whole school, I performed "Michael Rowed a Boat Ashore" and a self-composed song. Kevin didn't get to see it, but oh how I wished he had been there. The applause was spectacular. Since I had gone blind and could no longer draw, music became my new form of art.

I loved the people at AcSteven and in our neighborhood. I had so much fun when outside of the house and away from my family's cloud of dysfunction. My fifth-grade best friend was

Michael Mandozio, a white boy two houses down. We were joined at the hip. He had no problem guiding me around the school and taking me to the playground. In fact, he found it to be a badge of honor to help a blind person, let alone befriend one. I was a rather daring child. Eventually, I grew so confident of our neighborhood and woods that I could go and come safely, without using a cane. Michael and I loved water gun fights, playing Power Rangers and going around scaring people. But my Uncle George—truly an Earth-disturber I believed—helped put an uncomfortable dent in our innocent relationship.

"Michael," I said once he had answered the phone one afternoon in March, "You wanna go to the park?"

"Lemme ask my dad," Michael replied, the excitement in his voice already saying he'd loved to. "My dad says yes we can, but we could also play here, Mario."

I paused; Grandma had a big "no no" about me going into other houses, especially those of white folk.

"OK, that's fine, Michael."

"You sound unsure," he began, "Are you OK with playing here? We can still go out if you want."

"I just want to spend time with you. It doesn't matter to me."

"Alright, come right over then." I knew the way to Michael's house and could get there without help. Naturally, each house had a pathway leading up to the door, so I trailed the edge of the grass with my foot to gauge the change from grass to concrete, and at the second opening, I'd soon be at Michael's house. But when I returned home much later, though, I would find out just how prejudice and immature my crazed Uncle was.

As Michael and I played, the Mandozios' phone rang, and I was summoned.

"Where are you?" asked my brother Kevin when I took the phone from Michael's father. It was funny. Didn't he just call here? What did he mean where was I?

"I'm getting ready to go to the park with Michael."

"Why you in their house?" he quizzed.

"We're leaving."

"Y'all better be." Kevin knew the rule. A disappointed Michael and I trudged off to the park, briefly played there and then called it a night.

When I walked into my own house, my male cousins and my brothers began teasing me, calling me a homo. My Uncle George laughed a drunken man's laugh as he told them his story of eavesdropping on my conversation with Michael. I was stunned that he had listened to my conversation, and more so because he was calling the conversation and me gay.

"'I just want to spend time with you,'" he mimicked in an awful high-pitched imitation of my girly, youthful voice. They taunted me and called me an Oreo. I wasn't gay. What Michael and I said wasn't gay. My statement was innocent. I wanted nothing more than to crawl under the covers of my bed, put on my headphones and listen to track two of *Dangerous*. Michael Jackson sings with plenty of attitude: "Why you wanna trip on me? Why, why?" I imagined getting lost in the choir and strings of River Jordan, but I couldn't at this moment.

My Uncle George was having fun at my expense, trying to make my older brothers and cousins believe I was gay. They taunted me with "faggot in the making" insults. When I heard Shawn laughing, I wanted to wring his neck. Had he forgotten what he had done to me four years earlier? Nevertheless, I didn't want boys; I still missed Felis. Michael Mandozio was merely my best friend. They told me I could put an Oreo cookie out of business; I was black on the outside and too white in the inside.

"Mario growing into a fag. Am I right though, Nikk? Am I right though? Ha ha ha." The laughter continued for what seemed like an endless hour. For the rest of the evening, George would occasionally revisit the subject and I hated him for it. He craved attention and got it at the expense of a ten-year-old's heart. When I tried to speak with Shawn or Hasan in happy terms while watching TV, I was told: "Mario, you're not white. Stop talking like that. What's wrong with you, dawg? He really thinks he's white." I felt crushed, over and over again. I hated all of them. I cried and Grandma consoled me. She told me to ask for permission to go over someone else's house; I complied thereafter.

George's onslaught didn't stop with me. One day, he felt my sister Asia was disrespecting him, and he tried to take matters into his own hands. It was common knowledge that George was a druggy, a drunk and sick in the head. He still resented his Mother for taking custody of us. He would let all of the resentment build up and get to a point where he thought retaliatory payment was due to us, the children. I have no idea how the problem started, but I listened as George screamed, and Grandma screamed as my sister Asia sobbed.

"Why is he here? He's on drugs. Why you keep lettin' them do this?"

"Shut your mouth, girl," Grandma said in her usual defense of her biological children. I admit, when she did this despite our distress, it angered me and made me quite disappointed in her. We quickly found out that George had put his hands on Asia's neck. Being asthmatic, his strength had induced an attack. She wheezed and coughed as she sat on Grandma's bed. Her twin Adonis had supplied her with a paper bag to breathe into. I panicked and wanted George locked up. I rushed to the telephone, snatched it up and dialed 911.

"What's your emergency?" I couldn't speak. I was afraid that George would kill me for calling the police. I hung up the phone. It didn't matter;

within ten minutes, the police were there. This was one of the scariest moments of my young life.

"Yes, Officer?" said Grandma after answering the door.

"Did someone call the police?"

"No," said Grandma. By now, Adonis, Kevin, Marian, Maria and George were huddled on the first level stairs; Haily and her clan had gone out for the day. I stood at the top of the stairs, right outside the master bedroom where a coughing Asia still employed the paper bag.

"Someone did."

"Mario did," said Adonis.

"Can he come down here?" asked the officer. My heart pounded hard, as if it were seeking an escape from my chest. I shook violently as I stumbled blindly downstairs, over the legs and feet of my siblings.

"No, Grandma." I cried, thinking I was going to be arrested and afraid to divulge George's offenses.

"No."

"You called the police, young man."

"Yes," I sniffed, still shaking. I began playing Michael Jackson's "Black or White" in my head. "My uncle hurt my sister and she couldn't breathe."

"They just had an argument and ain't nothing wrong with that girl," said Grandma to my surprise. She was protecting George. What had been a firestorm just moments ago was now being reduced to an adult-to-child spat. I was stunned. Michael sang in my head: "Tell me if you agree with me, when I saw you kicking dirt in my eyes. Hee." Why was Grandma doing this again?

"So you're saying everything's OK, Ma'am?" the officer questioned.

"Yes," Grandma said, without hesitating. The police officer wished us a good day and left. Grandma only said one thing to me for the rest of the day: "Go on downstairs, Mario." I did so, and didn't show my face again until the next day. I cried, wanting to understand Grandma. Did she *like* drama? Did she *like* her kids abusing us? Did she enjoy the dysfunction? Of course she didn't, but I wanted to understand why yet again, Grandma's adult children were being allowed to emotionally abuse us. My desperation to understand this increased considerably when Haily became the reason why our stay in Martins, Virginia ended, leaving bitterness, heartbreak and a family stain in its wake.

Haily first caused our house to split when she—against Uncle Rick's wishes— decided to stay there. Uncle Rick's wife, Marsha, absolutely loathed Haily. Apparently, they'd had some misdealing in the past. In early April, Marsha and Uncle Rick traveled to Martins to check out the upkeep of the house, and to see to some maintenance work Grandma had requested. When Marsha saw Haily living there as well, she told Uncle Rick that she wanted Haily out of the house, or she would sell it. George had gone back to Maryland. Uncle Rick waited until he returned to Delaware to call and demand that Haily leave his house; Haily flatly refused. On the first of these calls from Uncle Rick, no one but Haily could hear what Uncle Rick said, but whatever it was, it sent her into a rage.

"You called down here to ask me to leave. Come down here and put me out, Rick. I dare your ugly ass wife to come down here, too. I will snap her neck."

Grandma tried to diffuse the situation by getting the phone from my aunt's grasp, but it was no use. Things would take a turn for the worse in the forthcoming days.

At about 12 o'clock one April night, everyone was in bed. My brothers were in their room, Grandma in hers and my sisters in their own sleeping quarters. I lay dozing in my bed in the basement family room, where my co-occupants Haily, her fiancé, Shawn and Hasan were also. Sefra slept in Marian and Maria's room. I heard it over Michael's "Keep It in the Closet." Out of nowhere came a loud noise, followed by thunderous footsteps as someone sprinted up the stairs.

"Haily," came her fiancé's voice. He raced after the inclining footsteps, adding his own "much too loud midnight noise" to the din.

"No." came my aunt's voice from the first level. She had been the one running first. She was shrieking.

CHAPTER 7– WHOE VIRGINIA

"Nooo. Can't believe they did that stuff to me. Let me go. *Nooooo.*" The rest of the house was up now, desperate to get to the bottom of this late-night hubbub. The upstairs occupants came down and the basement occupants came up.

"Get off me, Robert. No. Nooooo."

"She's trying to kill herself." Robert yelled, his voice thick with fearful desperation.

"Put the knife down," Grandma said. My throat was tight with fear. I wanted to disappear. I didn't like my aunt, but I also didn't want her to harm herself. Moreover, I was worried about Grandma's blood pressure, which had been out of control for some time. Somehow, Robert managed to get what I later learned was a butcher knife from her. Then, Haily broke down. She became inconsolable. Her voice became muffled as she cried and I knew she was burying her face in Robert's chest.

"He raped me. That goddamn Rick raped me." Her voice rose and her sobs became screeches. "I was a freakin' little girl. I was a little girl. Ma, he raped me." She kept sobbing.

"What are you talkin' about, Haily?" asked Grandma who had been loudly praying to Jesus.

"Rick." Haily screamed. "He raped me. Rick and Nathan did stuff to me. I was a little girl." She had lifted her head from Robert's body by now.

With this bomb shell, I didn't know what to do. Here Haily was, just captured from the threshold of suicide, crying and now saying that our religious pastor uncle had raped her when she was a little girl. Then, she accused my father of having a part in it. At this age, I knew my father had problems, but this news took my confusion about him to a whole new level. Did my family have an incestuous curse hanging over it? Why was this stuff happening? I hated being alive. Haily's news also had a huge effect on Grandma. Now, her "Mother Syndrome" kicked in and she became worried about her heartbroken daughter.

"Haily. What are you talkin' about?"

"They raped me. Every time you went out to church, they raped me. I was five-years-old, and Rick would have me sit on his lap going to church and would touch me while you drove. Aaah. Rick raped me until I was a teenager. I'ma kill that son of a bitch." She wailed some more.

Haily's story took me for a mental spin. Why did I have to hear, witness and suffer with these things at such a young age? Sure, this was my aunt's story, but I suffered as a result of witnessing a suicide attempt, and hearing the vile things she claimed were done to her. I was just a child. At this age, the adverse effect of my mental trauma as a result of my family was increasing.

Life became very strange in the house in the days that followed my aunt's suicide attempt and revelation of sibling molestation. I didn't know what to feel around her. Her presence made me very uncomfortable, as if she were a dangerous animal, poised to strike at any moment. One thing was clear: she and her family weren't going anywhere, no matter what Marsha and Uncle Rick said. She confronted Uncle Rick over the phone.

"I ain't never raped you, girl," Uncle Rick had yelled from the other end. She was using her accusation over him, daring him to remove her from the house. If he did, she would make him pay for it. Haily's fighting didn't just include Uncle Rick. My sister Asia soon got her own one-on-one match-up with Haily.

As Asia was already unhappy living in Martins, far away from her friends and her boyfriend in Maryland, she became more agitated when Haily and her crew moved in with us. After Haily's scary outbursts and suicide attempt, Asia had very little patience for her. Haily and my sister got into it in the worst way possible for a niece and aunt, something I wish my 10-year-old mind never witnessed. It started over the television in the basement.

Asia always watched TV in the morning in the basement, her ritual before Haily and her clan moved in with us. This day, she chose her channel, went to make her breakfast, and then returned to watch her TV program. As the basement's family room area had become the sleeping quarters for Haily, her fiancé and her kids, they thought they had dibs on the only other TV with cable in the house, especially in the morning. When Asia returned and found the TV channel had been turned, while Haily wasn't looking she hurriedly picked up the remote and turned it back to her channel of choice.

"Asia? What are you doin'?" asked Haily in her dramatic voice.

"I'm turning the TV back. I was watching it first and I always watch this channel at this time," Asia responded with a dismissive wave of the hand.

"Asia, turn the TV back. You weren't in here and we're watching something else. Turn it back."

"Y'all can watch TV somewhere else." Asia was clearly done with the conversation and rolled her eyes at Haily. After all, none of us had respect for her after many years of witnessing how she treated Grandma. I sat on the basement steps, fearing what would come next. Asia's last statement had pushed one of Haily's buttons. She got up and tried to take the remote control from Asia.

"Don't touch me. I don't even know why y'all here." A floodgate in Asia had opened.

"What?" screamed Haily, now in Asia's face.

"Get out my face, Haily. Get out my face."

"Or what?" Haily said.

"You need to learn some freakin' respect." By now, Grandma and the rest of the house's occupants were in the basement playing audience to this argument. "You aren't any of our mothers. You need to get your own place. You always

coming around thinking you running shit."
Grandma was shocked by Asia's cursing.

"Shut your mouth, Asia." Grandma screamed.

"You gonna take her side." said Asia, heading for the stairs now. "You ain't never gonna be nothing keep thriving off your mother."

"Bitch, you ain't *got* a mother. That bitch dead. I hated that bitch when she died," said Haily. At these words, my hatred for Haily peaked. I was filled with a relentless rage. Here she was, talking so terribly about my mother whom I had never properly met, and who had been dead for nearly ten years. Again, I wanted to rip Haily to shreds. Already, the raging, angry, retaliatory mentality of my family was rubbing off on me. How could she say something so horrible? I didn't understand.

"Well, at least I ain't trying to commit suicide, hollering with a knife to your own throat," Asia barked as she stormed off to her room two flights up, her twin Adonis following her. Asia and Haily continued to shout insults at one another. Within minutes, Haily had followed Asia all the way to her bedroom on the top floor.

"Get out of my way," I heard. Then, the unthinkable happened. Haily pushed Asia and Asia—full of rage—swung a defensive punch. From that moment, the physical fight began between aunt and niece. Adonis yelled, too.

"Get the fuck off my sister," Adonis's voice boomed, full of rage. As Haily pounced on Asia, pummeling her with punches, Adonis jacked Haily up by the collar, his strength remarkable. Grandma watched, powerless to stop any of it. Adonis, Asia and Haily thrashed about, papers flying and the room's furnishing being shoved and toppled. I waited on the first level, again wishing disappearing acts were possible. My young mind screamed, "Leave my sister alone. Get off of her." I was indescribably afraid.

"Why you letting her do this?" Asia shrieked at Grandma.

"Stop it. Stop it." Grandma screamed at the top of her lungs. She was panting and her voice was screechy. By then, I was standing on the upper landing, the whole ordeal making me still wish I could disappear, but I couldn't. I wanted to purge my memory of all of them. Finally, Haily exited Asia's room, still cursing.

"Them kids ain't got no damn respect, Ma. Told you, you should've given their asses away a long time ago."

Asia was crying and wheezing by now, her asthma now engaged. Someone had called the police. The children were ushered to the basement as the door was answered by Grandma. Moments later, a policeman came into the basement to apprehend Haily. He told her to get dressed.

"I will, Officer," she said, heading for the closet next to the stairs. "You gonna shoot me?" Haily snorted, her voice without fear. I was later told the officer had pointed his gun at her legs.

After all, she was heading for a closet. I was scared that he would kill her in front of me. I hated her, but I didn't want her dead. The policeman led her outside and she was taken to the police station. I'm not sure what became of her there, but she did return later that night.

My sister Asia and Adonis were furious over what had happened and were going to leave. They quickly packed their things, called Nancy to explain the situation to her, and in no time, they were on their way back to Maryland to stay with my grandmother on my Mom's side. They were disgusted with Grandma for putting them in a living situation with Haily again. Asia shouted her disappointments at Grandma, her fury impossible to quench. I heard Grandma talking to Jesus the entire time.

"Lordy." she would scream. "Lordy. They evil, Lord."

I didn't want Adonis and Asia to go. I wanted to beg them to stay but I knew I was inconsequential. I knew if they went, I wouldn't see them for a very long time, and I didn't want that. All of the drama took a toll on Grandma, and she sank into a massive depression. One day after school, my sister Maria and I sat on the basement stairs, listening to Grandma and Haily argue. Actually, it was more like listening to my aunt yell, while Grandma responded with quiet sobs.

"All this mess. I made a mistake," Grandma said, crying.

"What mistake Ma?" Haily yelled.

"With you. All this mess start with you. With you coming around."

"I ain't done shit. Uncle Rick raped me and Nathan's kids ain't got no respect. You gone sit up here and tell me that you don't see that Ma? Uh, Ma?"

Grandma wasn't listening anymore. Her responses told us that she had heard enough. "You. You too much, Haily. Too much."

"What." Haily screamed. "I'm too much? You can forget that. Me and my kids are out of here." She yelled for her kids to get their things together to leave. She vowed that they would find an apartment somewhere. She gave her usual disrespectful farewells: "I'm done. I mean it this time." They did leave that day, but not before Haily completed her ritual task during these unceremonious goodbyes: taking back all gifts she had given the kids and Grandma. She wasted no time taking the TV she had given Grandma for Christmas. Then, they were gone.

The house was now left to Grandma, Marian, Maria, Kevin and me. Kevin had the room to himself, and I had the basement family room to myself. I didn't like the emptiness, but I did enjoy having uninterrupted control of the cable television. I was glad my brother Kevin was still there. I looked up to him, after all, and his presence helped me bare the departure of Adonis and Asia. I did, however, feel sorry for him. He was constantly sad because he wanted to be with Adonis and Asia. Kevin did, however, have a plan to get exactly what he wanted.

At about 5:00 a.m. one Saturday morning in late April, I was up listening to cartoons, and thinking about my Michael Jackson CD that had been destroyed by Grandma a day before. I believe my brother Kevin thought I was asleep. He normally got up early to go to work at the local department store, but my talking clock told me that this hour was far too early. Nosily, I listened to him rummaging around and packing clothes into a bag. There was the "clink" of metal against metal, and the slap and dull rustle of cloth as he deposited his folded clothes and belts into a bag. I was very suspicious. I willed myself to believe that Kevin wouldn't be leaving me as well. I wanted to head for the stairs to get Grandma, but I didn't. I didn't want him to be mad at me for ruining his escape. At the same time, I didn't want him to go. I was rooted to the spot with shock as it dawned on me that Kevin did intend to steal away in the night. When it seemed he was satisfied with his packing, I heard the sound of a pen, scratching against paper resting on a wood surface. Then, without one word to his number-one fan, Kevin gathered his things, opened the outside basement door, and was gone.

I was only ten, but very analytical. Not seeing meant nothing. Per intuition, I knew my brother had just left for good, without Grandma's knowing. I quickly got up and sprinted up the basement and upper level stairs.

"Grandma," I yelled reaching the top landing. Foolishly, I thought she could catch him and persuade my hero not to disappear on me. I couldn't take it again. No father, no older siblings, and no Kevin, too?

"What?" Grandma questioned, sleep still in her voice.

"Kevin is leaving and it's too early for him to go to work," I said, my high voice desperate. She got up and followed me downstairs. I hoped Kevin hadn't gone far. In the end, Grandma didn't have to go after sixteen-year-old Kevin. Something else caught her attention first.

My brother had left Grandma a sweet, but strongly worded letter, bidding her a permanent farewell. He had apologized for doing it this way, but said he could no longer be without his brothers and sisters. I thought, "What about me, Mary and Maria, Kevin? Why are you leaving us?" Grandma remained solemn for a few moments, then she retired to her room, the letter in hand. After praying, she cried bitterly for how things had turned out. She now had three out of nine of the children she had promised to take care of. She had done the best she could, but her tolerance for her disruptive adult kids had split the God-fearing home she had intended to maintain. Indeed, she did cry bitterly.

The notification that Haily had finally moved out wasn't enough to dissuade Marsha from requesting that we leave her house too. She had decided that she wanted nothing more to do with her husband's crazed family, and she wanted to sell the house immediately. Under his wife's demand, Uncle Rick told Grandma that we had to leave at the end of the school year. He put his own mother out of a house with nowhere to go, and didn't give one recitation about it.

Michael was devastated when I told him we were moving. For the first time, I did dread having to lose new friends all over again, but, in the end, as usual, I told myself: "You'll get over it." Grandma got a moving truck, and in early June 1998, two days after the school year ended, everything was packed up, moved into a storage unit and we went off to North Carolina.

We spent several weeks at my Great Grandma's house, whom everyone called Grandma Suzy. She was seventy-five and as mean as a scorpion. She tried reprimanding us by trying to strike us with coffee cups and curse us out for not going outside, playing the same videos repeatedly, and more. This would be our home indefinitely, as there was nowhere for us back in Virginia, DC or Maryland. As kids, we really didn't know this. Grandma kept everything from us. This was probably a blessing, as it allowed us kids to have a blast in North Carolina. There were countless barbecues, lots of attention from my great aunts and uncles, and many movies to watch.

Grandma and Haily reconciled again and it was Haily who invited us to come stay with her family in an apartment they were renting in Martins. The mental trauma cycle was in replay, and I was wary. Before July had fully had its share of the calendar, Grandma, Marian, Maria and I were in a car with my Great Uncle Jerry, Grandma's brother, on the way to Virginia to meet Haily. He was escorting us, and would turn around to head straight back to North Carolina the day after.

It was a rather uncomfortable reunion. I hadn't forgotten the awful things she had done and I wondered why Grandma was subjecting us to her again after only three months. She felt she needed Haily, and, I knew to some degree, we did need her for somewhere to live. We had no one else.

We went to stay with Haily, Robert and her kids in a two-bedroom apartment on the outskirts of Martins. The days there are ones I wish I could forget. Here, we found out just how sadistic and troubled our cousins Hasan and Shawn were. First, Maria, Marian and I spent most of our days arguing with them, as they tried to remind us that we were deadbeats and had nobody that cared about us outside of their mother. They told us we'd be nothing without their mother, and sadly, I believed them. As a result of this knowledge, I cried bitterly. Shawn would blast DMX'X's music all day while Hasan plotted fun for his private part.

Within a week of staying there, Hasan approached us with an incestuous proposition, attempting to have sex with one of my sisters, and trying to force me to do the same. Had he been influenced by hearing what Uncle Rick had allegedly done to his Mother, Haily? Why was my family so messed up?

The stay in the apartment on the outskirts of Martins—like all the other places we had stayed—was fairly short. By early August, the whole occupancy of that apartment was staying with one of Haily's friends in Burgson, Virginia. On the first day of our stay with Haily's friend, we were dropped off at a nearby 7/11 and told to walk down the street to the house. Haily and Robert had business to take care of and drove away. Grandma purchased sandwiches with her food stamps for us, and we walked down to the stranger's home. We felt sorry for ourselves. I was reminded that we were very poor. At our new temporary living quarters, the family drama continued, but this time, with an outside audience.

The first two weeks at Haily's friend's house, Mary, were eventful. I quickly made friends with her son Chris, who was one year my junior. We went swimming, to the park and we loved to play video games together in the basement. I was blind and he considered it to be a badge of honor to be my friend and helper. Grandma put a stop to me going swimming with Chris and his British next-door neighbors because "we don't know them." It brings a smile to my face when I think of how I cried and begged to go, and as a gesture of consolation, nine-year-old Chris promised: "Mario, don't worry about it. I promise, watch, when we're older, I'm gonna take you to the pool everyday. I swear that. Watch."

My sisters and I buried ourselves in movies again to cope. We were stuck with Haily, with no way out. We watched *The Little Rascals*, Jim Carey's *Liar Liar*, *The Lion King* and Tina Turner's *What's Love Got to Do with It* over and over. For me, it was like going to a different place. *The Little Rascals* really gave me that feeling. I imagined I was in the romantic boat scene with the girl, or I was the stuck up rich kid with the golden singing voice. This movie became a vital medicine when things crumbled again in the aftermath of a sibling fight that temporarily split us all up again.

Marian, Maria, Chris, his five-year-old sister, and his two teenage female cousins and I were playing in the basement of Mary's three story, three-bedroom house one stifling summer night in mid-August. Grandma, Haily, Hasan, Shawn, Mary, Mary's Aunt Ethel and Sefra were watching TV in the upstairs family room. Marian and Maria were fighting and boy, were they throwing thick verbal mud. Maria had the tendency to lose all reason and control when she was angry. The Bonds' curse for dysfunction was rubbing off on us. In front of Chris and the others, Maria threatened to tell Grandma what Marian had almost done with Hasan. She was angry that Marian refused to give her a chance with the video game console. As I lay on the carpet, I hoped with every fiber of my being that Maria would calm down before she caused a thunderstorm. I knew my sister enough to know that if she got too angry, she would deliver on her threats. I wanted to forget all about that night. I got up and sat on the basement stairs.

"You better not. Shut up, Maria. That's not true."

"Yes it is," Maria said, her voice thick with a child's evil.

"Hasan put his ding ding inside Marian to have sex with her."

"What? Stop playing," said Chris's eldest female cousin who, prior to this moment, had been laughing at Marian and Maria's argument. She wasn't laughing now.

"Yep," Maria continued. "He did, twice, talkin' about how it was too big to go in." That did it. Marian was sent over the top.

To my utter horror, Marian raced past me up the stairs, bolted into the family room and without preamble, screamed, "Grandma, Maria down there telling Shanika and them that I had sex with Hasan." I knew that Hasan had unsuccessfully tried to have sex with Marian, and Maria knew this too. Why was she talking as if it had actually happened? Nothing could have prepared us for the shriek that came from Haily. Her "*What.*" could have awakened the sun, I was sure of it. I panicked, quickly leaving the stairs to find my way into the rec room. From what we could hear from the rec room, Haily pounced on Hasan immediately. There were series of slaps and smacks, mixed with Haily's crazed screaming. Grandma's voice, talking again to Jesus, joined the din as well. Within minutes, they were on their way downstairs.

Haily dragged Hasan into the only bedroom in the basement and closed the door as she continued thrashing him. He screamed: "They lying, Ma. They crazy, Ma. It was Mario and Maria that was doing that." Those words struck Haily and she came out of the room. I was now sitting on the carpet with my legs folded in the rec room, toying with my shirt. Haily walked in front of me and stood there. I could smell her sweat and perfume as she towered over me.

"Hasan said that it was you and Maria doing that stuff and not my son. Was it Hasan, Mario?"

I remained silent.

"Did it happen, Mario?" It took ages, but I told her yes. I wanted to say, "Yes your sick son did all of that and tried to get me to do things too." But I figured yes was as far as I needed to go.

"Shawn, Sefra." my aunt screamed. "Get down here and get in this room. Y'all ain't gonna have anything else to do with Nathan's nasty kids."

Nasty. My mind screamed, "But we didn't do anything. Sure, Maria forced Marian to spill the beans but, *your* kids were the sick ones." Haily believed her kids over us. This night broke

Grandma's heart, and caused her blood pressure to skyrocket. Shanika, her sister, Marian, Maria and I walked to the park later that night with Grandma. I couldn't find a way to lift this doom. It was all-consuming. Haily was livid and she was gathering her kids to leave right away.

"I hate myself. If I had never been born, and if we never came here, Grandma wouldn't have to deal with all of this," I said, tears flooding my eyes as I clung to Shanika's arm.

"Don't say that, Mario. Don't say that. Your Grandma loves you." It didn't matter what Shanika said. I wanted to die and disappear. I was worried more about Grandma than anything else. There was no staying in a child's place. I thought that if we disappeared, specifically me, all of her problems would go with the disappearance.

Somehow, in no time, Haily and Robert managed to score themselves an apartment in the heart of Burgson. She and her kids moved into it while Grandma, Marian, Maria and I remained at Mary's house. Haily was again "done" with all of us, including Grandma. Because it was shrouded in incestuous accusation, it was a painful fallout, but this time, instead of years, it lasted only a month. I believe Haily knew the truth, but it killed her inside because of what Uncle Rick had allegedly done to her as a child. Towards the end of August, I first learned of Haily's increasing change of heart when she secretly paid for a church dinner for us at an all-you-can-eat seafood restaurant.

By the start of the school year, a day after Labor Day, we were living in Haily's three-bedroom apartment, now forced to again be around the people who would throw us under the bus at a moment's notice. For much of the time at this apartment, I hardly interacted with my male cousins. I slept in the room with all girls and at times, I hated it. Haily made us feel like roaches and being there was akin to permanently living on eggshells. Nevertheless, this period in my journey would serve to be the most important, pivotal moment of my young life. I treasure the years that followed as they brought me to the people who had an immense influence on who I am today.

CHAPTER 8–THE UNSTOPPABLE FOURSOME

On the first day of school, Grandma registered my sisters and me at Rogerson Elementary, and Haily registered Sefra at the same school. All four of us were in the sixth grade. We triplets were on the threshold of turning eleven. I liked the school, even though I hardly did any work. Things were quite hard at home and Grandma did her best to give us lunch for school. Sometimes, all we had was bread; Grandma was afraid to ask Haily for anything.

I only spent a month at Rogerson before I was transferred to another elementary school. It took some serious convincing for Grandma to agree for me to attend a different school. In retrospect, changing schools was the appropriate thing to do at that point. At Rogerson, I didn't do any schoolwork because the school didn't have a permanent teacher of the blind on site. Instead, I was assigned a vision instructor from the Burgson County vision program named Ms. Mosamotee, who had several schools to which she had to report. It was she who suggested that I change schools this time.

"This school is just not set up to serve Mario. I mean, really, he could eventually thrive here, but he'd be behind most of the time. Tree Front is still a public school, Mrs. Bonds, and he would get one-on-one time with a vision teacher that's always at the school. I'm an itinerate instructor."

"I don't want him going to no special school without regular kids," Grandma had shot back during this conversation.

"Mrs. Bonds, it's *not* a special school. He'll still be assigned to a mainstream sixth-grade class, but he'll have a resource and technology lab with special technology available to him and a permanent instructor that'll be there all day."

For much of September, Grandma was quite conflicted about changing my school. Finally, she relented—well, almost. The Vision Program had persuaded her to at least bring me to tour the school. They told her that she could come and see the facility firsthand, and then judge. I will never forget the day we received a tour of Tree Front Elementary. It brought me to Zoey, Paul and Ciara.

Tree Front Elementary was a one-level, fairly small building that served first through sixth grades. Grandma guided me through the front doors, straight for a while and then into a room off to the right. My nose immediately picked up the distinct smell of electronics, markers and construction paper. Inside the room, I heard student voices off to the left and adults off to the right. I was first introduced to Ms. Goldberg, who would be my permanent vision teacher while at Tree Front. She told me that she would be there every day, all day to help me. I was shy and quiet. I hardly moved my hand as Ms. Goldberg tried to shake it.

"Hi Mario," she said excitedly. "Mario, I want you to meet some of the other students, OK? They're in the sixth grade as well." She took my hand and led me away from Grandma, off to the left of the room where I had heard the other voices. The marker smell got stronger.

"Zoey, Paul, Ciara. I want you guys to meet Mario. He might be coming here." Ms. Goldberg sat me down at what felt to be a rectangular table.

"Hi, I'm Zoey," said a girl's high voice directly across from me.

"Hi," I responded, my throat tight. I really didn't want to meet these kids. They all had visual impairments and I didn't like that. I didn't want to mingle with other handicapped kids. I wanted to be with my sighted peers. I was missing the few friends I recently made at Rogerson.

"I'm Paul Nguamsanith," said a boy's goofy voice to my right. His voice was very breathy, as if he were permanently hoarse. I shook his hand.

"And I am Ciara Khymes," said another female's voice, diagonally across from me. I took this to mean that she was seated to the left of Zoey, across from Paul.

"So, are you blind?" asked Zoey without preamble. I didn't answer right away. I was struck by her straightforwardness.

"Yes, totally blind." I responded, thinking this girl was quite nosy. I knew her question meant we all would start discussing our various vision issues and I didn't want to do that. I wanted to leave and return to Rogerson. Where was Grandma anyway?

"I still have vision," Zoey continued. "But it's a little difficult to explain. I don't have any peripheral vision and I have a few other issues, so I still need to read Braille and do everything else like kids like us."

"What's perifio vision?" I asked, confused by this new word.

"Well, I can't see out of the sides of my eyes so I have to turn my head to see things." she explained.

"Well, I'm Paul, as I said," began Paul. I noticed he was annoyingly fidgety. "I can see out of one eye so I'm legally blind. My right eye is a wax eye that I have to take out and wash from time to time." With that revelation, I felt like throwing up. I was thankful I had both of my real eyes still rolling in my head, even if the lights were out.

"It's nothing serious though," Paul continued. "And, Ciara, you."

"Oh, yup," Ciara began. She was quite animated and I despised her for it. "I have retinitis pigmentosa. I will eventually lose more vision, but now, I am legally blind and I read large print like Paul."

"Oh," I said, feeling silly, "I'm totally blind and I read Braille."

"Guys," cut in Ms. Goldberg, who had been standing behind me the entire time, "Mario's gonna go for a tour of the school with his Grandma.

He will probably attend school here." With that, we said our "Nice to meet yous" and I left with Grandma, Ms. Mosamotee and Ms. Goldberg to check out the rest of the school.

"This is Mario," said Ms. Goldberg. We had reached the last destination on our short tour of Tree Front, Mr. Parker's sixth-grade classroom. Funny that I wasn't even registered yet and they had already chosen a class for me.

"Hey Mario," said Mr. Parker. He towered above all of us. I took him to be probably over six feet tall. I later found out that my guess was correct. "I look forward to working with you Mario."

"Nice to meet you," I said shyly. I wanted to be with my sisters back at Rogerson so badly. Unfortunately, Grandma's mind had already been made up by the time we got to Mr. Parker's classroom. Attending school with my sisters was no longer a possibility. Apparently, while I met with my new co-blind associates, the staff of the Vision program and Tree Front had been brainwashing Grandma, or so I thought. I was registered that same day and started attending school at Tree Front two days later.

Within a week at Tree Front, I regretted how I treated Zoey, Paul and Ciara on the day I first met them. Moreover, I hated myself for my bad thoughts about them; it wasn't their fault they had visual impairments. They were awesome people. How could I have ever thought them to be revolting? They exhibited a sincere interest in me, my life and my disability. In the same week, I met Michele Weil, who was to be my orientation and mobility specialist. Michele, as I was told to call her, was kind and direct. She had a very strong inner-city Baltimore accent. It made her pronounce my name as "Mah-rio" instead of "Mar-io." She was the first instructor to teach me how to independently cross a street as a blind traveler, and she later became one of many mother figures for me in my teenage years and adulthood.

I was also introduced to Ms. Swenson, a small-framed, professorial vision instructor who worked one-on-one with Ciara three times a week. I met Ms. Kirsten, a rather plump, short white woman with long brown hair. I grew to really like Ms. Kirsten. She exuded a mother's energy in everything she did for me and every word she spoke. Lastly, I was reintroduced to Mr. Parker, my sixth-grade teacher. For some strange reason, I was kept from his class during my first few days at Tree Front. He would prove to be an awesome teacher. Zoey, Paul, Ciara and I would spend the start of our mornings in the resource room, go to Mr. Parker's class by mid-morning, through lunchtime and half of the afternoon, before returning to the resource room to complete our day.

Tree Front was a far cry from the school in Martins, and Hunsville County for that matter. I was introduced to a world of technology that I never knew existed. Moreover, the level of independence and accountability that Ms. Goldberg and her colleagues placed on us was vital. In no time, I became a technology whiz, acting as the resource room troubleshooter for the Braille N' Speak, a small note taker device, akin to a personal digital assistant, but configured with a Braille keyboard and a voice.

Zoey, Paul, Ciara and I became an unbreakable foursome. However, I became particularly close to Zoey, so close that her family was the first family ever allowed to pick me up, keep me out late, and to have me to their house. It was said that Zoey and I were joined at the hip. Our friendship was innocent and beautiful; I had made a female best friend. My first indication of this was Tree Front sixth-grade dance.

"Mario, are you going to the fall dance?" Michele had asked me in one of our mobility lessons. We were in front of the school building, practicing how to cross streets without traffic.

"No, we don't have a car. I won't be able to get here or home," I told her.

"Well, perhaps Zoey's mom can pick you up."

"I don't know," I replied. "I don't know her mom and I don't want to be a third wheel." I remembered the phrase "third wheel" from a TV show I watched a day earlier.

"I'm sure she wouldn't mind," said Michele, "I'll give her a call with you after our lesson."

"This isn't a good idea. I don't wanna be trouble for her."

"Mario," she said in an exasperated voice I had gotten used to. Back in the school, Michele and I went straight to the front office where we used the phone to call Zoey's mother at work.

"She just answered the phone. Are you gonna talk?" Michele asked, tapping my hand with the phone. I shook my head and repeated how much I didn't want to be a third wheel for Zoey's mother. I was so scared and nervous.

"Hi Karen," Michele began into the phone, her voice polite. "I've got Mario here, who you've met. He's a little shy and afraid to speak to you but, I'm calling because Mario would like to go to the dance tonight, but doesn't have a ride. He was wondering whether he could go with Zoey this evening, and if you could pick him up."

"Oh, I'd love to bring him along," came Mrs. Jacobs' voice from the other end.

"Great." replied Michele.

"He was afraid to ask me?" Mrs. Jacobs asked, the sound of a smile in her voice.

"Yes, he said he didn't wanna be a third wheel, but I explained to him that it doesn't hurt to ask."

"He's cute. He's not a third wheel. Anyways, absolutely, I have no problem with that at all. I will call Aubrey [Ms. Goldberg] and talk to his Grandma this afternoon to get his address."

"OK, great, Karen. Thanks so much."

"Thank you." I finally found my voice.

"Mario says thanks."

"Awww. He's a sweetie. Tell him he's welcome." Once Michele had terminated the call, I got a positive lecture on learning how to ask because asking could never hurt. Michele told me I should never be afraid to ask for anything. The next order of business was to ask Grandma.

Once the special ed bus had dropped me off, and my sister Marian had apprehended me, I was pumped up to ask Grandma about the dance that night. Truthfully, I resented coming home, but I would have to ignore those feelings tonight. Inside, I could taste that the apartment was full of a lot of tension and I despised being around it. Thanks to Haily, I was reminded in no time just how much I *should* resent coming home.

That evening, before I could ask Grandma about the dance, I had my feelings hurt worse than ever by Haily. She took my self-esteem and dashed it against the wall. While Grandma encouraged me and told me that she knew I would be just fine at Tree Front as we sat in the family room, Haily was cleaning in the kitchen and had overheard Grandma's praise.

"You got a good brain, boy," said Grandma. For some unfathomable reason, Haily abruptly joined the conversation, and her words shook my self-esteem.

"Momma, I don't know why you think that boy is smart. That boy ain't smart. He always walkin' around here screaming big words like 'indubitably' and all that and you sucking it up. Mario isn't smart, Momma. He is pretending."

I was absolutely stunned. I was eleven, listening to my aunt try to persuade my grandma that I was dumb. I sat in silence, my heart pounding my chest. Grandma merely sucked her teeth and said nothing.

"That boy isn't special and he ain't got the brain you think he does." Haily was calling me stupid. I wasn't the brightest child, but I had some intelligence worth remarking. Why didn't she know this? I loathed Haily with a passion during this conversation. She made me feel dumb as I started to believe her words. Perhaps I was in fact a blind, dumb and worthless boy. When Haily left for her bedroom, and Grandma and I retired to the room where she, my sisters, Sefra and I slept, I mustered all of the resolve I could to deflect Haily's dumbing-down of my brain. I had to discuss the dance with Grandma anyway.

"Grandma," I whined. Grandma was folding clothes as she watched Oprah. "They're having a dance tonight at the school and Zoey's mother said she can pick me up. Can I go?"

"Yes," Grandma said without hesitation. I was elated, but stunned. Was it because Zoey was also visually impaired that Grandma was relenting on her rule of me not leaving with people that she didn't know well? Naturally, I didn't press it. Now, I just had to wait to get picked up at 7:00 p.m., the time Mrs. Jacobs had agreed upon when she had spoken with Ms. Goldberg earlier that afternoon. When they arrived, I was happier than I could ever remember, but I was also afraid. Due to my family's constant remarks about white people, and how my family tried to make me understand that whites don't really care for blacks, I felt uneasy about being out with new white people again. Was I dumb like Haily had said? Was this why I was stupidly out with white people? Was this a dumb decision made by my eleven-year-old dumb brain? I knew Grandma wasn't prejudiced, but she considered herself making sure I never got too comfortable with whites when she would tell me these things. I understood the period in which Grandma grew up. I couldn't say much about Haily's prejudices, though. For much of the night, though I thoroughly enjoyed myself, I had to constantly tell myself that I shouldn't care about what my family told me about whites, or what Haily said about me being dumb. This wasn't the 1960s. Zoey was my friend and that's all that mattered.

I happily left the house as Grandma watched *Wheel of Fortune*, and my other family members all watched TV in their rooms. I was going out to have fun.

And I did. The sixth-grade dance was awesome. Zoey, her mother and her mother's best friend and I danced like crazed people, although at first, I was very nervous. Mrs. Jacobs worked to break me out of my uncomfortable shell, and once out, I let loose. We tangoed, twisted about, jumped and pumped our fists to every hit on the charts at that time.

After the dance, I was shocked to find out that they were going to feed me. We went to a restaurant named Artey's, which would become my favorite restaurant in later years. Zoey and I laughed at the sound of "chocolate moose." I had never heard of that and I sincerely thought it might have been moose meat, cooked in chocolate. On the way home, I got my first introduction to country music, Zoey's favorite genre. I heard a catchy tune playing in which the skilled country singer repeated the phrase: "Wide Open Spaces." I found out that the enjoyable music was that of the Dixie Chicks and the lead singer sang about a girl who needed wide open spaces, and room to make a big mistake. I liked that.

When I returned home, quite late, I was still excited and thankful for such a great time. I had the weekend to look forward to and the dance was a nice way to start it off. All was still in the apartment as I quietly felt my way down the hall to assume my place on the floor in the room where my sisters, cousin Sophia and Grandma slept. I put in my headphones and listened to Whitney Houston and Mariah Carey tell me to believe. I recognized the song from the *Prince of Egypt* film Zoey's parents had taken us to see two weeks

earlier. It was on this night that I decided Mariah
Carey would be my favorite female singer.

My friendship with Zoey grew for the rest of
1998 and well into 1999. Her parents had me over
for visits quite often. On one such visit in early
1999, as I had never seen the *Titanic* movie, and
Zoey was a Titanic fanatic, we planned to watch it.
Before watching the movie, she and I went upstairs
to check out her piano. I wasn't yet a skilled pianist,
so I was in awe of anyone who could play well.
Zoey astonished me with her playing of Celine
Dion's hit, "My Heart Will Go On." I was jealous and
didn't want to play for her once it was my turn.
Instead, I suggested that we go on to the basement
to see the movie. Her mom gave us quesadillas for
lunch and we were in heaven.

As 7:00 p.m. neared, Zoey and I started to
dread my departure. Mrs. Jacobs told Grandma
that Zoey's father, Keith, would drop me off once
he had returned from a flying trip. Zoey's father
was a pilot for American Airlines. As Mrs. Jacobs
busied herself upstairs, Zoey and I sat on the couch
in the basement. We knew it was only a matter of
moments before Mr. Jacobs would return home.
We laughed about silly things and goofily whined to
one another.

"I don't wanna go."

"I don't want you to go." Followed by more
fits of laughter.

"Hey, there's a way to show them that I
don't wanna go," I said to Zoey.

"How?" Zoey asked, hiccupping with laughter.

"Turn my way." Zoey and I positioned ourselves in a human knot. We sat at opposite ends of the couch with our legs on the couch, facing one another. We peculiarly intertwined our legs and grabbed hands. It was an innocent gesture. I had nothing inappropriate in mind when I suggested it and at first, I truly thought her mother would think nothing of it. I thought she'd get the joke. However, my feeling about our awkward position changed when my 11-year-old member became erect. I didn't understand it. Why was it happening? I was laughing and having innocent fun. I then realized that Zoey's hands were the softest hands I had ever touched. They were so soft that it seemed unbelievable. Her hands were the closest to silk that human flesh could get. In that moment, I realized that Zoey and I should stop this weird position right away. She didn't understand, but I did. Her mom would see the position to be sexual. We had to stop. When I left, I feared Zoey would tell her mom what had happened in innocent silliness, and her mom wouldn't understand. All weekend, I feared for what I would meet on Monday morning in school.

Monday morning did come but without trouble. Instead, school continued to be the blast it had been since I started at Tree Front. My interest in the school increased when I learned that Ms. Goldberg had a reading agenda for us. As I loved having books read to me, I was ecstatic. I was surprised to find out that we all would be made to read together each afternoon in our resource room. This would definitely force my Braille skills to improve. That year, we read *Libby* on Tuesday, and the *One Hundred Penny Box*. Both of these books are on my list of favorites.

At Tree Front, things were on the up-and-up. I had friends, great teachers and an escape from home. Michele cared for my educational and musical development as well. It was she who got me my first piano lesson.

"Mario, there's a program called Music Link. Blind students from George Mason University and other colleges will teach blind younger students for free and, they'll give you a piano to practice on. Do you wanna do it?" She asked this during a mobility lesson outside the school building one day.

"Yes, I guess," I said goofily and laughed. For some reason that I couldn't ever explain, nearly everything Michele said made me laugh. I loved her accent; therefore, the way she said certain things would crack me up. Nearly a week later, Michele had fantastic news for me regarding Music Link.

"Do the lessons start now?" I asked Michele one day when she pulled me from Mr. Parker's class.

"Yeah, the piano teacher is here. She just got here."

"My lessons will be here at Tree Front?" I questioned.

"Yeah, they agreed to allow Kara to teach you in the music room. That's her name. She's totally blind like you and her name is Kara." With that, Michele led me to the music room. As we approached the room, I could hear someone playing the piano and my heart pace increased.

"This lady's a professional," I said to Michele excitedly. Michele let out her all-too-famous laugh, which was more like a hiccup.

"Kara." Michele called out as we entered the room. The playing stopped.

"Michele." Kara said excitedly, "Is my student ready for his doom?" We all laughed.

"Mario this is Kara, Kara this is Mario Bonds. He's also totally blind." Michele helped me find Kara's hand. I was made to sit next to Kara on the piano bench and Michele left me to my first piano lesson.

The lesson started with Kara doing the most amazing thing I'd ever experienced up to that point in my life. She played "My Heart Will Go On" from the *Titanic* movie. I was stunned. Zoey had nothing on Kara. She made the piano sound like it took little effort at all to play it. Once she was finished with the song for the third time I had requested it, I begged her to teach me that as my first song. At first, she refused, thinking the song was too complex for me. Normally, she would have been right, but I had an ear and a thirst for music that no one would keep me from. She did begin teaching me the song that day and it paid off. I worked on the song tirelessly at home on the electric piano Music Link had lent me. Eventually, I could play it almost as well as Kara.

Conveniently, I began taking a violin class and for the 1999 spring concert. We were going to play "My Heart Will Go On," with the violins playing the melody of course. I begged the chorus teacher to allow me to play the piano part since I learned it in the key of G (the easiest key for me at that time), and the violinist were already playing it in G. Willing to give me a moment to shine, the chorus teacher agreed. Even though I hit a few wrong chords the first time I practiced with the violin class, she still allowed me to play. By the night of the spring concert, I was perfect.

Grandma, Maria, Marian and Sefra accompanied me to the concert. The concert was broadcasted on the school's closed-circuit television so that the other performers waiting in the classrooms could see it. Although I was nervous, I played like a champion. I was so happy that my family was there. Afterwards, I was told that I had gotten a standing ovation. At that time, I hadn't the foggiest idea what on earth a standing ovation was, but I was glad I had gotten one. I was on top of the world. My popularity increased dramatically after this concert.

My newfound joy of music and the urge to perform in front of people didn't stop at the spring concert. Zoey and I performed in two talent shows that year. In the first one, we performed our favorite country ballad, "From This Moment" by Shania Twain. In the second talent show, at the close of the school year, we performed "I Want it That Way" by the Backstreet Boys. I loved NSYNC and the Backstreet Boys. It didn't matter to me that my sisters called me a homo for this; I loved them and their music anyway. It was ironically Maria's fault why I loved these groups so much. She made me learn the lyrics to all of their songs, and she and I would sit for hours, recording ourselves singing with the Backstreet Boys and NSYNC. After recording each song on both boy-band albums, we would play them back and listen. We also would record ourselves reenacting our favorite movies. We used anything in the room to help us make sound effects and we would have fun for hours.

The music hysteria continued when the sixth grade class put on the production of *Lewis and Clark*. I even had a small part in it. I was bursting with excitement as I stood on the floor in front of the risers where my other classmates sat, and was later walked out to the microphone to deliver my lines. The gymnasium was filled to capacity with family and friends of every student in the sixth-grade chorus. That year, a musical me was born. I knew then that there was no other joy like performing, inspiring and giving people a good time.

Of course, my time at Tree Front came with its rough edges as well. At times, Mrs. Goldberg was a very tough instructor. As if we were five, she created Velcro cutouts of our hands and placed them on the tabletop in our resource room, and we were forced to place our hands on them at all times during instruction; she thought we were too fidgety. Zoey's mom complained and requested that the principal visit our room to assess the situation. When the principal did come, Ciara, Zoey, Paul and I let loose all of our frustrations about Mrs. Goldberg, her antics and her mean streaks. Needless to say, those Velcro hands came up and the principle gave her a good telling-off.

When I realized that the sixth grade would soon come to an end, I felt a little sad. I was so in love with Tree Front and my new friends that I didn't want us to part. Due to moving so much, I had already made and lost friends too many times. I wasn't sure whether I'd be moving again, but I definitely thought I'd be losing my new friends. My sadness left when I found out that I wouldn't be losing my closest friends Paul, Zoey and Ciara after all.

"You guys are gonna go to Hamax Secondary next year," said Mrs. Goldberg during instruction one day.

"What's that?" we all said in stereo.

"It's just like the set-up here, where your vision teacher will be with you all day instead of being itinerate. However, it is a secondary school which means it has middle school and high school in it. We are taking you guys on a field trip to see

Hamax tomorrow and your parents are coming too."

I fell in love with Hamax as soon as I stepped foot in it. It was massive and felt more like a college building rather than a public school. Since the county had struck gold by sending me to Tree Front, Grandma was more than happy to allow them to make the decision for my next school. Grandma loved Hamax as much as I did. Without hesitation, Paul and Zoey's parents agreed to send them to Hamax. We were stunned when Ciara's mom said that she'd rather Ciara go to the middle school in her neighborhood, Herndon Middle. Ciara's mom couldn't be dissuaded. She didn't want her child bussed across the county to Hamax. In the end, we had to accept that we wouldn't see Ciara in the seventh grade with us. Our foursome would be reduced by one.

When the end of the sixth grade did come, I met it with mixed feelings. I was going to Miss Zoey, Ciara and Paul over the summer. We had no phone where I lived, so there was no way to call them. I knew I was destined to spend my summer cooped up in the same room with my sisters and Cousin Sefra. I wasn't happy about that, but there wasn't anything to do about it. To my utter surprise, the summer of 1999 did bring a significant change, and the change came with serious consequences.

CHAPTER 9— SEVENTH GRADE MILLENNIUM

The summer of 1999 brought with it a huge surprise. At the end of July, Haily told my sisters and me that we would be moving into our own place. She had found a home in Oats, Virginia for Grandma and us. I was elated. I would get back all of my things in storage, or so I thought.

"Well, the storage unit was lost, Momma, and they sold everything," said Haily a day before the move. I was flabbergasted.

Because my cousin Sefra was so close to Marian and Maria, Grandma agreed that Sefra could stay with us, and by July 30, the move was underway. On this day, Haily and I drove to the new house, while my sisters, cousins and grandmother went to find moving materials.

"You hear that music Mario?" my aunt asked in her dramatic voice.

"Yes. I like it," I replied in the timid voice I often used when talking to Haily. I was always insecure and apprehensive around her.

"Can you tell me the instruments that are playin'?" she asked.

"Lead guitar, bass guitar, organ, drums and the sax."

"Very good. They have a bit of strings in the background."

"Well, finally you all have y'all wish: your own home." With that, I felt the car perform its familiar back-and-forth motion as my aunt parallel parked. I had know idea how Grandma and Haily were making a house possible for us. She and I headed into what would be my new home for the next three months.

I was elated to find that for the first time, I would have my own room. The house was a three-level townhome on the corner of the street. Grandma's, Sefra's and my room were on the very top floor. The middle floor housed the kitchen, dining room and the living room, while my sisters had the whole basement to themselves. I was in heaven knowing that I was living in a nice house and that it was ours—or so we thought. I was also glad that Sefra was there. Haily and Grandma had worked out a deal that Haily would pay for Sefra's boarding to help with the rent.

My glee in the new home increased when cable TV was installed and a telephone was turned on. I now felt in league with Zoey, Ciara and Paul. I had a house, cable TV and a telephone just like them. One day in early August, I headed up to the kitchen to use the phone for the first time. Paul had told me his telephone number several times during the school year, and by sheer luck, my brain hadn't deleted it. I dialed his number and heard: "Hello?" Bingo. It was Paul's hoarse and solemn voice.

"Paul. It's Mario."

"Mario... What, huh, hey. Hey. How are you?" I decided to rush the conversation; I wasn't sure whether I was allowed to use the phone anyway. Afterwards, I felt pumped up and couldn't wait to start seventh grade at Hamax Secondary. The conversation with Paul reminded me how much I missed my friends. School was due to start the day after Labor Day, and boy was I ready.

Grandma was quite content with her new living arrangements as well. She busied herself with cleaning, cooking, and washing clothes, unpacking things and arranging furniture. I was happy that she could again act as head of household, giving orders and making demands on the adolescent house slaves, we children. My sisters and Sefra were assigned weeks for kitchen duty and Grandma set up rules for when the telephone couldn't be used. For much of August, MTV, BET, Cartoon Network, WPGC 95.5 FM, 93.9 WKYS FM, Z-104 FM and Grandma's favorite, Heaven 1580 AM kept us entertained, although I was merely burying myself in these forms of entertainment to forget my growing depression. But at the end of August, I am pained to admit that I tried to commit suicide.

When I was watching cartoons, singing or sleeping, I was quite content, but when these activities weren't in full swing, I was miserable. During this period, my sisters were quite unkind to me. I felt like a worthless human being, living and breathing with no purpose. Actually, I felt like God's biggest accident. Most times when I ask my sisters to make me something to eat, or to help me with something I couldn't do myself, they complained, would refuse and sometimes even called me names. Grandma would be gone from the house, and I would sometimes sit hungry for hours, desperately hoping that my sisters would help me get something to eat.

"Hold on," would be their response sometimes, followed by another "Hold on" two or three hours later. I begged them at times, but to no avail.

I cried nearly every day, cursing God for making me and destining me for blindness. I wanted to disappear so that I could never be a burden on my preteen sisters and Grandma ever again. My sisters' annoyance with looking out for me was so transparent that oftentimes Sefra complained about their treatment of me and she occasionally stepped in to help. I understand now that my sisters were children too, coping with our tumultuous misfortunes in their own way. Nevertheless, the bevy of emotional strife caused by everyone from Haily on down had me calling for my grave.

One Saturday morning after watching the cartoon *A Pup Named Scooby Doo*, I ran a bath, put in bubbles and sank into the tub. I was singing Gloria Estefan's verse in the song "Music of My Heart" with NSYNC. I purposely deepened my prepubescent voice in order that I might imitate Gloria's impressive singing. "You were the one always on my side ..." My young mind was flooded with many thoughts of worthlessness, purposelessness and wanting to disappear forever. I laid down in the tub face first. I took a deep breath and plunged my head under water. I trembled as the hot water caressed my frame and flooded my ears. As I lay there, fully submerged, what I thought to be a beautiful decision came to me. Finally, I realized that I did have a painless way out. I decided that I could lay there without breathing until I fell unconscious. Then, when my body did the natural act of gulping for oxygen, the water would flood into my lungs and drown me and I wouldn't have to experience any of the associated pain of drowning. Determined to end the horror I thought my life to be, I willed myself to stay there under water, the bubbles crackling in my ears. I even started counting the seconds.

Once I'd counted to two and a half minutes, things changed; the danger mounted. I started to get dizzy and a loud whistling started in either my ears or my brain; I couldn't tell which. It seemed as if the water was closing in on me; I was becoming a part of the water. My throat constricted and bubbles began to pop from my nostrils and mouth. I could feel my heart begging for my lungs to do their job, but they wouldn't. I wouldn't let them. The whistling got louder and I could hear my heart beating in my ear and just as things began to spin and become impossible to bear, I splashed up for air. I sat, gasping with my back against the side of the bath tub, in disbelief of what I had almost done to myself. By the grace of God, I failed my suicide attempt. I had been seconds away from blacking out. I had almost reached death, an escape from my horrid life but, at the last minute, God handed me an ounce of reason.

A week before school started, Hamax Secondary held an orientation for seventh graders. Burgson County was even sending a bus to transport me to orientation. I was horrified. I was desperate to see Zoey and Paul again, yes, but anxious about starting a new school that had high-schoolers roaming around with seventh and eight graders. At Hamax for orientation, I was guided to the gym where I sat with other students who needed vision services. There, I met Tomoko Endo, a small-framed Japanese girl who would become a good friend while at Hamax. For some reason unknown to me, Paul and Zoey didn't attend orientation. Tomoko and I hit it off right away, talking and laughing about everything imaginable. Tomoko was sweet, funny, kindhearted, but very tough on herself. I later observed that Tomoko took academia seriously, and became quite depressed whenever she faltered with an academic task. In later years, her serious outlook on studies would become comical material amongst Zoey, Paul and me.

After the portion of orientation in the gym ended, Tomoko and I were taken to what would be our Resource/Vision room. There, we met Catherine Krebs and Tracy O'Maly. Zoey, Paul and I were to have Mrs. Krebs as our vision teacher, while Tomoko would have Mrs. O'Maly. Mrs. O'Maly also managed a few visually impaired high school students. Mrs. Krebs was a short, thin white woman who was the biggest bookworm I've ever known. She heavily influenced my love for reading. She was a very important figure during my seventh and eighth grade years.

The start of seventh grade turned out to be harder than I expected. I struggled with math and science. I hadn't yet learned how to best study for exams or how to retain information when my brain would rather sleep. Was this even possible? Thankfully, Zoey and I were placed in a one-on-one math class with Jane Smith, who also became an extremely important figure during my seventh and eighth grade years. Mrs. Smith modified the lesson plans as best she could, while Zoey and I did our best to comprehend Braille math. I hated math with a passion.

Before getting my textbooks in Braille later on in my seventh grade year, Mrs. Krebs, classmates and others recorded material on audio tape for me so that I would be prepared for class. It didn't make a difference. Retaining the boring information offered in school wasn't going to happen. I would turn on the tape to play back a chapter from my history book, and as soon as the reader got going, Mariah Carey, Michael Jackson or *The Simpsons* would flood my mind with a jealous force. Once the tape was done, there would be questions to answer, and of course, I would remember nothing and would have to rewind and start the tape again. Until Mrs. Krebs developed a strict study plan for me, school was a terrible drag. It wouldn't be until October when things finally settled and school became better, and I started to look forward to academia.

The month of September of 1999 was considerably better than August. I had friends, my own room, and it seemed like the happy days after my suicide attempt in August would stay. At home, I spent much of my time recording myself sing, pretending to have my own radio show and listening to playbacks of my favorite TV shows. When September 25th arrived, my sisters and I turned twelve. It was a birthday that I will never forget.

Paul, Ciara, Tomoko and I were invited to Zoey's house. I was surprised with a chocolate birthday cake and a brand new CD player boom box. I had never owned a CD player before; I felt on top of the world. Zoey's mom had purchased the machine and presented it to me while we played. She had even made my favorite dish at the time, chicken piccata, which seemed to bring heaven to Earth.

But then a plethora of problems arose in October of 1999. I got a better handle on school, but then things got weird. Zoey and I were closer than ever, and the assistant for the vision program couldn't handle it. Crisy Isen had been hired to be with us during class, as an aid for our class instruction. Eventually, she had been trained to Braille our work for us by scanning print materials into the computer, proofreading it for accuracy and then having it embossed on a Braille embosser. Quite often, we were undeservedly scolded by her. Some of Zoey's and my activity may have been annoying, but they didn't call for Ms. Isen to try separating us. Sure, we may have acted a little immature for our 12-year-old age, but we were having fun. The horrors in my childhood had me trapped in a protective, immature mind of elementary amusement. For example, while walking or standing against the corridor wall during class change, Zoey and I would count to three and then we would scream "Dozzee du." and then burst into uncontrolled laughter. I encouraged this behavior by saying to Zoey in her ear: "Let's say *whaaaaat*, dozzee du." and then the countdown would follow and we would shout it. I believed these elementary outbursts embarrassed Ms. Isen. She complained so much about Zoey and me being together that I finally brought the issue up with Grandma.

"That white lady probably ain't use to seeing a black boy and a white girl so close. She being racist."

The seventh grade counselor Mr. Berg met with Ms. Isen, Zoey, and me and he managed to quash the sad ordeal. Meanwhile, things at home, while generally happy when I was entertaining myself, were quite complicated. My sister Maria was on another mean streak. Like Haily, Maria had the power to emotionally destroy me. On one particular night, Maria was livid that I wouldn't let her use the phone. I had just gotten on the phone to talk to Paul and I wasn't going to be bullied into giving up my time. Maria wasn't having it. She wanted to talk to her friends. We all had phones in our rooms. I happily talked to Paul about school and other things, when suddenly Maria came on the line from in the basement.

"Get off the phone, Mario," she said.

"I'm using the phone, Maria, and I just got on it," I replied.

"Whatever, you stupid black critter," and with that, she hung up. I was stunned. Once again, she was making fun of my dark skin and I was so embarrassed that Paul, who was Asian, had to hear such mean language directed at me from my own sister. Some children may have been able to brush things like this off as typical sibling teasing or name calling, but I couldn't. It wasn't like that for me. I was blind, insecure and already thought myself to be worthless, ugly and too dark. When my family called me names or hurt me by commenting on my dark skin, it felt ten times worse than the teasing most kids receive. I cried and hung up the phone without a word to Paul, asking God why on earth he'd made me such a dark shade.

Zoey and her family were the force behind my being able to cope with life at home, my adolescent depression and my fears. Zoey was always cheerful, funny and treated me like her brother. Her support was immensely helpful when, at the start of November, Grandma, my sisters, Sefra and I had to move back in with Haily. For reasons still unclear, we were forced from the house in Oats and the things we had acquired while living there were placed in storage again. This included the piano from Music Link. My sisters and I should have known a move was coming. Nearly two weeks before being forced out, some strangers came into the house and asked us if we were ready to leave. I felt that the days of feeling like a cockroach had returned. Haily, Hasan and Shawn were now living in a townhome in Famhill, Virginia. Every minute, I longed to be with the Jacobs', laughing, singing and being cheerful at the movies or at one of Zoey's piano recitals.

Some help for the pressure at home came at school as well. Aware of my troubles at home, Mrs. Krebs thought she would step in and get me a teenage mentor. Through a high school mentoring program at Hamax, I was assigned an eleventh-grade high-schooler named Austin Williams. He was going to be my role model, a "Big Brother." Looking back, I admit that Austin was both a good and bad influence. For the time we spent together, he was the closest thing to a big brother I had since my real brothers were gone, but he had his flaws. Austin would come to the resource room to get me at 1:00 p.m. on Mondays and Wednesdays. At the start of our mentor/mentee relationship, we spent a lot of time walking around the school building and talking about girls and music. Austin told me all about the joys of sex with his girlfriend and was the first person to tell me what a condom was. He was elated that he didn't have to use one because his girlfriend was on what he told me was "the pill." Without going into too much detail, he told me that his girlfriend being on the pill meant he didn't have to worry about getting her pregnant. I was fascinated. One day, I too would be able to do the same.

Austin was a sixteen-year-old, 5-10, muscular half-black boy with well-defined arms, and a light-skinned complexion. His cologne smelled fantastic, and I found the masculine quality of his pubescent voice fascinating. I wondered what my voice would sound like at his age. He became a bad influence when he talked me into allowing him to steal some CDs for me. Austin loved music as much as I did and promised to shoplift CDs for me from Tower Records. I felt horrible about the idea, but the thought of having the music I loved to comfort me at home was too much to ignore. I could really put my CD player given to me by Mrs. Jacobs to good use. More importantly, I would have the music I loved as medicine. It could help me block out the drama from Haily and her kids.

In an act that I am ashamed of, I went home one night to type a list of albums I wanted Austin to get for me; I needed something to look forward to. He told me that he and his friends did it all the time and that it would be far too easy. On my Braille N. Speak, a Personal Digital Assistant for the blind at the time, I came up with nearly thirty CDs that included everything from Britney Spears to Michael Jackson. I felt evil caving into Austin's suggestion of stealing music, but that didn't stop me. I knew that I was going to be a part of a cool clan. In the end, he and his friends—so I was told—attempted to steal the materials and got caught but fled the store before authorities could get them. In our next session, he apologized to me and said that he felt bad that he couldn't deliver on his promise to get me the music. I told Austin not to worry, and that I had other plans for getting the music I wanted.

Then, in another act I am pained to admit, I went home and took all of Sefra's CDs. Of course, Grandma was too poor and religious to buy popular music for my sisters and me, but Sefra's mom had supplied her with music and she had plenty of CDs for the taking. She had everything from the Backstreet Boys to Lil Kim. I felt awful listening to Sefra complain night after night that her CDs were missing, while I kept them safely hidden in my book bag. I chose a different one to listen to every night, but eventually, I returned her CDs, unable to bear the guilt any longer. Instead, I decided to cling on to Shania Twain's *Come on Over* album I borrowed from Zoey. For much of my down time, I was lost in Shania's album, replaying each track until sleep came. I needed music like a drug to help me cope with home, and like an addict, I was willing to do anything to get it.

I saw Austin for nearly three months before our sessions ended. A week after they ended, I told Mrs. Krebs about the sex conversations and CD theft and she was aghast.

"I wish you had told me," she said in her dramatic, academic voice. I really liked Mrs. Krebs. She believed in me when I didn't believe in me. I resented not telling her. I didn't get another mentor from the same program, but instead, found my own later in the school year.

Things at home became quite difficult for me. One Friday night in early November, Grandma, Sefra and my two sisters drove into DC to attend Friday night church service, while I stayed home. Feigning sick, I was left behind with Haily, Hasan and Shawn. On this night, I overheard Haily, Hasan and Shawn talking about my sisters, Grandma and me as if we were uninvited dogs.

CHAPTER 10– WHERE DO WE GO

"And she always down here taking over the TV watching those religious programs," came Hasan's voice in a hushed whisper. Sefra, Grandma, Marian, Maria and me occupied a room in the basement that had a heavy door. Sefra and Grandma slept on the bed while we triplets slept on the floor. A large-screen television sat in the rec area of the basement where two sofas were. The heavy door to the bedroom was closed, but having sensitive hearing, I could hear everything. I got closer to the door and placed my ear to it.

"I know." began Shawn. "And if we wanna watch TV, nobody wants to keep seeing that crap. Plus, they be eatin' all of our stuff."

"What else is bothering y'all?" asked Haily.

"They don't need to be using the TV at a certain time and can't they get their own stuff."

"I know," began Haily. "My mother gets depressed and always starts eating. And that damn Mario, everything he eat go right to his damn butt. That boy got a big ass." I was stunned and in that moment, I had further confirmation that we were somewhere we weren't welcomed. I planned to tell Grandma what I overheard so that hopefully, she could find help elsewhere.

When Grandma returned, I told her everything I heard. She was heartbroken and did what I hoped she would do, vow to get help from Social Services and step out on her own. She promised that no longer would we be depended on Haily. She was going to contact Social Services to get help from them for a change that would go far past food stamps. I didn't know what it all meant, but I was excited to hear that Grandma was going to try and do better for us, independent of Haily. But I should have known better than to get my hopes up so fast.

To my utter astonishment, Grandma told Haily everything I'd said I'd heard and things got worse for me. Haily, Hasan and Shawn denied the entire exchange, calling me a liar and a troublemaker. What hurt worse was that Grandma believed them. She believed that I made the whole thing up just to "start something," as Haily said. Haily started treating me like I was an infectious disease that threatened to plague her and her children. She called me names like "big butt" and "jerk." Every time she called me a name, it would melt my self-esteem into nothingness.

"Mario, hurry up and walk upstairs, goddamn jerk," she would say or: "Your food is ready. Eat it and go right back downstairs. Damn troublemaking asshole. Everything you eat go straight to your damn butt. You got the biggest ass I've ever seen on a boy." I thought: "Grandma will never break away from this hellhole."

When Thanksgiving arrived that year, I felt alien. I was beyond uncomfortable when having to talk to, eat with or even be around Haily and her family. Zoey and her parents were my only refuge.

When one considers Haily's nasty attitude, I understood why she and her fiancé Robert had split up by that point. Nevertheless, it looked as if we would never split from Haily. By early December, the whole occupancy of the house in Famhill moved again. For some reason, after nearly three months of her and her sons living in the Famhill townhome, Haily had to move. Without a job and a known source of income, Haily had the green light for another place. We all crammed into an apartment on the opposite end of Famhill. It was a two-bedroom apartment with a loft. Once again, Sefra, Marian, Maria, Grandma and me occupied one room, while Hasan and Shawn shared another, and Haily had the loft.

This period was just the beginning of stranger days to come. As the special bussing for me had to be changed several times in the first half of the school year, the school was well aware that I had moved three times in five months. The school system was suspicious. This was primarily due to my family habitually forgetting to pick me up from the bus after school. Whether it be my cousins, aunt, sisters or Grandma, someone always forgot. On these occasions, the bus driver was forced to return me to school. Once there, Mrs. Krebs, my history teacher, or the seventh-grade counselor would give me something to eat and discuss my plight. Who would get Mario home this time? Why does this keep happening? Does his family love him? What was home life like? On a few occasions,

Mrs. Krebs drove me back home. The bus problem happened so many times that Mrs. Krebs and the counselor were eventually forced to report this form of neglect to Social Services. Grandma was stunned when she was briefed on the neglect accusation and told that a social worker would be coming to the apartment.

"Don't make no doggone sense," Grandma said one night, her voice thick with paranoia. "They got on this paper that I've been neglectful and ain't taking care of Mario. God knows." I sat in my sleeping area of the floor feeling awful. But I didn't feel awful for Grandma; I felt awful for me. I *wanted* Social Services to consider Grandma neglectful. I knew she was doing her best, but I wanted to be away from Haily. If it meant losing Grandma too, so be it. I wanted refuge. I wanted Social Services to come and find the truth, something bad to report. I wanted a way out from Haily and the foolish game she was running. And I have held this secret until now. But soon my family finally started to make sure someone met me at the bus, and nothing came of the ordeal with Social Services. Indeed, I was interviewed by a social worker named Linda Crouch, but I decided that I couldn't hurt Grandma like that. I made the decision to stay in the tough living conditions.

Christmas came and went, as uneventful as usual. But when December 31 came, I was horrified. I was one of those kids who worries until it drives them sick. The great Y2K was upon us and

Haily had done a good job scaring me six months earlier, when she told us of the doomsday to come.

"Yep, and the traffic lights and everything are gonna be out," she said. "People gonna be rioting and stealing and all that. The computers are gonna blow up and everything."

As usual, everyone, save Haily, Hasan and Shawn, went to Watch Night Service, the name given to church service on New Year's Eve. I sat bent over with my head in my lap—the way I often slept in church—listening to the loud singing, praising and organ music. I knew the 12:00 midnight mark loomed over us. Finally, the assistant pastor, Elder Fields came on the microphone and began praying, speaking in tongues and worshipping the Lord. He then announced that the New Year had come. The organ roared and spirit-filled praises surged from everywhere. I remained in the same state, my head in my lap. With amazement, I realized that the electricity was still on, the organ was still playing and that there were no loud bomb booms outside. With a relief, I sat up and began praising God, thankful for another chance to get things right. I knew once I turned thirteen my guarantee to go to heaven would lift, but I wasn't thirteen yet. When we returned home that night, I rushed to the radio, grabbed my headphones and spent the rest of the night listening to Z-104's Y2K countdown, where they counted down the top 2000 songs of the century.

I spent the first school week of the new century sick as a dog. I stayed home from school for five days with a severe chest cold. When I returned to school, I found out that I had been greatly missed. Zoey was elated to see me well and back. Mrs. Krebs and Ms. Isen were just as excited to know I had pulled through the winter cold. When the Martin Luther King holiday came, Zoey and I took the opportunity to hang out since we hadn't seen much of one another over the winter break. My family made me feel quite uncomfortable about spending Martin Luther King's birthday hanging out with white people. I wondered whether my family remembered that this was what Martin wanted: interracial unity.

Nevertheless, Zoey and I watched movies, played the piano, ate her mom's cooking and checked out Celine Dion's Greatest Hits CD, which included a brand new song, "That's the Way It Is." Zoey fell in love with this song and to this day, it's still one of my favorite Celine Dion tunes.

With the start of the new semester, Zoey and I found out that not only would we have math class together, but Introduction to Foreign Language as well. The course was divided into four different languages. The first few weeks of the semester would be spent on Latin, followed by a few weeks on Spanish, with French and German at the end. I was fascinated with Latin and loved practicing my pronunciation of "salve" and "salvete," which meant hello. When we started our introduction to Spanish, I was like a kid on Christmas.

The Intro to Foreign Language class time spent on Spanish sparked my obsession with this language. I loved all Hispanic accents and dialects. By the second week of Spanish, I had learned the days, weeks and seasons and felt like I knew the whole language. I drove Grandma and my sisters crazy with my Spanish outbursts. "Gracias. Hoy es martes." I would scream at random moments, only for my outbursts to be followed by Grandma's "Shut up, boy." These moments were so funny.

Things at home took a turn for both the better and worse, although the worse came first. One night, my sisters, Sefra and her brothers and I were home alone in the apartment watching TV. My aunt and Grandma's whereabouts were unknown. Suddenly, there came a knock at the front door, and Hasan answered it.

"Yeah?" came Hasan's voice, thick with feigned maturity.

"We from Domino's," replied a man with an Asian accent. I got excited, thinking Haily had purchased pizza for us again like she had during the previous week. I was wrong. "Dee check no good," the man continued.

"What?" laughed Hasan as the man sounded like he was unfolding paper.

"Dee check from uh ... Hailee...Uh, no good." Then, it hit us all like a ton of bricks. Haily had paid the Domino's pizza bill with a bad check, and this man was returning to get their money. I was in disbelief. Indeed, the pizza delivery man was at the door, but without a delivery. My aunt's check had bounced.

A few days after the pizza ordeal, my aunt and her children disappeared, and even Grandma wasn't sure where they were. One afternoon, a white man came to the apartment and asked when we were going to leave. Just like that. I was astonished. What was going on? The same night the white man came wondering why people were still in the apartment, Grandma gathered my sisters and me and we left. We had no choice. The apartment was up for eviction any minute and they were going to change the locks. We had absolutely nowhere to go. Grandma had temporarily reconciled with her estranged husband. She still had access to a car that my Grandfather had gotten her from an auction a week before and she packed all of our clothing into it and we drove to a nearby Safeway parking lot. Then, she told us to go to sleep. With nowhere to go, we spent the night in a miserably cold car. I pouted, blew my breath and let out pitiful sighs all night long. My mind went back to the neglect ordeal with Social Services, and I thought: "Why didn't I just tell the Social Worker the truth and get out of this situation?"

The next morning, Grandma drove to the gas station and one by one, we all had a turn washing in the station's bathroom. Then, she drove back to the apartment where we waited for my school bus. She said that she would be waiting for me when the bus came back at the end of the day. I got on the bus, and went to school, where I was to pretend all day as if everything was OK. Seeing Zoey and my other friends made it easier, but I was stressed not knowing what on earth would become of us once I left school for the day.

Nevertheless, I gave a first rate performance pretending everything was OK. I know that last night had to be hard on my grandmother. She had to have felt like a failure. I sincerely regret blowing my breath in exasperation and audibly pouting when she felt as bad as we did. Although she'd made a few mistakes, she tried her best. Back at the apartment and in Grandma's car after school, I learned that Grandma had contacted her second eldest daughter Shearl, and that we were going to stay with her and her friend Beverly for a few days. Unfortunately, we would have to miss a few days of school. The forecast of "a few days" was right, as by the fourth day, Beverly was eager for us to leave.

With our departure came the better half of the turn that things took in early 2000. Grandma had finally gotten in contact with Social Services to get help for us. Linda Crouch, the worker from the neglect case, worked on our behalf and found us a place to stay. We moved into a roach-infested, foul smelling motel on Lee Highway in Burgson. Social Services was paying for our stay while they helped Grandma get on the Section 8 housing list. I didn't know what to expect. I was, however, excited that I would be getting some of my things out of storage, or so I thought. Once we were settled in the motel, Haily visited us with news of our latest storage unit.

"Momma, they said that the roof of the storage caved in because of the rain and everything was lost," Haily said. My sisters and I were a little suspicious of being told for the second time that our things in storage wouldn't be coming back to us. Of course, we didn't expect to bring large couches into a motel room, but we thought we would have been able to retrieve clothes, electronics and keepsakes. Not a chance, though. I would have to find a way to tell Michele that the electronic piano from Music Link was gone now.

Life at the motel was a time of mixed blessings and hurt. It is a period in my young life that I still occasionally revisit in my sleep. School and home life seemed like night and day. At home, I felt less-than, a scum and a waste, while at school, I felt wanted, appreciated and cared for. If I could, I would have spent my nights and days at Hamax, and I would have been pleased with never having to go home. I felt embarrassed of my life as a poor boy, now living in a motel. It was bad enough that my personal business was paraded in front of the school because of our frequent address changes, but when Michele had to train me on how to get from the motel room to where the bus would pick me up in the mornings, my embarrassment grew. The special ed bussing made sure that I kept the same bus driver at every location I had lived since attending Hamax. Everyone knew that my family had trouble and I knew that I was the helpless, hopeless and poor black boy with a troubled family and no money.

Zoey, Paul and Michele were my inspirations. Michele encouraged me to attend the Valentine Day dance to take my mind off things. I asked Zoey to go with me and Michele was our escort, as both Zoey and I were having mobility difficulties. At the dance, I was very nervous but Michele talked me out of my nerves.

"If you need me, just stick your hand in the air," she said over the loud music.

"No, Michele." I said. "That's embarrassing." She laughed. In no time, Zoey and I were eating pizza and holding hands as we danced to all of the popular music of that time. I danced and sung loudly to each of my favorite tunes: Eiffel 65's "Blue," Britney Spears' "Crazy," 98-Degrees "I Do (Cherish You)," Christina Aguilera's "Genie in a Bottle," Lou Bega's one-hit-wonder song "Mambo No. 5" and more kept me oblivious to the other students. Eventually, the DJ called out a dance contest. Zoey and I were coaxed onto the stage by Michele. We grabbed hands and danced our own way to the music, not knowing or caring who we were competing against. To my astonishment, we won the dance contest. I knew we had won because of the student audience's probably thinking: "Aw. Look at the blind boy and half-blind girl," but it didn't matter. I had a blast. Moments like the seventh-grade dance made my home life seem miles away, distant, almost a bad dream. But it wasn't a dream; it was real. However, God sent me another therapeutic outlet to help me cope.

The nonprofit organization, Focus on the Family, changed my life and gave me another world to get lost in. In 1987, Focus on the Family started a Christian radio drama that took everyday struggles and tied them to biblical resolutions. The program is syndicated around the country on Christian talk and music radio. I accidentally found the program while browsing the radio one night in February of 2000. I was intrigued by the sound effects, first rate music and superb voice actors. I became obsessed and I tuned into the DC Christian station every night at 8:00 p.m. I never missed an episode. For the first time, I had an entertaining way to learn about all of the classic biblical stories.

In the show, Mr. Witiker, the town of Odyssey's resident Grandpa and ice cream shop owner, was the man who all the kids in the town went to in order to learn Christian principles and get help with resolving their problems. My favorite episodes were the ones about trips taken in the Imagination Station created by Mr. Witiker. In this contraption, kids could experience history and pretend to be a part of it. In one particular episode, one of the kids is sent back in time to experience Jesus Christ's crucifixion. Every time I heard an episode that involved a trip in the Imagination

Station, or one that retold a classic bible tale, I would excitedly tell Grandma what I learned about Jesus and other bible characters while listening to *Adventures in Odyssey*. I fell so deeply in love with this program that I just had to have copies of it for myself to listen to at any time. Mrs. Perry-Thibault, my seventh-grade science teacher, and later, my mentor, was instrumental in getting me copies of the show.

One day in late February, I told Mrs. Perry-Thibault that I needed to speak with her privately. While outside of her classroom, I asked her in a twelve-year-old's high voice whether she'd be willing to be my mentor. Without hesitation, she said yes. From that day, she began bringing me sweets, recording Spanish words on tape for me, and taking me on educational outings. One afternoon, I told her about *Adventures in Odyssey* and that it was possible to get copies of the show by calling them. She pulled me out of class one day and took me to the teacher's lounge to use the phone. I told her that I memorized the titles of all of the episodes I wanted.

"Hi, my name is Katherine Perry-Thibault. I'm calling on behalf of Mario Bonds, a twelve-year-old student of mine. He loves your radio program *Adventures in Odyssey* and I'd like to know how I can get copies of it for him."

"Sure thing. What are the names of the episodes he likes?" asked the voice from the other line. Ms. Perry-Thibault placed the phone in front of my mouth and I called out my list of twenty shows I wanted. Once I was done, Ms. Perry-Thibault took control of the conversation again.

"Great," began the voice on the phone. "Will you be paying the asking price or making any donation amount?" asked the voice on the phone.

"Oh," replied Ms. Perry-Thibault, "I didn't know a cost was associated. Could he get them complimentary?" I had no idea what the word "complimentary" meant, but I knew Ms. Perry-Thibault was working her magic.

"Oh, sure thing. That's not a problem. Um, one second please...OK, to which address can I send them?" Ms. Perry-Thibault gave her address and the rest was history. Nearly two weeks later, I had my own cassette copies of twenty of my favorite episodes. Whenever I wanted Focus on the Family material gratis, Ms. Perry-Thibault would order them for me.

Another therapeutic highlight of seventh-grade was the mobility lessons Zoey and I had together. Michele would take us to Baskin Robbins, park the car in front of the building and then tell us to find the door, order our ice cream and get seated without her help. Zoey and I would grab our canes, laughing and joking as we blundered along to find our way to an ice cream afternoon treat. We helped one another through the mildly difficult task. It was on one of these trips to Baskin Robbins that I realized my favorite ice cream was Rocky Road, packed with marshmallows. Zoey always got a soda with ice cream in it which I thought was gross. Once we were seated, only then would Michele come over and eat with us, and of course, also lecture about mobility travel, praising and correcting wherever needed. During one such ice cream afternoon in March, I thanked God for Zoey, her parents, Michele, Ms. Perry-Thibault and one of my other close female friends, Courtney Turner. I felt that these people were truly showing me what real love was like.

Zoey and I had met Courtney in the drama class we had taken last semester, and the three of us hit it off in no time. Courtney thought I was adorable and wasted no time telling me. She laughed at practically everything I said and I loved that about her. She and Zoey became so close that they started calling one another best friend in no time. Whenever Zoey and Courtney had a sleepover at Zoey's house, they recorded themselves singing along with Celine Dion. We all loved Celine's 2000 hit "That's the Way It Is" and I was given the recording as a gift. I had the hugest crush on Courtney, but seventh grade would definitely have to end without me telling her. Now that I was a little older, I didn't understand why I was suddenly somewhat uncomfortable around girls who found me cute.

CHAPTER 11— LEARN TO BE SOCIAL

Before the close of the school year in early May, fearing I would be stuck in a motel room all summer, Mrs. Krebs made it her business that I had camps lined up for the summer. She registered me for Beacon Lodge, a two-week overnight camp for visually impaired youth, located in the mountains of Pennsylvania. After beacon Lodge, she scheduled me to attend a three-week long day camp, the same one provided by the Lighthouse for the Blind that I used to attend when I was a younger child. I was elated that Zoey and I would be attending the Lighthouse day camp together, but I was on my own for Beacon Lodge.

While my sisters would be spending time at Haily's new house with her boyfriend and his son in Mitchellville, Maryland, I was heading off for a summer of learning to be social.

Michele and her husband Chuck drove me to Beacon Lodge. When we arrived, they wasted no time getting me unpacked, situated and trying their best to make sure I was comfortable. I hated for them to leave, but I wasn't stupid. Of course they had to go. Once I was unpacked and Michele oriented me to the cabin, the bathroom and my sleeping quarters, we went to the mess hall where I was handed over to the camp staff. Then, Michele and Chuck left.

I was introduced to Albert, the adult head of my cabin. Albert was Russian and had the coolest accent ever.

"I'm Albert, Mario and I want to introduce you to your other cabin mates. This is Joey." Albert helped me find Joey's hand to shake.

"Nice to meet you," said Joey, his voice hoarse and his handshake feeble.

"I'm Sam," said another boy, grabbing my hand. "I'm Dutch and sexy." He patted, no punched my shoulder hard several times. I wanted to smack him, but I remembered Mrs. Krebs wanting me to learn to be social. I'd never had anyone hit my shoulder before as a nicety.

"This is Kyle," said Albert, helping me shake another boy's hand. For the first time, I realized that the odd sounds I was trying to ignore while greeting the other boys were coming from Kyle, who was seated to my left.

"Diga diga dee, dee deee deed a dee dee dee. Ha-ha."

I laughed and Albert whispered in my ear that Kyle was autistic.

"What does he draw?" I asked.

"No, not artistic, autistic. it's a form of mental disadvantage."

My mouth opened in a big "Oh." Kyle beat on the table and continued his "diga diga dee" melody. I felt bad for having felt annoyed.

"And this is Chris. The last one," said Albert, helping me shake a boy's hand at the far end of the table.

"Hi," was all Chris said.

"Y'all ready to eat?" came a loud voice. It was the camp director. "Today, we have baked potato, broccoli and steaks." The mess hall erupted in applause and cheers as all of the campers praised the menu selection for our first night. Still uneasy and not wanting to give myself a full tank, I only ate the baked potato, lying that I was a vegetarian.

"Why don't you eat the broccoli too then?" asked Albert.

"I'm picky about which vegetables."

"But potato is a starch."

"Potato is his vegetable of choice," said the cheery Sam, seated to my right. Albert had gone off to sit with the other camp cabin heads.

I ate quietly as the rest of the boys talked about their lives. After dinner, we were led back to our cabins. Albert guided me while the other boys, still with some sight, walked of their own accord. We were expected to fool around chatting until bed time.

As I was already unpacked—thanks to the Weils—I found my bunk and climbed up on it, while discovering Kyle was my bunk mate. He had the bottom and I had the top. Even then, he continued his "diga diga deee" melody.

So I wouldn't have a hard time finding the bathroom in the middle of the night, Michele had chosen a bunk for me that was near it. My closet and drawers were next to the bunk.

"I'll be back later. You fellas behave." Said Albert, and with that, we were on our own. For hours, we had conversations about girls, our homes, our talents and what we wanted to be, and surprisingly, I opened up. We talked until we realized it was nearly 1:00 a.m. We continually told each other, "Go to sleep." then, we would laugh. A couple minutes of silence would follow before someone would start talking again. I was loving it. I was feeling comfortable. Sam, laughing and lying in his bunk to the right of Kyle and me, said: "Ha ha. Everyone go to sleep, really." And then he did something that made it very hard for me to remain social. He walked over to each boy in turn, laughed and repeated his "Go to sleep," then he spit in each of our faces. He got to me last. My Bonds blood boiled and although I knew the Dutch white boy was playing, my rage couldn't be quenched. Before he could step down from my bunk after his spitting, I grabbed him by the collar and pulled him up, his throat pressed against the sideboard and his air restricted from the pressure.

"Don't freakin' do that," I said in a slow, evil droll, and then I let him drop to the floor, coughing and gulping for air. With my rage subsiding, I quickly went to wash my face. I couldn't believe the nerve of Sam. This was how some people said "you're cool with me," or how some people were social?

By mid-morning the next day, I was elated that I would be spending thirteen more days in my newfound heaven. The food was amazing and the activities were fantastic. I felt at home, which made my fear of strange toilets subside. We were offered swimming twice a day, nature trails with "Nature Pat," arts and crafts and social time.

My ability to be social was tested again by a totally blind kid named Joshua. Joshua was only eight years old, and was as evil as anything. At least, I thought he was evil.

"I wanna go to the freakin' pool," I heard him yelling to his cabin head.

"Josh, you're gonna go to the pool but if you keep talking like that, you won't." Once everyone was finally in the pool, I had my own run-in with Joshua. He was screaming his head off about how much he didn't like me since he hadn't been invited to play Marco Polo. In three feet, he began violently splashing the water, screaming that eh hated me. During his splashing fit, his left arm struck me on its way down to the water, and I saw a flash of blue light. Like a crazed child, he shouted "Fuck you everybody." Once I was struck a second time, a rage filled me and I grabbed Joshua's arm with all of my might. I squeezed and twisted his arm, rage coursing through my fingers.

"You crazy boy. Don't … do … that." I said, continuing to twist his arm, my teeth gritted with the effort. Albert called my name and I relinquished my hold on him.

Joshua yelled, "Stupid fucker. Why you do that?" His cabin head helped him from the pool. I was scolded for my actions, but I didn't care. I was sick of people doing things to me. Later, I did feel bad for losing control.

The following day, we had a real camp night out. We slept in sleeping bags in an on-campus camp site. I used that time to get back at Joshua. Once ghost stories and chocolate time was over, everyone retired to a large board that had been placed over some grass. A pavilion was placed over us and we all got into our sleeping bags. As Joshua lay there, trying to get to sleep, I whispered in his ear.

"I am the devil," I said, making my voice deep and scary. "I have come to get you."

"Ryan." yelled Joshua, "The devil's here. The devil's here." The occupants of the sleeping area laughed.

"No he's not," replied Ryan, trying to control the amusement in his voice.

"Only you can hear me. No one else can. You're going to die."

Joshua screamed like a mad child, flailing his arms. He managed to accidentally hit my nose, but it didn't bleed. I laughed and backed away to our sleeping bags.

"Mario, quit it." said Albert. And so I was done torturing Joshua.

A day before the camp ended, there was a talent show. I was elated. I loved singing and playing the piano and now was my time to show everyone. To everyone's surprise, Kyle was an excellent piano player. For the talent show, he performed "Miami" by Will Smith. Due to his slurred speech and him playing and rapping the song too fast, no one could understand a thing he said.. He played the heck out of the piano though.

I was the last contestant, and I went on right after Kyle.

First, I played my piano version of Celine Dion's "My Heart Will Go On, and then I sung NSYNC's "It's Gonna be Me." For some reason, I was crowned the winner of the talent show. I was floating.

The next day, Saturday, Mrs. Krebs picked me up and drove me home to the motel in Virginia. She quizzed me all the way home about my experience at Beacon Lodge.

"Was it a good social experience, Mario?"

"Yes." All I felt like giving was one word answers.

I also had a blast at the Lighthouse day camp, which started on the Monday after my return from Beacon Lodge. The camp was held from 9:00 a.m. to 3:30 p.m. at Sitwell Friends in Washington, DC. The campers in DC, Montgomery County and Hunsville County, Maryland, were bused to camp each day, while the Virginia kids were transported via cabs. Zoey and I had the pleasure of riding in the same cab.

The highlights of the camp were the great lunches, swimming and the trip to Six Flags America.

Each blind camper had a designated volunteer, a teenager who was there to complete his/her high school community service hours. I had a fourteen-year-old boy named Marvin as my volunteer, while Zoey had a 17-year-old girl named Rachel. Thankfully, Rachel and Marvin kept Zoey and me together. At this point, Zoey and I were truly best friends. Michele often said "Mario and Zoey are joined at the hip." We thought and said the same things all the time. We needed only to turn towards one another, and we would burst out laughing, knowing what the other was thinking about any given situation. Forget Mrs. Krebs' desire for me to learn to be social. Zoey was all I needed.

"OK guys," the camp director, Will, would say: "Good morning. This time, we'll start with if you're 'Happy and You Know It.'" All of the younger campers clapped and cheered. Zoey and I turned towards each other and said: "Oy gevalt." We laughed, wondering what on earth we had gotten ourselves into. We had learned "Oy gevalt" from Michele who was Jewish. It became a word we used whenever we felt bemused, amused, upset, indifferent, silly or otherwise.

While at the camp, I saw Eli, an old friend from my younger childhood days at the Lighthouse camps. Eli was a year and a half older than me. Eli developed an enormous crush on Zoey and gave an awkward notification of it on one of the swimming trips.

As Sidwell didn't have a pool, we were bussed on Thursdays and Tuesdays to an indoor pool elsewhere in DC to swim from 10:00 a.m. to 12:00 p.m. There was one small and one very large pool. At first, Eli, Zoey and I contented ourselves with playing in the small pool, until we convinced our volunteers that we could handle the large pool. Eli and Zoey were telling the truth; I was lying. Zoey swam expertly around the large pool, treading water and all the while a jealous me trailed the walls. It wasn't until my volunteer handed me a life jacket that I had the courage to abandon the wall. Zoey, Eli and I swam to the twelve-foot deep end of the pool. Of course, Zoey and Eli were faster than me.

"Guys, wait up," I screamed, splashing the water as if it were attacking me.

"Ha-ha, Mario, you're making too much noise," Eli laughed.

"Come on Mario." Zoey teased. I was so jealous of these expert swimmers. Finally, all three of us reached the wall on the twelve-foot side of the pool. Our volunteers kept watch on us from the shallow end.

"Hey," began Eli, sounding to blow water out of his nose: "It's fun to dive all the way down to the floor of the pool and come back up."

"Yeah, let's do it," Zoey said excitedly.

"What? I mean, OK," I said, pretending to be game. Eli counted and he and Zoey plunged into the water. I clung to the wall, too afraid to join the game. Once they resurfaced, Eli, the one with the best vision, saw my pitiful form, still clutching the edge of the wall.

"Mario, you didn't even do it."

"I'm scared." I said.

"Dude, it's fun. Take off the life jacket and put it on the edge. I'll go down with you." Eli swam over to me and grabbed my hand. I removed my life jacket, and with one hand still firmly planted on the edge, I counted to three and plunged into the water with Eli. I allowed my hand to bang against the wall as we plummeted. I was fascinated with how deep we were going. Once we hit the pool floor, an excitement filled me.

Unfortunately, it was quickly replaced with panic when I realized the number of feet of water above my head. I let go of Eli's hand and desperately felt for the wall, as I had floated a few inches from it during my temporary moment of bold excitement. Once I found it, I used the wall to rush myself back to the surface. It seemed as if the amount of water surrounding me was endless, and when I broke the surface, I heard Eli and Zoey laughing. I felt so weak; Eli had beaten me to the surface, and he didn't have to use the wall. Panting for air, I said "Let's do it again."

Again Zoey stayed behind while Eli and I dropped to the pool's floor. This time, I stayed under a longtime. I could stand it, and I was loving the floor of the pool. Quickly, I became obsessed with it and the three of us submerged and surfaced ourselves for nearly twenty minutes. Once the in-pool diving frenzy had gotten old, we swam back to the shallow end of the pool, which was only three and a half feet. I was wearing my life jacket again. It was then that Eli delivered his news.

"I really, really, really, really like Zoey," Eli whispered in my ear. My heart froze.

"You do?" I mused as we leaned against the edge of the pool as Zoey swam with Rachel.

"Yeah, she's really pretty." I wanted to punch Eli's lights out. Zoey was *my* girl. Didn't he know this? Well really, Zoey and I were just friends and nothing more, but she was still my girl. She had no room for other close guy friends or a boyfriend. I was her unofficial friendly boyfriend.

"You mean like, or like like?" I asked.

"Like like like like," Eli exaggerated, splashing water.

"Wow."

"Does she have a boyfriend?" asked Eli.

"Yeah," I insisted. "Me."

I ruined Eli's hope to get with Zoey. For a short time after his embarrassing revelation, He avoided us like the plague. I knew I shouldn't have lied but, I was being possessive and wanted to look like the bigger man. During the ride home, I told

Zoey about Eli's crush and she said what we always said about awkward stuff: "Oy gevalt." Oy gevalt was right: Zoey was my girl.

Needless to say, Zoey and I became closer during our day camping adventures. Overcome with sentimental feelings for Zoey, on the last day of camp, during Arts and Crafts, I made a special birdhouse with a bird on top for her. The house and bird were made out of clay, and then hardened. I knew we would be friends forever and I wanted to give her a token of our never-ending friendship. When I presented her with the house, I had the mind to break it, but Zoey stopped me.

"No, I like it." she giggled, "It's my birdhouse." I was relieved that Zoey liked the crudely made birdhouse. She kept it for years.

I spent the last few weeks of my summer vacation at Haily and Marcus' house. Haily and Marcus had gotten married during my absence, and Haily was keen on my becoming friends with Marcus' son Justin. We did become friends afterall. Haily had told him of my piano playing, singing and drumming, and Justin was intrigued with meeting a juvenile Stevie Wonder. We spent much of our time together inexpertly playing the piano and having jam sessions on the drum set that Justin owned.

By the end of August, my sisters and I were back in the motel, preparing for the new school year. Although I would miss Justin, I was ready for the school year, although this school year would bring many changes that put my love for my family to the ultimate test.

CHAPTER 12— EIGHTH GRADE WITH THE SMITHS

The eighth grade started normally enough, with Zoey, Paul and I ecstatic to see one another. To our delight, Ciara's mom had changed her mind and now she was attending Hamax as well. At last, the foursome was back together. Mrs. Krebs was still Zoey's, Paul's and my vision teacher, while Ciara and Tomoko had Mrs. O'Malley in the high school resource room. Ciara was still her goofy *Harry Potter* and *Sailor Moon*-loving self, and we were glad to have her back. My classes were satisfactorily scheduled as well—and, well, that was because of Zoey. She and I had the same math, English and civics classes, which were back to back. Naturally, I was quite pleased, as this meant I would be seeing my best friend a lot. We had lunch together every other day.

Life was looking up now that I was back in school. With my more-than-fun summer and coming back to school on top of the world, I thought the good times would stay. Thanks to Mrs. Krebs, I was now a model student, making great grades. I had fantastic study habits and I had developed a great memory for all things trivial. This came in handy for history and science exams. Math was still a work in progress; poor Mrs. Smith.

The assistant, Mrs. Isen, didn't return, and in her place, we received a new aid named Mrs. Leach. She was a frail white woman with the spirit of an angel. She fell right into place, and Zoey and I adored her. It was Mrs. Leach who introduced me to what became one of my favorite candy bars, a Heath Bar.

At home, I dug into music more than ever. With my thirteenth birthday approaching, my endurance for my frustrating living conditions was fading fast. A teenage boy with an irritable attitude was near. For my birthday, Courtney—my crush from seventh-grade—bought me Savage Garden's *Affirmation* CD. I fell in love with songs like "The Animal Song," where the chorus tells of a man wishing he were an animal, careless and free. I also fell in love with "Gunning Down Romance," "I Don't Know You Anymore," "You Can Still Be Free" and "Crash and Burn." For my birthday, Grandma purchased a load of blank cassette tapes for me to use with my portable recorder, my favorite Pop-Tarts and gave me $10. Stupidly, I was grumpy at first that she gave me such a small birthday present. Hadn't she realized that we hardly get anything? Why couldn't she have gone all out for the birthday at least? My grandmother was doing the best she could, but at thirteen, I still couldn't fully understand or appreciate that.

Zoey, Paul, Ciara and I spent a lot of time together during what we called get-togethers. During these, I was always armed with my tape recorder, pretending that I was broadcasting the "Mario Arnauz Bonds Show," which Zoey nicknamed the MAB Show. The name of each show depended on whose house we were visiting. If it was at Paul's, the recording was called "Life at Paul's House." If we were at Zoey's house, it was "Life at Zoey's House." I would stock up on blank cassette tapes and record us having random fun throughout the day. Before turning off the tape, I would say: "You're listening to the MAB Show, 'Life at Paul's House.' We'll be right back." Zoey's mom didn't like seeing a running tape recorder in my hand.

"Turn the tape recorder off," she'd always whisper to Zoey on such occasions.

Zoey's parents were staunch Republicans and therefore avid supporters of George W. Bush's run for the White House. I was in favor of Al Gore because...well, because my family and all of the blacks I knew were. The eighth grade held a mock trial in which the entire student body cast their vote for their favorite candidate. George Bush won with a convincing marginal lead. Whether it was the news or special late night programs, everyone was talking about Clinton's departure, and who would be his successor. Who would the country trust to maintain the surplus Clinton left behind? Zoey and I got in countless arguments over politics.

"Zoey, you only like George Bush because your Dad does."

"No, I like him because Gore and Clinton are disgusting men. The media loves him and we don't. CNN stands for the Clinton News Network."

"Well, what did he do wrong? Wait, is it that private stuff that's the issue?"

"Yeah, and others. He's just a gross person."

I couldn't believe she didn't like Bill Clinton. I couldn't understand why anyone in their right mind wouldn't like Clinton. "Well, Zoey, I think Clinton was great and he has the country in a great money spot and Al Gore was under him so you know you're gonna get a continuance of what Clinton did."

"Yeah yeah." Our political arguments always ended with Zoey catching an attitude and saying: "I don't really care anyway, Mario." My eighth grade English teacher made it mandatory that students read at least one book a month. She didn't care what the book was, as long as we were reading and of course, able to provide a substantive book report on what we had read. Somehow, Ciara convinced me to start reading *Harry Potter books*, and to my surprise, I fell in love. She gave me her audio copy of *Harry Potter and the Chamber of Secrets*, the second installment in the Potter series. Thank God for books on tape. The narrator was a British guy named Jim Dale, and he was incredible. He used a different animated voice for each character, making the read that much more entertaining. The plot was entertaining and the idea of using magic was interesting. I became obsessed with *Harry Potter*, but not quite like Ciara did though. Ecstatic that I too was now a fan, Ciara would give me the next Potter book once I had finished and returned the previous one.

When I wasn't listening to *Adventures in Odyssey*, I was listening to J.K. Rowling's brilliant literary work. Her stories were quite therapeutic during the bomb shell that October, 2000 brought.

"Mario, you know I been trying to find a place that take Section 8 all this time?" Grandma said one afternoon after school. "Social Services been paying for this motel since we been here and they don't want to do it no more. They've been spending a lot of money each day for us to stay here."

"I know," I replied.

"Well, we gonna move back to Maryland. Linda Crouch gonna see to it that our Section 8 is transferred to Hunsville County."

My heart seemed to stop its beating. It felt as if my lungs had forgotten their job as well. Moving? *Again,* we were going to move? I was going to lose friends *again*? This seemed impossible. I couldn't lose Zoey, Paul and Ciara and Tomoko. This wasn't happening.

"We gotta move?" I asked weakly.

"Yeah, we do," Grandma replied, folding newly washed clothes.

"Oh well," said Marian, climbing in bed. I was stunned. Maria and Marian didn't care. Did anyone know that Grandma had just shattered my world? How could I tell Zoey? What would I tell her? This would doubtless break her heart. It was already breaking mine.

On Halloween morning, Zoey and I saw one another in math class. I had forgotten to get my Braille math book from my locker I was now being forced to use. Mrs. Krebs insisted on us being normal students, so it was mandated that we each got a locker and equip it with a special lock. I grabbed my cane and asked Mrs. Smith if Zoey could accompany me. Once we rounded the corner out of sight of the resource room, I waited until we were in front of my locker before telling her.

"Zoey," I began, fidgeting as she clung to my arm, still holding her own cane, "I have to leave."

"What do you mean?" she asked goofily. I didn't feel funny. That wasn't at all funny.

"I have to leave."

"Oy gevalt, what are you talking about?"

"My grandma said last night that we have to move back to Maryland."

Silence ... and more silence. I could sense that Zoey was at a loss for words. She was probably more surprised than I had been. The news had shocked her into absolute silence. Her best friend, her partner in crime was leaving. I was moving, and the news of this ripped a hole in her heart. "Why?" she finally asked.

"Zoey, you know we're poor. I could never repay you guys for what you've done for me, so you know we're poor."

"All that doesn't matter to my parents and me, Mario. We love you. No, you can't be moving."

She began to tear up, her voice thick with her impending sobs.

"Zoey, please don't cry. We will talk later." I grabbed her arm and we felt our way back to the vision room as Zoey tried to sniff away her sobs that were eager to escape. Once back in the vision room, Mrs. Smith, always able to make us laugh, told us how happy she was to see us.

"Now guys," she said in her happy smoker's voice, "Did you all finish your math work yesterday night." Then she giggled. Mrs. Smith had such a rich and infectious giggle. Her laugh made you want to laugh. I would miss that laugh, but right now, it was out of place. Mrs. Smith noticed Zoey's face and asked: "Zoey, what's wrong? You look as if you've been crying."

"Uh ." I said, wishing I had cautioned Zoey not to tell anyone. Instead, I chimed in as Zoey's sobs took hold. She cried as I told Mrs. Smith that I was going back to no-good Hunsville County, leaving Hamax for good. Mrs. Smith too was stunned into a brief silence. There was nothing to be done, nothing to be said right away. Mrs. Smith was going to lose a good student whose mathematical skills she so anxiously looked forward to developing. Everyone knew that Burgson County's vision program was much better than that of Hunsville County. What would become of me back in Maryland?

That night, I was so devastated about moving that I called my mentor Mrs. Perry-

Thibault to vent about the move. I also had Michele to talk to and Mrs. Krebs. I was in a pitiful state over having to leave and I didn't think my grandmother knew it. On November 2nd, back in Mrs. Smith's classroom, I got another surprise. Mrs. Smith had news of her own.

"Mario, I've been bothered since I found out that you are going to move. It kills me and has been on my mind since Tuesday. We cannot see you taken out of a great program like this. You need development and all of the technology and materials you need are here. Sure, I know Hunsville has some, but it's not what you need. It's a very under-developed program there. We have the best here and I can't see you ripped out of school like this." She paused for what seemed like an eternity. "Therefore, I talked with my husband Brian and we're gonna see if we can get you to stay with us to at least finish the school year." The room was filled with the loudest silence I had ever heard. Even Mrs. Krebs' ticking clock seemed to be protesting so much silence.

I was shocked and amused. Was this white woman nuts? Sure, I knew she was kind and nice, but did she truly think my grandmother would allow such a plan to take place? No, she didn't know my grandmother. There was no way my grandmother would agree to let me stay behind in Burgson and live with another family while she and my sisters went back to Maryland. Mrs. Smith was a complete stranger to Grandma anyway, *and* she was white. I didn't have a problem with any of it, but Grandma ... oh my goodness, Grandma? This was their plan? It wasn't going to work and I was sure of it.

"I'm not sure how things would work Mario, but I have decided that I'm going to try. A bunch of us have spoken, including Zoey's mother, and we're going to see what we can do to get your grandmother to agree to this." They didn't know my grandmother. She wouldn't agree to anything crazy like this. Sure, it was an option for me to stay and still be with my friends with access to the best materials, but how would Grandma see that?

Later that day, I talked over the situation with Michele during our mobility lesson. "Don't repeat this, Mario," said Michele, "But we're gonna have Zoey's mom talk to your grandmother since she trusts Zoey's mom."

"When?" I asked.

"We don't know. We're still figuring things out." I felt so happy to know so many people were pulling for me to stay in Burgson. Boy, I was loved. A teacher was offering her home to me. Nevertheless, I knew I was kidding myself; Grandma would never agree to this.

On November 4th, a Saturday, Zoey, Ciara and I went over to Paul's house. We knew it would probably be the last time we spent time together, the four of us before I left for Maryland at the end of the month. It was on this day that Mrs. Jacobs intended to speak with my grandmother. While I played at Paul's house, she was going to take Grandma out to lunch and bring up the proposition. While at Paul's house, I recorded every moment of another episode of "Life at Paul's House," but my mind continually dwelled on the conversation Mrs. Jacobs could be having with my grandmother. Was it going well?

I was deeply pained when Ciara sang a song called "I'm Only a Memory Away." In that instant when her beautiful voice delivered the lyrics, I knew no matter what, I was leaving Burgson.

Mrs. Jacobs had news when she picked Zoey and me up from Paul's house. For events and house gatherings, the Jacobs always picked me up and took me back home.

"Well Mario," she said as she drove me back to the motel, "I had lunch with your Grandma and I brought the stay with Mrs. Smith up."

"Yeah?" I said apprehensively. Oh no, Grandma dug into Mrs. Jacobs. "How'd the conversation go?"

"It went well. She said she'd think on it." Think on it was probably my grandmother's way of being polite until she had run the whole thing past Haily.

"What did she act like though?"

"She seemed very receptive," said Mrs. Jacobs, turning the corner.

Receptive? Really? My grandma receptive?

"She said she would talk to you and the family and I expect she'll let us know."

I knew the county had been a little frustrated with my grandmother. The school system had found a Section 8 apartment for Grandma a few months earlier and she turned it down, saying she wanted a house, not an apartment. It was then that the county really turned their back on her. No one understood how an impoverished woman with three teenagers to take care of could be picky over whether she had a house or an apartment. But, Haily was responsible for my grandmother's awkward refusal. Now, the only option was to leave Burgson and have the Section 8 voucher transferred before it could expire. I didn't care. I hoped to God a miracle could happen and Grandma would somehow be persuaded to let me stay with the Smiths until the end of the school year.

When Mrs. Jacobs dropped me off, I was uneasy with suspicion. Grandma said nothing to me about the doubtless strange conversation she had with Mrs. Jacobs over lunch. Had I underestimated her? Did I even know my own grandmother?

On Sunday, two days before the 2000 Presidential Election Day, I overheard Grandma talking on the phone. From the way she spoke, I was quite sure it was Haily on the other end. "I know. Well, they say they wanna keep Mario until the end of the school year so he ain't ripped out of school. They say the system down here is better for the blind folk and I know that's right but ... I don't know." Grandma paused, quietly sucking her teeth

as she listened. "I know that. I just don't want them
to have him on *Oprah* someday talkin' bout all they
done for him and I won't get any credit." I was
stunned as I pretended to be asleep on the motel
bed. Grandma had been considering allowing me to
stay but, her only hesitation was that if I became
something one day, the teachers in Burgson would
claim credit and she wouldn't be recognized? I
didn't understand. She was contemplating making
me leave Burgson still because she was afraid
others would be credited for my success. I thought
this to be quite confusing and inconsequential.
Sure, Grandma was a God-fearing woman, but she
had her mistakes. This seemed like it would be one
of them. It wasn't until the second conversation I
overheard after church did I realize Grandma was
actually considering the idea of allowing me to stay
with the Smiths.

Grandma was talking to Uncle Rick from
Delaware. He told her in flat terms that she should
consider the proposition. Thankfully, he put it in
religious terms and said: "Momma, you could be
blocking that boy's blessing. I don't think you
wanna do that." This statement stuck with
Grandma because she repeated it to Haily later
that night.

Grandma never discussed the arrangement
or her indecision with me until her mind was set.

"Alright, I'm gonna let it happen Mario,"
she said to my relief and excitement. "I don't
wanna block any blessings God got for you. Marian,

Maria and me going to live in Maryland with Haily until we find a Section 8 place to move into. I guess they'll let us know what to do next." I was again feeling like a kid on Christmas with all of my favorite toys around me. I wasn't leaving Zoey. I didn't have to leave Hamax and lose this group of friends that I loved so much. More importantly, I wasn't going back to a county that had me labeled dumb all those years ago. Sure, I knew it was just until the end of the school year, but that didn't matter right now. It was only November and school didn't end until June, six months into the New Year.

It was the end of the first quarter of the school year, and teachers were processing their grades. The students had Monday off, and Tuesday was Election Day. I was thankful for the four-day weekend. I listened to the third installment of Harry Potter, *the Prisoner of Azkaban* during my time off. I felt quite depressed not knowing how things would really work out. I ate a bag of Reese's peanut butter cups Mrs. Jacobs had given me on Saturday and I tried to get lost in a world of elementary pleasure. I had an entertaining book on tape and sweets to boot.

I sat, hungrily eating piece after piece of the savory candy. I loved Oreo cookies, donuts and candy as well. As I listened to the radio and Harry Potter, sitting atop the corner bed in the motel room, I ate myself to a sugar high.

"Mario, my God. Stop," came Grandma's voice.

"Huh? What I do?" I questioned, amused.

"I don't want you to eat all that candy tonight. You can't keep eating like that."

"Grandma, I'm small."

"Yeah, now you are," Grandma retorted, fixing the pillows on her bed in the opposite corner of the motel room. "You ain't gonna stay that way if you keep eating like that. I want you to have your pick of women."

"Grandma." I giggled bashfully.

"I'm serious, boy. You gonna have to stop that or make sure you exercise. Ain't no woman gonna want a fat blind man swingin' on her arm."

"I know, Grandma. I won't get fat."

CHAPTER 13– NEW BEGINNINGS IN BURGSON

For much of November, after the unprecedented Florida voting crisis on Election Day, Grandma prepared to leave for Maryland. She packed, had meetings at the school about me and finalized the Section 8 transfer with Linda Crouch. Burgson County even gave Grandma a car. She had transportation and Section 8 eligibility, which was a good way to start in Maryland. The teachers, Linda Crouch and I still didn't understand why Section 8 housing had been so difficult for my grandmother in Burgson. It was still unfathomable that she turned down so many apartments.

By Thanksgiving, we were out of the motel. In fact, we had completed the move the day before. Surprisingly, we didn't go to Maryland to stay with Haily as planned. We moved into a one-bedroom apartment above our church's dining hall. I was confused that Grandma took this but didn't take the multiple-room apartments Burgson had found for us. In the end, the county had gotten frustrated with her, pulled out the funding for the motel and I guess Grandma was taking whatever she could get now. Grandma had solicited assistance from our church, and they agreed to house us.

The apartment was small, and became known as "the Box" by the family. There was a small kitchen, a small living room, one bathroom and a one large, long bedroom. Grandma and my sisters slept in the large room while I slept in the living room on a futon.

On Thanksgiving Day, we went over to Haily's house to eat. My sister Asia, who was now living with Haily, was there to eat, along with Kevin, cousins and friends of the family. I was told that Haily and Asia had made up after their 1998 Aunt vs. Niece physical altercation. I played with Justin on the keyboard and on his video games for much of the day. Everyone was consuming every fattening food imaginable. Marian couldn't wait to get her hands on the chitterlings Grandma had made. I was repulsed by the smell, taste and texture of chitterlings.

"I just can't eat my food with something that smells like stuff on my plate. Oops," I said as I ate at the table with my cousins. Sefra, Shawn and Justin burst into loud laughs. "Grandma, Mario cussing."

"No I didn't," I said desperately.

As I knew I was going back to Burgson the next day, I couldn't help but feel anxious. Everyone wanted to know why I wanted to go back so soon, but the Jacobs, Mrs. Smith and Michele all convinced Grandma this was necessary. It would give me time to get acclimated to being in Burgson without my family. However, I wouldn't be going to the Smiths' house just yet. Instead, I was going to spend a week with the Jacobs. I was excited, but nervous. I had never spent the night at Zoey's house before, and now, I would be at their home for an entire week. Zoey and I would eat together, and go to school together? Would I be OK with using their bathroom? Sure, I knew they were clean, but I didn't want them smelling my processed food, nor did I want to smell theirs.

Once goodbyes were done the next day, I was picked up by the school's social worker, Mr. Johnson, and he and his girlfriend drove me to Zoey's house. Zoey's grandparents, aunt and uncles were there. "Great, strangers to gawk at the black boy and his sad situation," I thought. But they turned out to be nice people. Zoey and I had a great time that weekend, eating sandwich after sandwich filled with rich turkey meat. It was a joy eating the Jacobs' left over sweet potatoes with marshmallows, stuffing and cranberry sauce. My stay was comfortable, and I enjoyed the week of sleeping at their house, and going to school on the bus with Zoey.

When Sunday night of the following week arrived, my anxiety had mounted. As planned, Mr. Jacobs drove me to the Smiths' house and gave me a pep talk. "Mario, we know you're a great kid," he said. "We wanna make sure you understand why you aren't staying with us for the school year." The truth is, I had been wondering why the Jacobs hadn't stepped in and offered me to stay with them. "You and Zoey are getting older, and we don't want a situation to arise where you might like Zoey, and Zoey isn't interested." I thought to myself, *What if Zoey's the one doing the liking?*

"We just don't want anything to interfere with your friendship." What was Mr. Jacobs talking about? What could possibly end our friendship or make things complicated? Was he thinking I would try to do something with Zoey? Of course, he didn't know the prospect horrified me.

After putting my things in my new room, the Smiths took me to their family room to have a talk. I was more nervous than ever meeting Brian Smith. He was a tall, husky, powerfully built man with a deep, commanding voice. Both Mr. and Mrs. Smith were huge smokers. I had guessed in school that Mrs. Smith smoked, but I never had the actual proof. Here was the proof though. The house reeked of cigarette smoke. Not only were they smokers, they were indoor smokers. As they talked to me, both of them lit a tar stick.

"Now Mario," said Brian, coughing between sentences. *Put down the cigarette.* I thought. "Jane told me all about your situation. We want you to know that this is your home until the end of the school year. We will do any and everything to make you comfortable."

"Yup, you know this Mario," giggled Mrs. Smith, "There are three floors. There are four bedrooms upstairs. There is a bathroom in your room with two doors. Brian's study shares that same bathroom." Great, Mr. Smith will hear me in the bathroom. We moved into the kitchen for donuts and the "welcome talk" continued.

As I sat eating a chocolate donut and nursing a glass of Coke, I had the strange sense that something was in front of my face. A faint stream of air would hit me in the nose and mouth and then stop. Occasionally, I would throw my hand in front of my face confused.

"Thanks, Fido," said Mrs. Smith now sitting at the table. "Our cat. We have three of them. There's Fido who is ten, Sparky who's four and Spot who is one. They're all females."

"Huh. All of your cats have dog names."

"Yeah, we're those kind of people. Sparky acts like a dog. Fido's the wiser, more relaxed cat." I had never lived with cats before so I knew this was going to be an adventure.

Back in my room, I was so exhausted and filled with anxiety that I dozed off several times while reading my Braille textbook for my civics class. I was in a large, quiet house and Mr. and Mrs. Smith did their own thing while I was supposed to be studying. With my slight feeling of loneliness, I really missed my family. If I hadn't had *Adventures in Odyssey*, I would have gone mad with boredom. Nevertheless, missing my family or not, I certainly didn't want to leave. This was only the first night and I knew I had to give the house and the Smiths a chance. I wished that my sisters had been given the same opportunity to stay with the Smiths, but I knew I was being ridiculous. When I finally gave up on homework, having dozed off four times, I climbed into bed and prayed that whatever this new situation was, it would turn out alright.

I was abruptly awakened in the middle of the night and at first I didn't know why. It wasn't until I felt something moving on me did I realize why I had awakened. Oh God, was I having an evil nightmare? I was afraid to move. I lay stock still on my back as whatever it was positioned itself on the left side of my stomach and stayed there. Then, it dawned on me: one of the damn cats. I was annoyed now. In order to keep the cat comfortable, I would have to stay in the same position. No chance, I had to move eventually. When I did, the cat ran for its life. Dumb animal. I guessed this would be the beginning of more adventures to come with the three house cats.

As things turned out, I didn't score a friendship with any of the cats. Within the first week of being there, the cats hated me. As Sparky and Spot loved to hangout on the stairs, after flattening each of them twice with my large-booted feet, they got the hint that I was dangerous, however unintentionally. Whenever the cats sensed me emerging from my room, or coming down the stairs, they would scatter as if a dinosaur were coming. It was quite comical to me, but the Smiths were concerned that when I appeared, the animals hid. I felt a little bad. Sure, I hadn't stepped on them on purpose, but I wished it hadn't happened. My thudding feet interspersed with the jingle of the cat collars as the cats ran for cover became a routine sound track.

As the Smiths lived fairly close to the Jacobs, Zoey and I still got to ride the same bus to school.

The first few weeks of December were blissful. I felt like a new person in my new home with the Smiths. I pretended as if I had always been their kid, although I was told to call Mr. Smith by his first name. Mrs. Leach, the vision assistant was a great help as well. She always had something funny to tell us and continually brought Heath Bars.

I had Harry *Potter*, Zoey, and the Smiths on my side, and I was making good grades. Life was so good in Burgson that I wasn't at all anxious to visit my family at the Box on the weekends as planned.

The first weekend in December, I lied to my grandmother and said that there was a school function for which I needed to stay in Burgson. I also lied to the Smiths, telling them that Grandma couldn't pick me up. As they had planned a weekend of sightseeing at several Civil War memorial museums, the Smiths were quite furious. I didn't care that they were upset. I was just glad that I didn't have to leave my new home. I was in love with the Smiths, and the new life they were giving me, but I knew that my lying stunt to avoid going to DC would never work again. I would have to go home on the weekends as agreed. The plan was that Grandma would pick me up on Fridays with the car Grandpa -- with who she had reconciled -- had gotten for her from an auction, and Michele would take me back on Sunday evenings.

"I love it here Zoey. That's why I lied," I told Zoey on the phone the day it was announced that George Bush won the presidency. Zoey and I had just finished arguing about it.

"I don't wanna go home but I know I have to."

Within a month of staying with the Smiths, I was spoiled. You couldn't blame me. Before coming here, all I had known was poor people's living, and going to be in the Box for the weekend would be revisiting that life. For the first time, I would have a sense of stability. To my frustration, nothing could stop my having to go home for the entire Christmas break, oy gevalt. It turned out to be the Christmas to miss the Smiths.

Instead of sleeping at the Box for Christmas, my sisters and I went to stay at Haily and Marcus's house. I felt so out of place being with my family.

"Why Mario act like that?" Asia said to Haily on Christmas Eve as I sat on the basement couch listening to a CD player.

"He can hear you," replied Haily.

"Yeah, Mario, why you act like that?"

"How do I act?" I asked, my throat tight with nerves.

"You act and talk like you white. You act like you're better than us." Here we go again. I was sick of this "you act white" stuff. I'd heard it all my life and now that I was living with white people, they were really attacking me with this color nonsense. "Well, I hope you know you coming home at the end of the school year. Those people can think they keepin' you if they want. But nah, you coming home." I tried to ignore my sister as I listened to the *Titanic* soundtrack CD my cousin Hasan had given me as a Christmas gift. I wasn't acting white. I didn't want to think about the end of the year because I didn't want to consider having to ever leave Hamax and my friends. Actually, I hoped that the Smiths would change their minds and allow me to stay past eighth grade, but I knew they wouldn't. That would be too complicated. More importantly, Grandma would never agree to that. They had gotten her to relent and support my one-year stay in Burgson with the promise that it was only until the end of the school year.

Before I left for Christmas break, Brian had let slip that the only way for me to legally stay in Burgson past the current school year would be for someone to adopt me or assume custody of me. I knew this would never happen, but maybe, just maybe, the Smiths could help me develop a plan.

The day after Christmas, things got stranger for me. Marcus's son, Justin, and I were the only ones home for much of the day. For the first half of the day, Justin and I busied ourselves with me trying to teach him how to play the *Titanic* theme song, "My Heart Will Go On." After taking a break for lunch, I sat on the couch in front of the big-screen television in Haily's basement. Without preamble, Justin began walking in circles around the couch I was sitting on, talking in a wannabe scary voice.

"So Mario," he said, making his voice deeper and scratchy, as if he were trying to imitate a monster. "How have you been," he continued, "without being able to hang out with your family? Really, I wanna know, how is ... how is." Then, he stopped speaking and continued walking in circles. In this awkward moment, the shuffle and thud of his feet was far too loud for the dull quiet of the basement. I wondered what the heck was Justin doing? "I wanna know about your ... ." Then, Justin walked over to me, grabbed the front of my jeans, and violated me. I just sat there, frozen. It was as if I had no control of my arms or legs. Misreading my unresponsiveness, Justin continued his violation. My brain was stuck, as if someone had pressed the pause button. The freeze held me. After some time, He stopped. I hurriedly fixed myself, and got off the couch to head for the piano keyboard. I felt dirty. I wondered why Justin had suddenly decided to violate me. Oh God was I confused. Why did I let him do that to me? Every relevant memory from my younger childhood revisited me, worsening my internal torment.

By New Year's Eve, I was back in the Smith's large home. Briefly, I felt down that I wasn't in church with my family, listening to Elder Michael

Fields preach the congregation into a new year, like he always does. I still had a great night watching cable television and drinking wine. Well, Mrs. Smith let me take one sip of her wine glass after 12:00 midnight and I felt so grown up.

The new year brought with it a few surprises. "You're going to get your own computer," Mrs. Smith began one afternoon after school in early January, "WTOP, the DC FM news radio station had a contest going on during Christmas about giving start-up computers to less fortunate people. I wrote in about you and you're one of the stories that won." I was stunned that Mrs. Smith had done something so nice. She then went on to say that a church had donated $1,000 for purchasing a copy of Jobs Access with Speech, or JAWS for me. JAWS is a screen-reading software that converts all text displayed on a computer screen to speech. In short, it makes the computer talk. With JAWS, a trained blind person can perform most tasks a sighted person can do with the mouse just by using the keyboard. It's just a matter of learning the hotkey combinations such as Control-P for print or, Alt-F4 to close a program. I had been initially introduced to JAWS during the seventh grade when Mrs. Krebs made it her priority that I was familiarized with all assistive technology. She made all of the blind students get email accounts, and that we checked it on a regular basis. I had gotten so good that I was providing technology training for my peers and teachers. Nevertheless, I only possessed a rudimentary knowledge of JAWS and the PC computer. I wasn't sure whether I knew enough to own my own computer.

"The church is also paying for four hours of one-on-one JAWS training with a computer trainer." Said Mrs. Smith.

"Wow. Thank you, thank you, thank you." I was beyond elated. I couldn't wait to get my new computer.

Two days later, Mrs. Smith, Brian and I schlepped to DC to the WTOP studios, where in addition to picking up the new computer, I got a tour of the broadcast facilities, and I was permitted to sit in the room as the reporters went on the air. Although I was young, I had been listening to WTOP at night and I knew most of the reporters.

"I've never met a teenager like you who'd rather be listening to us rather than the hit music stations like Z104 or Hot 99.5." said the Program Director.

Brian was an information and technology expert, so it was only fitting that he set my computer up, and installed all of the Microsoft Office applications and JAWS. In no time, I was on the computer, acclimating myself to my new digital friend. Sure, I wasn't a JAWS expert, but I somehow managed to download Napster and join in the hysteria of online music pirating.

Although I was on a 56k modem, I downloaded one hundred songs in the first week. It was a good thing I was due to have JAWS training because less than a week later, Brian was trying to fix the computer. Stupidly, I had renamed all of my important drives and folders "Mario." This was obviously something Windows 98 wasn't built to handle. I named my computer, my documents, my files, music, and all of my system drives Mario. That, coupled with the music downloads -- no wonder the computer went haywire. Brian was understandably upset that it took him hours to reinstall Windows and all of the essential applications. He told me that all of my downloaded music was gone. I was sad, but smart enough to not make the same stupid mistakes again.

When I finally did get the four hours of JAWS training that took place in the resource room at Hamax one day after school, I was all ears. As a totally blind computer user, I learned how to browse the Internet, add pictures to a document and how to email and word process. I spent hours on my computer at home familiarizing myself with the Windows system and Internet browser. In no time, I was a damn good troubleshooter myself, eventually able to undo any new problems I caused along the way. I would panic that Brian would find out that I messed up the computer again, and after hours of working at it, I would manage to fix the problems.

In addition to the computer, the new year brought a new instrument into my life. The Smiths, although they complained of Grandma not sending very much money for me, used the amount Grandma did send to pay for guitar lessons. I was now taking guitar as an elective and I wanted to get private lessons from the guitar teacher. My lessons were $15 for an hour, and I had a lesson every Monday after school. I was amazed that the school furnished me with a practice guitar to use at home. I studied the guitar like there was no tomorrow: in the morning before school, late at night before bed. I was best friends with my guitar.

I also joined the student body news team. We broadcasted on our closed circuit channel every Tuesday morning at 11. The whole school watched. I was put on to do the weather with a Spanish girl, and I loved the experience. I discovered my passion for broadcasting, which led to my sister Maria and me recording our own radio shows on the weekend.

This period in my teenage life is when my body started changing dramatically, and I had no one with whom I could discuss my frustrations. I would sometimes lie against my bed and slide my frame across it, desperately trying to put out the annoying feeling that kept me awake. Fathers are supposed to talk to their sons about their bodies, but I was fatherless.

As I had gotten quite good at the guitar, the Smiths thought I was nuts for not performing a song on the guitar for the eighth grade talent show tryouts. Instead, I decided to sing a catchy song I absolutely loved. Unfortunately, I didn't really know the meaning of the song's lyrics. The song was "Misery" by Green Day. It has an infectious melody and the lead vocals are well done. In the end, the song got me reprimands from Mrs. Krebs, her daughter Sarah, and the Smiths. On the day of tryouts in one of the middle school classrooms, and after Zoey had sung Jessica Andrews' country hit, "Who I am," I handed my CD to the talent show head and was guided to the front of the room. Happily, I sang along with Green Day: "And they're gonna get high high high, when they're low, low, low. The fire burns from better days."

"Sarah said that the song is about bludgeoning someone and getting high Mario." Mrs. Krebs said disgustedly back in the resource room once the talent show tryout results were out. Tomoko and Zoey had made it into the show, and I hadn't. I felt so stupid. Nevertheless, I was there with Zoey's family on talent show night in late February, cheering her on. She got a standing ovation. I was truly happy for, but very envious of my best friend. I should have been on that stage. Tomoko and Zoey were stunning. In the end, a Green Day song still made it into the talent show after all. Another kid performed Green Day's "Time of Your Life" and played the guitar for himself. This song isn't about drugs and bludgeoning someone. God -- I wish I had known the meaning of "misery" song before auditioning.

The end of something great can come when you least expect it. As May approached, the Smiths, Mrs. Krebs, and Ms. Perry-Thibault started talking at length about the end of the school year for me. No one wanted to see me return to Maryland, nor did I want to return. My life belonged in Burgson. I loved the escape from my family. I was focused, stronger, happier and doing phenomenally in school. The plan was that Mrs. Krebs would seek custody of me so that I could legally stay in Burgson to attend school. No longer would I have to worry about moving all the time, poverty and a bad school system. Burgson County had changed my life. I was now using a computer regularly, excelling in school and without stress. The thing was to figure out a way to get Grandma to agree. Grandma didn't know their plan yet, and I was glad. She would probably take me out of Hamax in a flash if she knew. The social worker told Mrs. Krebs to get in contact with my father. If a living parent gave their consent, then the county could move forward somehow with custodial talks. Mrs. Krebs was able to reach my father and one day in mid-April, I spoke with him for the first time since he had been arrested several years back.

CHAPTER 14– OUTSIDE A CHILD'S PLACE

"Hey son." Said my father ecstatically. I guessed prison had Jesused and sobered him down a bit.

"Yes."

"They told me about what's going on, son, and I know it's a fantastic opportunity for you. You know, my Mother, your grandmother, can be very afraid sometimes, 'cause she ain't able to understand. I always knew you was real intelligent ... huh, like you was real smart even coming up. I know this is good for you so I'm gonna tell Grandma that she need to go on and let these people do what they trying to do for you."

"OK," I replied, stunned into silence that my father was on the phone. Damn it. I was that eight-year-old little boy again. I wanted him to say sorry.

"I got to go, but you know I love you, right son?"

"I love you also," I said, feeling as if I were telling this to an absolute stranger. I didn't know him, how could I love him? I was ecstatic though, that it looked as if our plan would work. Hopefully, with my father on our side and willing to reason with Grandma, I would have a chance of staying in my new life. Not really. When I went home for the weekend, Grandma was up in arms about a call she had gotten from my father.

"Those white folk called Nathan in prison and told him some bull story about Mario to get him to agree. He says now he feels like he was lied to." What on earth was Grandma talking about? Mrs. Krebs hadn't lied. No one lied about anything. Now, from the looks of things, my father had decided against trying to change Grandma's mind.

"Anyway, he gave custody to me," Grandma continued. "They should have left that man alone. He in there doing his time and they come bothering him with some mess. I can't wait until the end of this school year so I can get Mario out of there."

A thick dread filled me. Grandma would be unmovable this time.

Back in Burgson the following week, late one school evening, I vented to Ms. Perry-Thibault over the phone about my grandmother, and how I knew she wouldn't let me stay.

"Well, we're going to figure out something. That is not a good school system, Mario, and I won't see you having to go back there. We may have to take your grandmother to court. At your age, a judge will side with you regarding where you'd like to live. It would mean breaking your grandmother's heart though." I didn't know whether I had heard Ms. Perry-Thibault correctly. She was suggesting that I break Grandma's heart and tell her I didn't want to be with her anymore in the court of law. A part of me knew that this exercise might be necessary, but the other half of me feared breaking Grandma's heart.

As Ms. Perry-Thibault continued to talk, a sorrow filled me. I cursed God for making me blind and putting me in the position to have to make decisions like this. I was a thirteen-year-old boy, torn between the world I wanted to be in, and the world that refused to let me go. Tears fell and before I could stop myself I said miserably: "I want to be in my grave." and then, I hung up on Ms. Perry-Thibault.

After hanging up on her, I practiced the guitar and then climbed into bed. All of my family would hate me if I broke Grandma's heart and agreed to go to court to voice my wish to no longer live with her. Ms. Perry-Thibault said that the court could order that I go home on the weekends and that it could be a joint custody venture between Mrs. Krebs and Grandma. I knew that would never work. What with my grandma's belief that I'd be on *Oprah* without giving her credit, I knew she would see this as her fear coming true. After all, I had overheard her telling Haily that she believed the white folks were brainwashing me and trying to take me. She thought my mind was gone and that I seemed to be ashamed of her. It broke my heart to hear Grandma think I was ashamed of her, so I definitely couldn't break her heart like this.

But what about Hamax? The good technology, great curriculum and my friends who loved me. I was happiest here. I had stability. That's all Mrs. Krebs and the rest involved wanted me to have, stability. All of this was an impossible ordeal for a 13-year-old to weigh.

The next morning during breakfast, Brian was quite standoffish. He gave me my bowl of Lucky Charms—an every morning delicacy for me—without a word. When the bus came, he guided me to it without talking to me or saying goodbye. What had I done? After school, Brian's strange behavior continued. Mrs. Smith was also standoffish. After dinner, I went up to browse the Internet when she called me down to the family room.

"Do you have something to tell us Mario?" My throat tightened. I didn't know what she was talking about.

"No I don't." I replied weakly, "Is something wrong?"

"We got a call from Ms. Thibault last night," said Brian, coughing his smoker's cough. My throat tightened even more.

"So, do you have anything to tell us Mario?" asked Mrs. Smith again.

"No, I don't."

"You had a conversation with her about what's going on we know, but what did you say to her?" After a very long silence, I lifted my head from the sofa arm where I had been resting it.

"I told her ... I told her that I wanted to be in my grave." A painful silence filled the room.

"I'm not happy," said Mrs. Smith, and I could hear it in her voice. It wasn't anger I heard in her quiet voice, it was utter disappointment. I had greatly disappointed her and she couldn't handle it.

"You are a thirteen-year-old little boy," Brian began, "You can't go around saying things like this. You have at least sixty or seventy years left and you shouldn't be saying things like this and scaring people, Mario." I felt embarrassed. Did they truly think I said it for real? I didn't say I'd kill myself; I just felt powerless and spoke those words. Mrs. Smith, on the other hand, stayed quiet as Brian lectured.

"You are a smart boy. Why would you wanna scare people like that when you've got your whole life ahead of you? You've got a brilliant brain. We are so disappointed." Brian's simple words cut like a knife.

Mrs. Smith stood, walked over to me and said "I am not happy. No, I'm not happy at all." And with that, she left for bed.

"You've got some thinking to do," said Brian, turning off the television and then he too left me to sit alone. I was stuck there, frozen in time.

The next few weeks at the Smiths were quite uncomfortable. I didn't know how to make them feel good about me again. They repeatedly had talks with me about taking Grandma to court all the way into the month of May.

"The school year ends soon, Mario. Unfortunately, because of where we are in our lives, we can only keep you until the end of the school year as you well know. In order for you to legally stay in the county, someone has to have custody. Mrs. Krebs is willing and we will still be a part of your life, but you've got a decision to make. There are too many hands involved and we must be careful."

"I know," I said.

"You've got to decide whether you're strong enough to tell a judge that you no longer want to be with your grandmother. I mean, of course, they will probably paint her unfit to take care of a blind child and in comparison, they will see Burgson as heaven for you. Nevertheless, your testimony is what will matter." I hated this part of things. Why did they have to bring the court stuff up? It made me feel very scared whenever someone talked about it. How could I take Grandma to court? I didn't want to lose my friends and Hamax. I didn't want to go back to the county that labeled me a troublemaker and malfunctioned. I was so confused, torn in 50 million pieces. In the end, though, I would never get to decide whether I would be for or against the court request for custody.

While at the Box one weekend in mid-May, I could tell something was bothering Grandma. She was noticeably distraught. She continually reminded me that I was a Bonds. "Those people ain't done nothing for you and I don't care what they say, you ain't staying. I know what they want and I'm not gonna let it happen." Before church on Sunday, the phone in the Box rang and Grandma answered it. As my sisters and I dressed for church, I listened hard. I recognized the loud voice coming through the telephone. It was Ms. Perry-Thibault, doing as she promised. She warned that she would call my grandmother to give her a piece of her mind, and it sounded like that's exactly what she was doing.

"You are holding him back and trying to hinder him," Ms. Perry-Thibault said passionately. "That's not right, Pearl. He's got a great opportunity here in Burgson."

"Mario ain't staying in Burgson."

"But why not, Ms. Bonds? Why are you trying to hold him back? I tell you what, we're gonna do what we have to do to make sure he doesn't have to stay with you anymore. He deserves a greater education than Hunsville and we won't let you hold him back."

"Oh, you're not, huh?" said Grandma, now obviously upset. "We'll see." And with that, Grandma put down the phone. Grandma then dialed Haily and told her everything. Seething with rage, Grandma talked slowly and deliberately. "I knew that's what they were trying to do. The white woman called here and basically gonna tell me that they gonna do what they have to do to take Mario from me."

"What?" I heard Haily scream. I had heard enough. I walked down the Box's front stairs, out the door and waited outside. My sisters came out moments later and attempted to help me to the church. I turned them down. I was too upset. When Grandma emerged from the Box, she said: "You ain't goin' back to Hamax, Mario. I'm going down there next week and I'm gonna withdraw you. I ain't having this mess." I panicked. Everything was falling apart quickly. Inwardly, I cursed Ms. Perry-Thibault for complicating things. Grandma and I walked into the church, the distress visible on my face. She couldn't be serious. She was going to pull me out of school with less than a month left?

After church, using my cane, I found my way back to the Box and hurried upstairs to the phone. I frantically dialed the Smiths. Brian answered on the second ring.

"I'm not coming back," I said, my voice shaking and eyes tearful.

"What do you mean?" Brian asked.

"Ms. Perry-Thibault called my grandmother and told her that the county was prepared to do whatever they needed to do."

"What? This is what I mean that too many hands are involved. I don't believe this." I couldn't believe it either. "Can her mind be changed?"

"No, Brian. She's serious."

"Oh God, you've gotta decide whether you'd like to proceed with a case." I tuned out. I wanted to stay in Burgson, but I knew I didn't have the strength or courage to hurt Grandma.

The next day, my sisters went to Haily's house and to my utter surprise; Grandma and I drove to North Carolina with a Deacon from the church. She was going down to visit her mother and had decided to take me with her. Yeah. It was

Monday morning and instead of being in school at Hamax, I wasn't going to any school. She was taking me to North Carolina with her until she could figure what to do next. The next morning, I awoke from a restless sleep. For a few seconds, I had no idea where I was. Then, my plight and where I was hit me like a ton of bricks. Impossible. Grandma couldn't be serious about taking me away from Hamax and Zoey a month before school ends. I got up and went into the room where my grandmother had slept for the night.

"Come here Mario," she said softly. I walked to where I heard her voice. She was sitting on a couch. I sat on the floor in front of her, my legs folded.

"Now Mario, you ain't going back to Hamax. When we get back, I'm gonna register you at Livist Middle School where Marian and Maria are. You coming back to Maryland with your family. Kevin, Adonis, everybody is in Maryland and you will be too." As she spoke those words, I melted. Furious tears fell from my eyes as I sobbed hopelessly. The truth was finally setting in. She was taking me away from Zoey, Paul, Ciara and Tomoko. I had to go back to Hunsville County.

"I'm sorry Mario. I'm so sorry." But her sorry didn't mean anything. We sat there for what seemed like an eternity. Me, crying inconsolably, Grandma troubled but determined.

Two weeks later, my grandmother and I walked into Livist Middle School in Mitchville, MD.

"How can I help you?" asked the front desk secretary.

"I want to register him for school," replied my grandmother confidently.

"What?" said the secretary before she could catch herself, "Ma'am, you do know that there's only a few weeks left of school?"

"Yes I do," replied Grandma. I was embarrassed. We must have looked like fools. There I was, my grandma registering me in a middle school that would be out of session in less than three weeks. I had spent the previous two weeks lying around the Box during the day while my sisters went to school, and Grandma looked for a house. The next day, I got up, got dressed and drove with my sisters and Grandma from DC to Mitchville for my first day at my new middle school. If it hadn't been for Zoey and my radio programs, I would have lost my mind. Thank God I could get lost in other worlds when I listened to my cassettes.

It took me years to understand Grandma's actions. Had she been wrong or right about what she had done? Had she acted selfishly or simply on impulse?

Livist was a far cry from Hamax. First, it wasn't a secondary school, and the students were out of control. A school where 99 percent of the population was black, for some reason, Livist was more of a playground than a place of preparatory academia. It was at Livist where, for the first time, I met a boy who identified as being gay.

"Mario, I'll buy the candy for you," said Jack Edison one day in class. He passed a boy selling fundraiser candy bars $2 on my behalf. A second later, I had two nice chocolate almond candy bars in my hand.

"Ay, buy one for me man," said a boy in the front of the class. Jack and I were seated next to one another in the back of the classroom, one row behind the kid with the candy.

"Nooo." said Jack dramatically. His voice was quite feminine, as if he were trying to imitate a woman.

"Why you buy one for him then?" asked the boy.

"Cause, Mario special," Jack replied, briefly rubbing my arm.

Uncomfortable, I began humming "La la la la la. It goes around the world."

"Oh my God," began Jack, "I love that song. It's so magical."

Later that day during lunch, Jack's interest in other boys was the topic for discussion.

"Yes I am gay, and I love it," he told the group of us seated with him.

"Oh my God," I said, amazed. "I've never met a gay person before. How is that possible? You call guys your boy friend?" With all that had happened to me in my younger years, I was amazed that I was meeting a real person who was claiming to be gay. This was a first.

"Yes. I am a bottom."

I was utterly confused. What the heck was a bottom? "What's that?" I asked as the other students at our table laughed at me.

"It means he let guys use their thangs to do nasty things to him. said a loud, dismissive girl, slamming down her lunch and taking a seat at our table.

"Girl, shut it up," said Jack. "Psych you out. It does mean that though. Lemme try to clear that up. During those kinds of moments ... well ... the bottom is the woman and the top is the man Hint hint." With that, he giggled.

"And you do those things?" I asked, realizing what Jack meant. Jack's words left me feeling slightly repulsed, but amazed just the same. The more Jack talked about it, my amazement and repulsion turn to intrigue. I didn't want to experience any of it myself, but I was rather amused by Jack's obsession with the subject.

"So, you're the girl in your relationships?" I asked.

"Yeah, I am."

Later that evening, I was so intrigued by the conversation with Jack that I recounted it to a laughing Maria. She asked for more details as her laughter grew.

"Marian, come here. Listen to what Mario said this gay boy told him at school." Then, I recounted the exchange with Jack again and Marian had her share of laughter. I started to laugh also. To my horror, my sisters, overcome with amusement, told Grandma about Jack and the things he told me. Grandma, however, wasn't laughing. She was furious.

"What else that little boy say?" I heard Grandma ask Maria. Marian and Maria continued to laugh, but Grandma wasn't at all amused. She vowed to march into Livist's front office and tell the principal about the pervert Jack. Jack wasn't a pervert. I thought he was just a kind guy that was answering questions I asked him, but Grandma was so sure Jack had been preying on me. Maybe he was with the "Mario is special" and candy purchases, but that wasn't anything conclusive. Nevertheless, true to her word, and to my dismay, Grandma did march into the front office and tell them. Jack was first reprimanded, suspended, and then forced to join a gay teen private support group. I felt awful for him, but I couldn't let anyone else know about my participation in the conversation with Jack. Shamefully, I pretended to be upset by Jack's words so that my sisters wouldn't think me gay.

In front of the principal, I said, "And what repulses me more was how comfortable he was in telling me." In truth, Jack's words had planted a bitter seed in me. I wondered how boys could do those things to one another. Why weren't women enough? God, I was so confused.

Saying goodbye to Zoey was the most painful thing I had to do. I was invited to her house for the third weekend in June. Burgson County was having a picnic for all of its visually impaired students and their teachers. Zoey, her mom and I attended the picnic on Saturday, and then Zoey and I spent Sunday together before Michele picked me up to take me back to the Box. Zoey had already spent much of the weekend crying, but she wasn't yet out of tears. As 6:00 loomed, I began my goodbye.

"Well, Zoey, Michele will be here any minute. Zoey?"

"Yeah ... this is too hard for me Mario," Zoey said, grabbing my hands. We were sitting in her room atop her well-cushioned bed.

"I know, Zoey. You and your parents have done everything in the world for me. I don't know how we will talk."

"That's just it," she interrupted, squeezing my hand. "How will we contact you? I'm gonna miss you." With that, her tears fell more freely. I cried too, my sobs inaudible. I didn't know how I would talk to Zoey once I was back in Maryland. I always thought we would go to high school together, but that wasn't going to happen. Zoey rested her head on my right shoulder, and I toyed with her hair as I always did when we goofed off. Male and female best friends, brother and sister. Zoey straightened, wiped her face and then grabbed my hands again. We sat in silence, squeezing each other's hands, silently crying and never wanting the moment to end.

CHAPTER 15— GAIN A BLESSING

Since leaving Burgson back in November of 2000, Grandma had been working with the Hunsville County Social Services in Maryland to find a Section 8 home for us. Their efforts were eventually successful and on July 4, 2001, Maria, Marian, Grandma, my Aunt Lisa and her three-year-old daughter Bria and I moved into a three-floor, three-room townhouse in Tanville, MD. George and their other two kids were living elsewhere.

"Happy Independence Day, Mario and welcome home," Grandma said as I stepped into the house behind her on moving day. Since my goodbye to Zoey after the Vision Picnic in early June, I was still upset with Grandma for taking me from my Burgson heaven. On this day, however, I couldn't help smiling at my grandma's "welcome home," and it was nice to see her happy.

Maria and Marian were going to share a room, while Grandma and I had our own, and Lisa had the basement. I was surprised and elated to have my own room again. Bitterly, I thought of how much of a far cry the size of my current subsidized room was from the spacious one I'd had at the Smiths. Boy, had a poor boy been spoiled in Virginia. God had finally blessed us with our own place. no one in our family had anything to do with it, and no one in the family could take it away from us, or so I thought.

For Grandma's sake, I decided that I would give our new home a chance, and finally give up on my prayer to return to Burgson. She busied herself with unpacking the few things we did have and organizing the house. There wasn't too much to organize since once again, all of the things Grandma put into storage when she and my sisters left Virginia was, according to Haily, destroyed. We didn't have beds, but I was glad to have a home, and I hoped we would stay for a while.

After only two weeks in Tanville, Haily's children were living with us for what was said to be just for the summer. The electricity bill hadn't been paid at their house, so they were now with us. Haily always boasted about how much money she and Marcus had, so where was the money?

Shawn and Hasan slept on the living room floor, while Sefra slept in my grandmother's room, the only room with a bed. Justin was visiting his mom for the summer.

As usual, Shawn spent all day being entertained by his Play Station. Although I was blind, I played some of the fighting games with him, but he was always a sore loser. Even when we were younger, he would be excited by the challenge of playing a fighting game with a blind person, until I started winning.

Whenever Shawn was around, he and I got along like brothers. We would talk about rap music, or rather, Shawn would talk. Most of the time, I just listened, wishing I knew as much about DMX,

Fifty-Cent and Dr. Dre as he did. At the start of August, our talk switched to topics I had never discussed before. I had wished for someone to discuss these things with, but being fatherless, and with my older brothers gone, that was difficult. Shawn was a typical 15-year-old boy obsessed with girls. He told me countless stories about his encounters with girls, and the x-rated films he watched. Although I didn't let on, I was confused and ignorant. Whenever he talked about wanting a girl, he'd say: "Man, I wanna smash." I was only thirteen and I was highly jealous of him. I knew nothing about girls or what it meant for a guy to "smash."

Shawn's porn stories left me fascinated and grossed out all at once.

With all the talk about Shawn's encounters with girls, the strangest thing began happening to me in my sleep. Most mornings, I was horrified that I had wet my pants in the middle of the night. When I would touch just inside my underwear, I was shocked to find that what I thought was urine was dotted on the front. I thought something was severely wrong with me. I didn't understand why at age thirteen, I was urinating in my sleep. I realized one day that I always seem to wet my pants on the nights I had dreams about the girls in Shawn's stories, and girls I met at Livist Middle. I dreamt of kissing them, and during those dreams, I would feel like I was urinating at the same time. One morning, I awoke right after having one of those dreams.

"Oh my God, what is this God?" I would say, ashamed. Fatherless, and my older brothers living elsewhere, I didn't have any trustworthy male to ask about what was happening with me. I definitely couldn't ask Grandma. One night, I gathered up the courage to tell Shawn about my issue. Shawn, overcome with laughter, let me know what was up with me.

"Ha-ha, Mario having wet dreams." I didn't laugh with him. It wasn't funny. "Dude," began Shawn once his fit of laughter was over. "You having wet dreams. Dudes have wet dreams when they first start puberty. It's when sperm comes out while you're sleep. Ha-ha, who you thinkin' 'bout doin'?" He started laughing again. "When you start wanking, or doing things with a girl, it will stop."

I hadn't the foggiest what it meant to wank. "What's that?" I asked.

"Dawg, you don't know what wanking is? Beatin' off." he laughed again, making me feel more stupid. He told me how one does it and honestly, I was intrigued. Shawn was telling me that I wasn't wetting my pants during my dreams, but rather, I was having a normal response to them. He said that I could make myself experience the same thing while awake.

"Every dude does it. If a dude says he doesn't, he lying." He explained the mechanics to me, and then he left to sleep downstairs in the living room. It was nearly 4:00 a.m. and I wasn't interested in going to sleep now. Shawn and I had been up talking for hours, and before I went to bed, I was eager to experiment with the things he told me. I wanted to be a normal guy, and I needed confirmation that I wasn't wetting my pants.

I was fearful as I left my room, heading for the bathroom. There were two doors to the hall bathroom, one in the hall and the other in Grandma's room. I made sure both doors were locked before sitting on the edge of the tub. I listened to my grandmother snore, the sound akin to a truck stalling. Boy would she be ashamed of me if she knew what I was doing. But actually, I didn't really know what I was doing.

I did everything Shawn told me to do, and the experience frightened me to tears. In the aftermath, I longed for a father to better explain what I had done. I so badly wanted to talk to a grown-up about this, but there was no one. Fearful, my heart beating in my throat, I hurriedly washed my hands.

"This is weird," I said aloud." I was deeply frightened of what I had just done. I dried my hands, and quickly rushed from the bathroom, cursing Shawn for telling me about this stuff.

"Mario, what you doing boy?" came Grandma's sleepy voice, but I didn't answer. I went in my room and hurriedly closed the door.

"Am I a man now?" I said aloud, "What the heck did you just do?" Had I just done what Shawn was talking about? Again, I wished for a father to talk to about this. My fright was mixed with inquisition. Would I have to try again to understand what really happened? I went to bed, indifferent about what according to Shawn, all guys, to now include me were doing to themselves. Now, was I supposed to find a girl?

In the weeks and months that followed, I became a fanatic for the new thing I was doing. I did it six, seven, sometimes ten times a day. I felt like telling the whole world: "I'm a man. I'm worth something. When my grandmother handed me my first pair of boxers, again, I wanted to shout to the world that I was a man.

Shawn, Sefra and Hasan moved back home a week before school started. The day before my sisters and I started ninth grade at Tanville High, Haily came over to gather things her kids had left behind. We didn't have a phone, but Haily had a cell. While she chatted in the living room with Grandma, I snuck her cell phone and called the Jacobs'. As she hadn't heard from me in nearly three months and she and her parents' had been worried sick, Zoey was in tears. I felt loved and thankful that someone missed me.

At the start of ninth grade at Tanville High, I was frustrated. Sure, it was great that I was now a high-schooler, and that I was now wearing boxers like a real teenager, but I hated the fact that I wasn't in Burgson with my friends. On the first day of school, I was accidently placed in a classroom with mentally challenged students. The school thought that because I was blind, I belonged with them. It wasn't until a smart guidance counselor thought to call the Vision Program to let them know about me was I rescued from the classroom of yelling, snotting kids. The guidance counselor took me to the library where I was told to wait for my vision teacher. God, I hoped I would like my new vision teacher. When she walked into the library and spoke, I got a blast from the past.

"Well, hi Mario. It's Ms. Betz-Zachery."

My heartbeat was fierce, but not from fear. I was amazed. This was the woman from elementary school that I thought had been so mean to me. I had Ms. Betz-Zachery again? This was going to be a rollercoaster; I was sure of it.

To my surprise, things weren't that bad with Ms. Betz-Zachery. She supported me in everything I did and she also wasn't satisfied with the level of assistive services Hunsville County provided.

"Am I gonna get to use the computer with JAWS?"

"Maybe not this year," she replied.

"But, in Burgson, I used it all the time and even scanned and Brailled my own work." This was true. In Burgson, the resource rooms had Braille embossers, which are massive Braille printers. One could take a Microsoft Word document, use a Braille translation software and emboss the document with the Braille printer.

"We don't have the funds for that right now." I went home and complained to Grandma about Hunsville County. Doubtless exhausted with the Burgson vs. Hunsville County argument, Grandma called Haily, and to my surprise, Haily got results. She threatened to sue Hunsville County and its Vision Program if I wasn't given adequate access to technology. My aunt could be quite scary. Within a week of Haily's threat, however empty it may have been, there was a computer with JAWS installed in the resource room of the library where Ms. Betz-Zachery and I worked when I wasn't in class. I didn't get the Braille embosser, but the computer was a start, especially since the computer Mrs. Smith won for me from the radio station was in disrepair, and was with Uncle Rick in Delaware for him to fix. He promised to have it fixed and returned by the end of September.

The eleventh day of September 2001 brought with it a horror that shook the core of the world's existence, and mine. At the start of school on this day, I was requested to come to the school gym to be photographed for my high school identification card. Once that was completed, Ms. Betz-Zachery and I walked to my first period class, Local, State and National Government with Mr. Brown. At 09:03 a.m., we entered the classroom, and I rejoiced when I heard that the TV was on. I was ecstatic in my assumption that the class was obviously watching a movie today. My ignorant ecstasy was extinguished immediately as I took my seat and really understood the sounds I was hearing. Sounds of screaming, emergency vehicles, and news reporting flooded my ears.

"What's going on?" I asked, a rising panic in me.

"Oh my God. Somebody ... some terrorists blew up the World Trade Center. They crashed planes into them. Oh my God," came a girl's voice to my left. My heart dropped and my throat tightened. I was gripped with an inescapable, paralyzing fear. Were there more planes? I was sure that the end of all of our lives had come. Listening to the horror on live television, I cried, unable to ignore the yells of terror coming from the TV. Those were real people. This was not a movie. Those were not artificial sound effects perfected and timed by the hands of a Hollywood audio engineer. I was frightened and could only think of my family.

"Attention teachers and students. Hunsville County schools will be letting out for the day. Please keep students in your rooms until buses have arrived, or someone has indicated a pick-up." The announcement of school closing early increased fear for everyone.

Ms. Betz-Zachery took me to our resource room. In vain, she desperately tried to reach her sons.

"You see. It's that old arrogance of Bush," she said angrily, setting her phone on the table. I didn't know much about Bush's arrogance, but I knew that things were bad for the country. Grandma picked us up from school and we fought major traffic trying to get home.

"What do you think is gonna happen?" I asked my Aunt Renee as the family gathered in the living room that night. I was ecstatic to see her.

"The end of the world is getting ready to come." With her words, I was frozen with fear.

My family returned to business as usual after September 11, but I remained glued to C-Span radio, and Washington, DC's only FM all-day news radio station, WTOP. It took me several days to pick myself up. Wars and the threat of bombings were things that typically frightened me to silence for days on end when I let them. Grandma told me that I had to keep going and focus on school. Somehow, I did pick myself up again. It took weeks, but I was back.

"I've only stayed all day for the first few weeks because you're getting acclimated," said Ms. Betz-Zachery one day in her academic voice, "But, I'm an itinerate instructor. I will be here on certain days. OK, Mario." So, no embosser and no vision teacher around all day. What a far cry from Burgson. No more having all-day access to my vision instructor. Well … truthfully, I knew I didn't really need all-day access to a vision instructor. Burgson had made me quite an independent student. All I needed was the electronic PDA Braille note Ms. Betz-Zachery brought from the county, my Braille textbooks, the computer with JAWS in the library, and I was set. Ms. Betz-Zachery turned out to be more supportive than she realized for a vision teacher that couldn't stay all day.

When I joined the mock trial team headed by Mr. Brown, my National, State and Local Government teacher, Ms. Betz-Zachery attended nearly all practices after school, and never missed any of the mock trial tournaments that took place in real court rooms in Hunsville County, where I loved being the leading lawyer for the prosecution. She always drove me home after these tournaments while I devoured her son's snacks in the back seat.

After Haily's children left at the end of the summer, for a brief spell, it was just Grandma, us triplets and Lisa in the house. In late September, after we triplets turned fourteen, Renee and her kids came to stay. Renee was again trying to leave her husband Albert, and it was said that she was having issues again. Grandma always knew when Renee was having problems, and again, made herself available. We all knew that whenever Renee had that certain medical complication, it was her own fault.

In October, more people came to stay. George, O'Mon and J.R. became occupants of our Tanville home. Now, there were a total of twelve people in the house, and I was flabbergasted. Finally, after years of bouncing from place to place, Grandma had been blessed with a home for her, my sisters and me, and she was now compromising it by having more occupants than were allowed by our subsidized housing agreement. More drama and abuse was sure to ensue, and it did.

Even Haily had the nerve to complain about the extra houseguests compromising our blessing: "Ma, it don't make no sense that George living with y'all again. You got this house for you and those triplets. Not the whole world." it's funny that Haily didn't think this way when her electricity was off and she had sent her kids to stay with us during the summer. I don't know whether it was as a result of her marriage or something else, but I began to see a different side of Haily. Also, I didn't know whether it was temporary or here to stay, but Haily was actually becoming a lot of fun.

By November, I started to spend most weekends over her house, where Grandma and she thought it best for me to be able to hang out with Shawn, Hasan, and most importantly, Justin. I really did love the time I spent over there, mainly because Haily cursed like a sailor and that made practically everything she said hilariously funny. We would watch movies together, sing together and eat all types of food. I even began to develop small friendships with some of Shawn and Hasan's friends from their high school. Occasionally, my sisters would come on the weekends as well to hang out with Sefra. My sister Asia was long gone, living in her own apartment Haily had helped her secure several months earlier. On a number of our visits, Haily would give her opinion about our extra houseguests. Although I felt bad about doing it, I agreed with her, but regretted it every time I went home and saw O'Mon and J.R., whom I was really close to.

Most of the time, O'Mon and J.R. slept in my room with me. We each had a place on the floor and we would listen to *Harry Potter* and all of the music I liked. Aaron Carter, Billy Gilman, Michael Jackson, and Mariah Carey were in heavy rotation. At times, things were OK, and at other times, they annoyed me and I wanted them out.

By November, Uncle Rick returned my now-functional computer. Haily helped me set up the America Online free service disc. This was the time when America Online had these discs littered everywhere. It became routine for me to take my computer with me when I visited Haily's house on the weekends, so that everyone could take turns using the Internet. Hasan spent most of his time looking for girls on online, while Justin, Shawn and I focused on downloading music. By Thanksgiving, I had an impressive music library. thank goodness I was rebuilding the music library I lost the first time I crashed the computer back at the Smiths' in eighth grade.

Since I was also spending a lot of time playing the keyboard, my piano skills were quickly improving. My sisters and I were even writing songs together. We performed our songs for Haily, our older brothers and sisters, and Grandma. If she didn't praise anything else, Haily always praised our musical abilities, although she sometimes tried to lord her own children's lesser talents over ours. She thought I was a piano genius and always praised the vibrato in my voice.

"Boy, where you get that much vibrato at age fourteen?" She would say. Haily was so enthused about our song writing that she wanted to record a song Maria had written called "Savior." Something possessed Maria to write a gospel song to piano chords Kevin taught me during one of his visits, and it turned out beautifully. Kevin was famous for writing great music for songs for which he couldn't find words. George tried to join in the music frenzy as well. Rather annoyingly, he would sing to his daughter: "Pretty Bria," in an off-key, deep and scratchy droll.

"I can sing Mario. I'm telling you, back when I was in school, I could sing just like Kevin. I used to be singing so good that girls would hit me and say boy, you better stop. Ladies love me." I'd never have the guts to tell George that I wished he'd give up on his "Pretty Bria" song, and that his voice was horrid. I think even little Bria despised the song.

After several months of practicing with the Tanville Gospel Choir, my high school enjoyment was in full swing. The lead pianist for the choir was very talented, and I needed a lot of work. Mr. Prior, Tanville's music instructor, had a horn section, a bass guitarist, and for some reason, put me on keys alongside the other piano player. When the night of our Christmas/winter concert came, I surprised myself and the rest of the school with a piano solo at the end of a loud and upbeat gospel song, "The Battle." Truthfully, I had no idea what the heck I was doing; I was just going with the flow. I also accompanied the band on a song called "Now Behold the Lamb" by Kirk Franklin. The concert excitement went up to the next level when Maria and Marian sang as a duet the solo at the beginning of "Joyful, Joyful" from the movie *Sister Act II*. It was the first time the family realized that my sisters were really, really good vocalists. They got a standing ovation.

With the month of December came a telephone for our house. Grandma had received a financial settlement from a car accident case, and she allocated money for a phone. Although it was long distance, I made an effort to talk to the Jacobs, and I was glad I did. We decided that we would get together soon. During Christmas break, I went to visit them. They drove all the way from Virginia to get me, and I was so happy to see them. Zoey and I spent time playing the piano, eating our favorite foods, talking, laughing and watching movies like we used to do. Zoey wanted to make sure I listened to Toby Keith sing, "We'll put a boot in your ass, it's the American way," words from his "Courtesy of the Red, White and Blue" smash hit of 2001. I loved it. For a Christmas gift, the Jacobs gave me an external hard-drive so that I could burn my own CDs. Just as she had done back in June after the vision picnic, Zoey cried when it was time to say goodbye. We didn't get to talk that often since phone calls were long distance, but whenever we did talk, Zoey had to do the calling.

I was truly happy and thankful for the gift the Jacobs had given me, especially since Haily had promised me the same gift and it never appeared. Haily had a habit of making promises and never delivering, and even worse, wouldn't give you an update or explanation as to why what she promised wasn't happening. If she promised to take us to Six Flags on a given day, we would sit around all day wondering when we were going to leave for Six Flags. When 8 or 9:00 p.m. arrived, it was safe to guess that Six Flags wasn't happening. She was famous for telling you that she had done or purchased something great for you, when she knew she hadn't done a thing.

The Jacobs returned me home two days before the New Year. God, I would miss them. There was no telling the next time I would be able to visit. I hoped Zoey had her way, so it would be soon.

By January 2002, tensions in the house in Tanville were high, and per usual, drama and abuse ensued. Renee had moved back home, but George, Lisa, Bria, O'Mon and J.R. still remained. George and Lisa had become the house guests from hell. George would smoke marijuana in the backyard, prompting neighbors to complain to our landlord. He was emotionally and verbally abusive to everyone in the house. Maria and Marian got into big arguments with Lisa quite often. The friction and stress from all of the arguing and dysfunction sent Grandma's blood pressure through the roof. Again, she didn't have control of her household. Most of the time, Grandma seemed to side with Lisa and George during the spats and arguing. Indeed, Maria and Marian were fourteen, but they had had enough of George and Lisa controlling our home. Before George arrived, Lisa had been rather quiet, however, with his arrival arose a new side of her. Much of the fighting between Lisa and Maria would start over the heating system.

"Why she keep coming up here turning off the heat?" Maria asked loudly one night as we sat on Grandma's Rent-a-Center sofas in the living room after Lisa had closed the basement door and started to descend the stairs.

"What you say Maria?" said Lisa, pausing her descent. She'd overheard Maria after all. Lisa sounded to be ascending the stairs now. The basement door opened and Lisa repeated: "What you say?"

"You heard what I said. You keep on turning up the heat. We are burning up because of you. This ain't even your house."

Lisa exploded. "You need to learn some respect, Maria. I turn up the heat because it's cold down here."

"Well, you need to put on some more clothes cuz that ain't fair to us." I agreed with

Maria because I was terribly uncomfortable having to burn up on account of Lisa. However, I didn't want her to freeze. God, I hated those arguments.

George was basically an overgrown child and he did very stupid things. When he wanted to use the phone while I was using the Dial-up AOL service, he would quietly come upstairs and silently unplug the phone from the socket. I would try in vain to connect to the Internet, and not understand why JAWS continually said: "No dial tone." Investigatively, I used the telephone software through my computer to make a call. When the telephone line would come on through the computer speakers, sure enough, I would hear George enjoying a conversation with one of his street thugs. It wasn't his home, nor his phone line, so why didn't he just ask me to get off the Internet instead of trying to make me think the Internet wasn't functioning? His stupidity in thinking I wouldn't know what was happening was frustrating. Why was George so petty?

For weeks, George screamed at Grandma, continued to smoke outside and take our things. He was complicating relations between Grandma and the landlord. Maria and Marian continued to fight with Lisa over everything. George and Lisa were definitely running our house. However, to Grandma, it was Maria and Marian who was causing her stress by supposedly not being respectful. Because of Lisa and George, Maria and Marian argued with Grandma a lot as well.

One Sunday at church in early February, things got so terrible that Grandma's blood pressure rose to a dangerous level. This gave me a massive scare.

CHAPTER 16– LOSE A BLESSING

"What's wrong, Mother Bonds?" asked a missionary.

"My head hurt like I don't know what. I'll be alright. I just need to sit for a while in the Social Hall."

"At least let me take your blood pressure, Mother Bonds," said the missionary, placing the blood pressure device around Grandma's arm. "Oh Lord," said the missionary, "Mother Bonds, we need to call 911. Your blood pressure is 200/111."

Once at the hospital, Grandma's blood pressure was confirmed to be over stroke level. She wanted to leave, but the hospital refused to let her go. "Ms. Bonds, if you go, you're more than likely going to have a stroke."

Grandma stayed in the hospital for several days. She blamed her condition on Maria and Marian. This shocked me. It was George and his minions that were causing the problems, not us. Again, Grandma was siding with George—there goes that damn Mother's Syndrome again. Had Grandma forgotten the week before when I told her I was worried about her blood pressure? She had been arguing and screaming nonstop with George about his drug use and attitude. Nevertheless, because my sisters spoke their minds to George and Lisa, she was claiming it to be their fault. Sure, I agree they said a few disrespectful things to Grandma, but didn't she understand that they were frustrated to be going through the drama with her abusive, overgrown adult son with the mind of a sixteen-year-old boy? It wasn't fair.

During Grandma's time in the hospital, I stayed at Haily's house. Several times, I overheard Haily telling Grandma that she was messing with her blessing.

"Ma, the Lord gave you that house like you say you wanted for you and those triplets. You getting complaints and George over there causing mayhem. You need to put George out before he 'cause you and them triplets to lose that house. People already telling the landlord that you got a whole bunch of people living there."

Although I didn't know what would become of them, I hoped that Grandma would put George and his family out. I didn't want to be back on the street, bouncing around and I didn't want to lose what we had because of them. I thought, And this is the chaos for which I was taken from Burgson?

Occasionally, my sisters and I got a break from the drama by visiting our sister Nancy, who was now living with our Aunt Diane on our mother's side out in Alexandria, Virginia. Nancy had just had a baby at the end of 2001. We would tell her of all of the frustrating things happening at home.

"And Lisa be running stuff like it's her house. George be taking our food and smoking. Before Grandma went in the hospital, he punched a big hole in the wall downstairs, and he punched a hole in Grandma's bedroom door."

"That don't make no sense," Nancy said in her typical ghetto drag, "Why is Grandma allowing that to happen? She got God and all that, but damn."

I agreed with Nancy: Damn.

Another coping mechanism was the field trips we took with the gospel choir at Tanville High. We performed everywhere from nursing homes to other high schools, singing our hearts out to God, under the leadership of a great director. Tanville was quite lucky to have Mr. Prior. He was the only reason we had a music program. However, after I left Tanville, Mr. Prior went on to do other things with Bowie State University, and Tanville converted to a military academy.

In March, Haily started a family band that included some of her son's friends. She purchased guitars and keyboards and the band would have practice jam sessions on Fridays and Saturdays. My sisters and Sefra were background and lead singers while Hasan, Shawn, their friends JC, Chris and Deric were instrumentalists. Shawn would also rap sometimes. I wasn't happy about being placed on lead guitar while Hasan was placed on piano. I thought I played the piano tons times better than Hasan, but I guess Haily was smart. For the sophisticated gospel songs we covered, she put me on the piano, and used Hasan for the easier songs.

Haily had us learning songs from the gospel group Commissioned. I had to play and sing "Love is The Way," an upbeat tune where Commissioned sings about Christians knowing and operating in love. Practicing the high level songs Haily put in my lap is probably why I was able to get into Dugson High School for the Visual and Performing Arts.

During a choir practice in late March, Mr. Prior told the chorus students about Dugson's performing arts program. My sisters and I got applications, filled them out and sent them in. In early April, we received a response informing us of our audition dates. Haily was more excited than we were. When audition day came, an ecstatic Haily drove us to Dugson. While waiting to register, we met a woman who had been best friends with my mother when she was alive.

"Look at you," the woman began after Haily told her who I was. Haily had recognized the woman at once.

"You are far too cute. Look at him. I see he got those Bonds' men's thighs."

"Ha-ha," laughed Haily. "Yup. All of the Bonds men got big fatty thighs."

My sisters were auditioning as vocal majors, while I on the other hand as a piano major. My sisters went off somewhere else, while a student helped me to the piano major audition waiting area.

The waiting room was full of several acoustic pianos, and I was elated. Some students were playing piano, while others sat in chairs, waiting. Classical and popular music songs were being played. When one of the students started playing Alicia Keys' "Falling," I joined right in. Although I didn't mean to do so, I ended up stealing the moment from the boy that had started the song. When we were done, there was a "Go ahead, son" and "Damn, he can play" and "Ay, he blind. Wow."

For my actual audition, I played two original songs and Alicia Keys' R&B ballad "Falling," adding my own dramatic ending. When I was done, Professor Babit, a short and professorial woman said, "You can learn Braille music, right?"

"Yes."

She sounded friendly. "OK Mario, we'll be in contact."

For two weeks, we waited to hear from Dugson with the results of our auditions. When the results did come, the family was relieved to learn that the triplets had succeeded in getting accepted to Dugson High School's Visual and Performing Arts program.

With glee, Haily gave the good news to the rest of the band during practice one day: "And ya'll, your lead guitarist Mario has just been accepted to Dugson. His sisters are going, too," she had said in her most dramatic tone.

Unfortunately, Haily's band never got off the ground. Not only did we never get off the ground, we never made it out of Haily's basement.

Although Haily had talked a good game about gigs, going on tour, logos and T-shirts, nothing came to pass. The band was dismantled by late May, the same time at which drama hit an all-time high in my family.

One Saturday night in late May, Grandma and I were over at Haily's house, while Maria and Marian were at home. Grandma was well aware that there had been worse friction between Lisa, George, Marian and Maria all week long. Therefore, it was no surprise when Haily's phone rang that night.

"*What*?" Haily shrieked when she answered the phone. "George did *what*? Ma, George is over there beatin' on Maria." I was stunned. George had gone to another level and was putting his hands on Maria? I was afraid of the frenzy this would cause. Maria and Marian had doubtless called Adonis, Kevin, Asia and Nancy by now. What was going on?

"Shawn, Hasan, y'all come on," said Haily. Immediately, Grandma started to panic. Everyone in Haily's house hurried to the garage to leave. I walked with Grandma.

"What is he doing?" I heard Grandma murmur. "He gets a stick to take over there to hit my son with? Who does Marcus think he is?" A chill ran through my spine. Haily's husband, obviously feeling a part of the family now, was getting a stick so that he could help in the onslaught against George. This was going to be bad. I wished I could stop what I knew would be a family horror, but there was nothing to do. I was blind, fourteen and powerless.

When we arrived at the house in Tanville, there were several cars in front of the house. We heard yells and sobs coming from the house as Grandma and I walked in. Once the front door opened, I heard Maria crying: "Grandma." as she tried to get to Grandma. I was separated from Grandma as she headed up the front interior stairs that led to the living room. There were bodies moving everywhere. I could hear Kevin's, Adonis's, Shawn's, Hasan's, O'Mon's, J.R.'s, Marcus', Haily's, Lisa's, and Asia's voices as they all shouted, one side of the family against the other. I was jostled in the chaos and commotion, trying to work my way through the frenzied crowd of family members to get to the kitchen.

As I passed, I could feel that they had George pinned up against Grandma's deep freezer. Adonis and Kevin were swearing, jeering at George, "You gonna hit a little girl, George? A little girl."

"Be careful y'all. Don't break this woman's house up. Watch out for the balcony door glass," said Haily from somewhere in the living room. "They gonna take him right through the glass." The entire time, Grandma was sitting in the living room, clutching her heart, her blood pressure quite high by now. She was screaming to the Lord: "They evil Lord. Lord, what's wrong with them? They evil Lord." There was a series of slaps and punches as each young male—save George's sons—all took swipes at him. My mind was racing. I wanted to disappear again. I hated my feeling, hated the reality, and hated the fighting. I wish I were Aaron Carter, way out in Florida singing for the Disney channel. No one could hear me. Working my way away from the frenzy this time, I found my way to Grandma and just stood next to her where she sat on the couch, misery clouding my mind.

What would become of us? If the neighbors complained before to the landlord, they would definitely do it again. This disturbance would almost certainly make her not renew the lease. I was sure we would lose the house. Through George and the family, our blessing had been compromised. We were going to lose it.

At some point, the violence subsided and George retreated to the basement, just as the front door opened again, and in walked Nancy. Lisa cringed with Nancy's appearance. Nancy had driven all the way from Virginia at midnight to see about her young sister.

The next day, we triplets sat on the stairs at Haily's house as she tried her best to persuade the landlord to allow us to stay.

"He is leaving and will not live there any longer, Ms. Wright," said Haily, her voice quite professional, "OK. I do understand. Alright, bye." and with that, Haily ended the call. I knew she had bad news. "Well Ma, she said no," sighed Haily, downcast, "She said the neighbors complained too much and that she now knows that she is no longer cut out to be a landlord. She won't renew the lease. She wants ya'll out by August." Maria, Marian and I sucked in our breaths at the same time. I felt as if a load of bricks had just been placed on my head, and in my stomach. The reality of which many people had warned Grandma was clear. Her allowing George to stay in our home with his destructive, drugging ways, coupled with the far-too conspicuous family spat the previous night had caused us a problem. If something else didn't come along, we were going to be homeless again by August. It had taken years for Grandma to find and get approved for Section 8 subsidized housing, and just like that, we had lost it.

Ironically, the following week, George and his family moved into their own apartment. So unfair were the odds. They stayed long enough to get us put out of our home, and then moved into their own in no time.

The only thing that helped me cope with our impending home loss was the camps Ms. Betz-Zachery had lined up for me during the summer. By the close of school in June, I was preparing for The Living Learning summer program at the Maryland School for the Blind. For the entire month of July, the Maryland School for the Blind taught me how to cook, clean, wash dishes and clothes, iron, grocery shop and thus helped enhance my independent traveling skills. Although it was a residential summer program, it didn't include weekends. Kevin was asked to take me to meet the

MSB bus on Monday mornings, and he would pick me up on Friday afternoons at the bus station. The camp was a fantastic social experience since Antoine Banks, who became my best friend, was there as well.

Antoine and I were the most popular blind people on campus. My popularity was sustained due to one Beth Anne Krug, one of my MSB instructors. One day in the hall, overhearing me and a few of the other guys singing, Ms. Beth was astonished. She loved our version of NSYNC's "Gone" and approached us with the proposition of recording our own version. A week after her discovery of our singing, Antoine, Earl Distance, Thomas Chafy, Nathan Chant and I went to a recording studio. I was amazed to be standing in a studio for the first time. I delivered crisp, pop lead vocals for our recording of "Gone." I swore to myself that I would one day have a life where I could spend every day in the studio. Once back at the school, we were treated to a congratulatory party where Ms. Beth sold the CD for five dollars to the other students.

Although MSB was a load of fun, my battle with teenage self-worth and self-esteem was still alive. After all of the name-calling and teasing from my family, I truly believed myself to be an unattractive, funny-looking boy. My sisters always told me that my big toes looked like thumbs, and as a result, I refused to walk in sandals or bare feet for years. My sisters told me that my legs look like girl legs. As a result, I refused to wear shorts for years. When I visited Zoey earlier that year, her mother had tried in vain to get me to work on the exercise bike with shorts on; I flatly refused. Maria had teased me so much about being dark that I truly thought my complexion was the worst thing God had done to me. It didn't matter that Grandma would say: "Maria just as black as you are so she need to quit her crap. You are a good-looking chocolate boy."

While at MSB, as a defense mechanism, it was routine for me to crack jokes about myself and my experiences. On one such self-insulting occasion, Ms. Beth said: "Mario, if you could see yourself, you'd be conceited." I was shocked. Were my sisters wrong? I now understand that Maria's intention was to make me feel bad because I couldn't see myself, but she didn't mean anything she said or did. She was immature and holding on to very deep anger, brought about by our misfortunes. I only mean to illustrate the effect harsh words and name calling had on the build-up of my emotional volcano. Naturally, at times, I didn't care whether she meant it or not. The words, names and actions destroyed me and caused problems in my social environments. I'm thankful for the short time I had with Ms. Beth. She was the first person outside the family to tell me something kind about my personality, appearance and talents.

When the MSB program concluded, I spent the first seven days of August at an overnight camp put on by the Lighthouse for the Blind. We traveled to Shenandoah, Virginia to a camp site owned by the Lions Club. I had a blast at the camp, although I spent most of it starving myself to make sure I hardly had to use the camp restrooms. The only thing worth noting about this camping experience as it relates to my problem with socializing was the time one of the campers decided to purposely throw a rock at my head.

"Ow." I screamed, throwing my hand up to my forehead.

"What?" asked Chitora Johnson, a fellow camper, giggling, obviously assuming that I was still goofing off as I always did around her. She also became a good friend.

"Somebody threw something at me."

"What, I didn't throw anything at you, Mario."

I was livid. I was so angry I could have ripped the perpetrator apart.

"Michael did it," said Chitora.

Michael Spriggs, forever my enemy for no apparent reason, had struck me with a rock. What had I done to deserve that? Since a few blind teen support group sessions at the Lighthouse during the school year, Michael hated my guts. He said I thought I was all that and a bag of chips. If he only knew the sexual, self-esteem, self-worth and depression battles I was fighting. I was glad I had

Antoine at the overnight camp to keep me cool. I
was so jealous of Antoine and his fearlessness
around females.

"Man, I brought rubbers just in case we can
get some play."

"You're crazy, Antoine," I replied. Privately,
I was fascinated. This was my opportunity to see
what a rubber felt like. No one had ever shown me
one.

"Psych, give me one."

"Alright," said Antoine as he guided me to
the mess hall for dinner. I closely examined the
circular object.

"We'll see if you get lucky before me."
Antoine said, laughing. He was just kidding, but I
hoped I'd be lucky one day, although I knew it
wouldn't be before him. I longed to try on the
rubber to see what they were like. Antoine was
three years older than me and I wanted to be him
so badly. Antoine always said: "You're the singer,
musician, writer, person that can change his voice,
plus you got pretty skin, why do you want to be
me?" With little self-worth, positive words from
friends won't do any good for anyone.

On the day I returned from, my grandma
and sisters had packed up nearly all of our things
and we were ready to move stuff into storage yet
again. We were going to start moving things the
next day. For the rest of that day, however, we
triplets were to spend time with our older siblings,
who were taking us to see Martin Lawrence's live

comedy flick, *Run Tell That*. It was in Martin's film that I heard invaluable, therapeutic advice for handling life: "Life is too short, so ride this motherblanker until the wheels fall off," said an ecstatic Martin. He was right. The help from these words didn't take effect immediately, but they gave me food for thought.

CHAPTER 17— DUGSON HIGH

Once all of our things from the house in Tanville were packed away in storage, we moved back into the Box. The church made it available to us again. I felt like I was stepping back in the past when I sat down on the sofa I'd slept on every night during our previous stay in the Box one year before. As there were still two weeks left before the start of school, Grandma allowed us to go to Aunt Diane's house in Alexandria, Virginia to spend the rest of our summer break. We were concerned about where we would live so that we could still attend the performing arts School in Maryland. Because the Visual and Performing Arts was a magnet program, we could be bussed from anywhere in Hunsville County to Dugson, but the Box was in DC.

Maria and I spoke with Asia, who was living in Hilson, Maryland at the time—just eighteen minutes from Dugson—and we begged her to help us. After several long, persuasive conversations, she agreed that we could stay with her. We were relieved. We had been given the invaluable opportunity to attend a great Performing Arts High School, and we almost lost the chance if it hadn't been for Asia coming to our rescue. With no other alternative, Grandma immediately agreed to this plan.

Four days before school started, Maria, Marian and I moved into Asia's one-bedroom apartment. The three of us slept in the living room while Asia and her daughter Erica had the bedroom. Once again, I was stuck with girls, girls, and girls. A new roof, but the same environment.

"Won't y'all hangout with Mario, sometimes Kevin?" Asia said on one of Kevin's visits as she, Maria and Marian played cards. She either understood my loneliness, or was sick of having her little brother around all the time. Truthfully, it was agonizing to hear my sisters fret over cute boys, their sexy lips, nice bodies and stylish hats. I was fatigued with the boy talk. Stupidly, I sometimes wished I could join in the conversations somehow, but how could I? I was supposed to act as if I didn't care, as if I wasn't listening. The constant talk about cute boys, light-skinned brothers with cornrows, and dark-skinned men with muscles, made me feel drowned in a world of the forbidden. I wished there were someone around who talked about girls like that. I would rather feel uncomfortable hearing about girls than feeding my building fear of thinking I was gay.

To my surprise, Dugson High School turned out to be full of the type of boys Grandma didn't want me to befriend. The Dugson boys and girls wore their sexuality on their sleeves. I had never been anywhere like this. To my sisters' and Grandma's dislike, I did make friends with a number of the gay students. I felt most comfortable around them. They seem to be the most upfront and friendly people I had ever met.

Grandma feared that the homosexual boys were so nice to me because they wanted me.

"I keep having dreams about one of them taking advantage of you, Mario," Grandma would constantly tell me.

The Visual and Performing Arts Program, which was called VPA for short, was comprised of TV production, dance, an orchestra, band instrumentalists, and piano and vocal majors. The piano and vocal majors were a part of the concert chorus, which had practice Mondays and Wednesdays during and after school. Additionally, piano and vocal majors had to attend an applied music course during the day with the chorus director. Dugson had an alternating class schedule so that students didn't have the same course each day. All VPA students were required to take courses in piano theory. It is in piano theory class where I met Mr. Allen, who is responsible for teaching me everything scientific I know about the piano and elevating my music skills. He taught me all of the scales, simple and complex chords, and proper music terminology. He had never taught a blind student before and at first might have thought it challenging to work with a student with a visual impairment, but I proved otherwise.

I was a very fast learner. Mr. Allen and I developed a fine working relationship and he became a valuable mentor to me. I'll never forget his style when teaching me something new or his disappointment when it was obvious that I hadn't practiced, and as a result got a bad grade on a scale test.

"What are you doing boy?" he would say in his polite voice. Because it was the only class where I could put on headphones and lose my mind in the keyboard, I loved piano theory class. When I should have been paying attention to the lesson, I would be playing songs I learned on the radio.

My sisters and I wasted no time joining the Voices of Victory, VPA's gospel choir. Student led Voices of Victory was a powerful student group singing praises to the Lord. It is because of Voices of Victory that my attention was brought to Reginald Anderson, a dwarfish, scratchy voiced ninth-grader whose talent, at the time, gave me a run for my money. Reginald was a phenomenal pianist, and to this day, is the only musician who has ever made me nervous to play in his presence, albeit this hasn't happened since high school.

The Voices of Victory performed in all of the school's talent shows, and ventured out to perform at several youth services held by area churches during the school year. With my piano playing getting better and the constant pressure to improve all around me, I was quite happy that music was in full swing. My sisters and I didn't stop at just joining the gospel group. We auditioned for nearly every variety, talent and pep show held. The first show we auditioned for was the pep rally for Homecoming in late October, and it was at this audition where I met Patric.

As my sisters and I stood outside the school's auditorium with the rest of the students waiting to audition, we chatted with Patric about music. Although he also was a VPA student, this was our first time speaking to him. I found out that Patric was a seventeen-year-old vocal major and a senior. My sisters were going through the list of all of my talents, and Patric was very excited.

"Mario can rap, too." said an ecstatic Maria. Maria may have said terrible things to me about my appearance and all, but she sure enjoyed showing my talents off to other people. Likewise, although my sisters drove me crazy, I loved an opportunity to showcase their flawless voices.

"Oh yeah? Rap something," replied Patric, who was clearly very gay. Remembering the ordeal with Jack back in middle school, I was surprised that my sisters weren't put off by Patric's sexuality. Perhaps, they were just excited to be auditioning. Nevertheless, pumped up by all of the attention from the surrounding students, I rapped: "Now I would never diss my own momma just to get recognition. Take a second to listen who you think this record is dissin', but put yourself in my position. Just try to envision witnessing your momma poppin' proscription pills in the kitchen." Recognizing it as a verse from Eminem's "Cleaning Out My Closet," the students cheered, especially Patric.

In the end, my sisters and I were not chosen to perform in the pep show. At first, I was rather down about this, but I understood why we weren't picked. We had auditioned with the song "Ready for Love" by India Arie, which I now admit was an odd choice. "Ready for Love" is a very slow, love ballad completely inappropriate for a pep rally. We lost that opportunity, but I connected with someone I thought would be a good friend.

Patric showed an interest in getting to know me after we left the auditorium following the audition. He had waited outside during the audition, his fingers crossed hoping that we got in. He was the biggest enthusiast of the crowd that day.

After the unsuccessful audition, Patric and I spoke on the phone nearly everyday after school. We became friends fast, or so I thought. Eventually, he admitted he was gay, and asked me whether I was comfortable with having a gay friend. At first, I disregarded his questions, finding some clever way to change the subject, but in time, I did let him know that although I didn't have a problem with him being gay, my family would. One day, obviously feeling bolder, he decided to tell me about what it was like to be gay. Just as Jack had done back in Middle School, Patric tried to explain boy-on-boy affection to me. I was still surprised that some guys liked that sort of thing, but I didn't stop him from talking about it. Sometimes, during his unceremonious boy-on-boy talks, Patric would add: "Mario, you are so cute. Boy, I can show you." Then, he would laugh. Quite often, he would have his favorite song at the time, Missy Elliott's "Work It" playing in the background. "I'm serious," he would say. "When can you come over here?"

"I don't know," I would reply. Still a naive boy, I was just glad to have someone to call a friend in Maryland, someone who acted as if I was the most important person to them.

"Yes, let me show you."

For the rest of October and much of November during our phone conversations, Patric begged me to come over his house. We had been having repeated conversations about my insecurities, and how hard it was for me to trust anyone. Patric reassured me that he was my friend. Honestly, it felt good having someone admire how I looked. The world was invisible to me, but being told I was cute made me feel very visible. Whenever someone said I was cute, temporarily, it made me feel empowered and as if I was "all-that and a bag of chips."

By Thanksgiving break, certain I had made a best friend, I decided that I would visit Patric at his house for a day. The day before Thanksgiving, I made a reservation to get picked up by Metro Access, a Para-transit organization that provides door-to-door car service for disabled persons who are unable to use public transportation. With Metro Access, I could get transported anywhere in the DC metropolitan area. As we were spending Thanksgiving break with Grandma at the Box, I had

Metro Access pick me up from there to travel to where Patric lived.

Despite my family's worry that I could be taken advantage of by gay boys, I thought it was OK to be friends with them. No matter how much of an internal conflict Patric's praise of my looks brought me, I wasn't gay, and I thought that was enough. Nevertheless, while waiting for MetroAccess, I went into the bathroom and sat on the edge of the bathtub to talk with God.

"Is this wrong?" I asked out loud. "Should I be hanging out with Patric? I'm not gay. What am I doing? What am I doing?" I could cancel the trip, but I knew I wouldn't. Patric would be annoyed with me if I canceled, and he would probably never compliment me again. He made me feel important, and his words made me feel needed. Why was I having reservations? Wasn't the most important thing the fact that I didn't feel like scum when I spoke to him? It seemed that he needed me as a friend as much as I needed him. In my mind, Patric's praise, and his constant efforts to talk to me meant he really cared for me, the person, Mario. I decided that I couldn't afford not to hang out with Patric. He was well known and very popular and I wouldn't forfeit his friendship by canceling, or turning my back after he'd told me so many of his dark secrets. He was important in Dugson's student body support group, Brothers and Sisters United, which everyone called BASU for short. I wanted to join that group. I needed to join that group so I could feel more visible. Perhaps I'd become a permanent part in Patric's group of friends?

"Marian, you clean those dishes up," came Grandma's voice, her voice bringing me back to reality. After all Grandma had worked for, and after all she had taught me about God, here I was lying to her. I'd told her I was going to Zoey's house, when I was actually going to visit a gay boy that no one knew I had befriended. To hurt my feelings, for years, Maria called me a faggot and a gay boy. None of it was true, but here I was, seemingly at the whim of a gay guy. Hearing Grandma's voice again was making me lose my nerve.

"I could stay here and adopt my family's homophobia, or I could spend the day with a friend," I thought. Just then, the phone rang. Metro Access was here. It was too late to even consider a cancelation.

An hour later, as Patric guided me into his house and into the basement, my nerves had my heart beating fiercely. Again, Patric told me how much of a good time we would have, and he reminded me that he thought I was cute. A bell went off in my head. I was horrified at the idea of Patric trying to do something to me, but he was a friend, right? I wondered whether I should have come at all, but there was no turning around now. Metro Access wouldn't be back for hours. Patric would think I was immature, stupid and a little, confused boy if I showed him my uncomfort. I was two years his junior, me a tenth grader, him a twelfth grader; I had to pretend to be on his level. My very low self-worth had my thirst for affirmation winning the internal conflict.

"I'm not gay," I whispered to myself. What about my older macho brothers? What would they think of me fraternizing with a gay guy who likes the way I look? As if on cue with my thoughts, Patric undid my belt, and then waited, observing my response. I was frozen again. The freeze. That damn freeze was back. The freeze owned me as Patric removed my clothes, and then his own. He pushed me onto the bed, and I lay there, with no sense how to stop whatever he had planned.

"You scared?" asked Patric. The freeze wouldn't let me speak, and Patric wasn't going to wait for an answer. My fright and self-hatred mounted as Patric began violating me.

"You're a homo. This is all you've ever been worth." a voice said to me in my head. I lay there, frozen in time, wishing to be elsewhere. "Why am I here? God please forgive me. I hate myself for this." These statements flooded my mind until Patric finally stopped, his plan completed.

In the weeks and months that followed, I progressively sank into a deep depression. After the Thanksgiving break, Patric wasn't interested in being friends with me anymore. He wouldn't answer the phone when I called. I was panicked that I may have gotten HIV from him. I knew nothing about sex, but I knew HIV was something dangerous associated with it. The one time I did get him on the phone, I asked, "Did you get checked yet?"

"Yes I did," Patric yelled into the phone. "Don't ask me that." And then he would hang up on me. Then, it was really clear to me that I had been used. All phone calls stopped permanently and he stopped speaking to me in school. I couldn't believe I had been used like that. Not only was I hurting because another boy had done something sexual to me, I hated myself that I had been so desperate for someone's friendship. I cursed myself for freezing that day with Patric. He had only been excited with the idea that he could turn me gay. I wasn't gay, but I don't know why I couldn't stop what happened. I hated the experience anyway, and then Patric treats me like I never mattered. After having his way, he turned his back on me. I was used.

Zoey unknowingly came to my emotional rescue. I didn't tell her about my gay experience and the degree to which I was ashamed, but I did let her know about the depression I felt. She was truly still my best friend.

Zoey and I were only allowed to talk on the phone on the weekends. We spent Friday and Saturday nights talking into the early hours of the morning, or at least until I fell asleep. Zoey was always annoyed when I fell asleep on her but she understood that I wasn't doing it on purpose. Neither of us had the sense to say: "I'll call you tomorrow." I was thankful for the Christmas break as it meant I could talk to Zoey every day, and this was a time where I really needed her friendship.

Tenth grade charged on without much incident at school. Of course, there were still the choral concerts, Voices of Victory and various talent shows to keep my sisters and me musically busy. Of particular enjoyment was the variety show in early spring 2003, when Maria, Marian and I performed India Arie's "He Is the Truth." The night before the show, I had gone with Kevin to his best friend Lemur's house and recorded a special track for our performance. Kevin, Asia and her boyfriend Thomas all came to see the performance. The audience sat with rapt attention as my sisters sang, waiting for the best part of the song when the music pauses, and India says in a very deep voice: "Y'all know what I'm talking about." This line had been given to Marian, and when she said it, the auditorium erupted.

At home, I turned on *Harry Potter* or *Adventures in Odyssey* to get a world away from my home experience. This was because things were changing quickly. Our stay with Asia ended abruptly when she and Grandma had a falling out, and Asia demanded that Maria, Marian and I leave her house immediately. I was in disbelief that Asia put us out in a flash. Our other sister, Nancy, was now living in a bedroom apartment in Oxmon,

Maryland. After hearing that Asia was putting us out, she invited us to stay with her for the rest of the school year. Grandma, left with no choice, agreed. Thank God Nancy came to our rescue. We finished the school year with Nancy without a problem, and when summer arrived, we headed back to the Box for a fairly uneventful summer. Grandma's focus was to find us somewhere to live when our eleventh-grade school year started at the end of August.

Haily and her family were now living in a three-bedroom condo in Larmon, MD, and Grandma hoped we could stay there for school. I was fearful of moving into Haily's condo with her children, while Grandma was to remain at the Box. Sure, Haily had gotten a little better over the years, but I knew this was probably because we hadn't been living with her, just visiting. Now, for the first time in years, we were going to have another extended stay with her. Just how long would this last before a blow up?

Meanwhile, to everyone's surprise, our choral instructor, Ms. Shawks decided to give Dugson another chance, despite the tumultuous time she had with the choir the year before. Honestly, I was happy to see that she was being a warrior, hoping to make a difference in the lives of a prominently black performing arts program. During the first week of school, I gave her an encouraging letter, and thanked her for returning to give Dugson another go.

My eleventh-grade classes were quite enjoyable. I was elated that I would have Mrs. Neale for my World history class. She and I had bonded well during the previous year when I took her U.S. History course, and I knew she'd be looking out for me again. I was placed in Mr. Allen's piano theory II course, which made me quite happy. Mrs. Edwards, a Virgin Island woman, was my English teacher and I loved her teaching style. The only class I despised, although I liked the teacher, was of course, math. I was now in algebra II with Ms. Pitman, the same math instructor from the previous year. Mrs. Pitman was a great lady. Whenever I had trouble with math, she would set up one-on-one tutoring sessions during my lunch time or after school. She and I would work for an hour or two, trying to get me to understand angles, degrees and the like with the use of tactile materials given to us by Ms. Betz-Zachery. I got through math by the skin of my teeth.

To my surprise, Jack Edison from Livist Middle, was now a student at Dugson, and he even road the same bus. Oddly, my sisters didn't remember Jack, but of course I did. We actually became friends. He wasn't at all bothered by what had happened years earlier. He even dismissed the memory when I brought it up when he and I walked to the bus one afternoon after school. Even more surprising, Jack didn't lapse into his enthusiasm over being gay. I guess being sixteen made a huge difference. Soon, Jack became an extreme comfort when my familial problems struck again.

On the first night living in Haily's Larmon apartment, she made it clear that she was feuding with our sister Asia, and that we were never to invite her over. In October, Haily got into it with Maria over this very same subject. One night, Maria needed something important from a store, and knowing Haily would not have taken her to get it, she called Asia. Asia agreed and drove to Haily's apartment to drop off the item.

"What were you just doing?" Haily asked Maria as she returned inside.

"Asia brought me something," Maria said innocently.

"You know what. I can't believe this. You invited that girl to my house after I specifically told you not to. Y'all gotta go." With that, Haily called Grandma at the Box and continued. "Ma, they can't stay here." She was wailing into the phone now. "After I told them not to do it, Maria done invited Asia over to my house. They have to go. I'm sorry." As I sat in the walk-in closet in the hallway where Justin had his music keyboard, my heart dropped to my knees. I felt worthless all over again. Just like that, Haily was putting us out. How would we get to school? Grandma didn't have a car anymore, and it was going to be impossible for us to get to Dugson High School from DC. Why was Haily doing this? I didn't think it would be this soon that something was causing us to move again. I called

Jack on my cell phone and deluged him with the woes of my family. Once again, I felt like a worthless, stinking ragdoll, inconsequential to my family. He consoled me and told me things would be alright. Even though I didn't know if things would be alright, hearing his soft voice say it with pure peace and calm settled me for a bit.

In the month that followed, Kevin came to our rescue. He drove all the way from Maryland to get us in DC, and then drove us back to Haily's in time enough to meet the bus outside Haily's house. Everyone knew that this was far too taxing for Kevin. A new plan would have to come, and I prayed that it didn't involve me leaving Dugson. I couldn't lose my friends again. To my surprise, we ended up doing what one would have thought we would have done at the beginning of the year; we moved in with Nancy. I hoped to God that nothing would mess this up. Although we were in tight quarters in Nancy's one-bedroom apartment, and I was in a deep depression over my family's dysfunction, I found happiness in my obsession with reading books on tape and writing. These things were highly therapeutic in the months that followed. They are what truly helped me through the days of Mr. Robins.

The recollections that follow had the deepest adverse impact on me, and trapped me in a massive prison of depression for years. I share these memories to again illustrate my deck of cards, and to show that overcoming any adversity is doable.

I met Mr. Robins in mid-October at an afterschool audition for the vocal ensemble in Dugson's BASU student organization. He was the faculty person in charge of it, although he was only a long-term, permanent-placement substitute. My sister Marian and I auditioned, she for singing and me for piano playing. As Mr. Robins played the audition song, I was seated at another piano and told to pick up the song by Claira, the student head of the vocal group. As Mr. Robins and I played, Claira turned to each auditioning singer and had them sing the audition song "Great is Your Mercy." At some point, she had everyone break into harmonies before making them do solos again. Eventually, Mr. Robins stopped playing the piano and let me play alone. Once the audition was over and the room was filled with the hubbub of student chatter, Mr. Robins introduced himself.

"I'm Jon," he began, "I'm in charge of the group. I've heard a lot about you, Mario and I really, really, really enjoyed your playing. We'd love to have you in the group." Surprised by his praise, I offered an awkward smile and thanked him.

"You ever worked with a blind person before?" I asked in an attempt to change the subject.

"Um, I can't say that I have, but this is definitely a start." Mr. Robins had a very strange speaking voice. It sounded as if he had a sock clogging his throat. He also seemed to use a "kkkhhhh" sound with his Cs and Ks, like Daffy Duck.

"You gonna bring him to the bus?" asked Marian.

"Yeah, I'll walk him," replied Mr. Robins. Checking my talking watch, I realized that there was some time before the bus would come. Marian obviously was heading off to be with her friends.

When the time to leave for the afterschool bus did come, Mr. Robins guided me as we talked about music. Halfway down the chorus room hallway, near the back of the school, he stopped, turned towards me, took my left hand and placed it on the front area of his jeans. It wasn't immediately clear what he was doing. Then, when realization setting in, I yanked my hand away. All of this takes time to explain, but it happened in seconds.

"This is what you do to me," he said. I was stunned. He was a teacher. In an attempt to deflate my feeling of shock, Mr. Robins said: "Mario, I think you are really, really cute, and for real, I'm really glad you're going to be playing with us because, you got a nice touch on the piano, and ... did I say you are cute as heck so ... ."

"You think I'm cute?" I asked, genuinely surprised. No one had told me this since the days of Patric, who had graduated the prior year. I was in disbelief. I thought I was ugly, but here it was, a teacher telling me I was cute. His praise made me feel oddly special.

"Yeah," Mr. Robins said. "You got really sexy lips, nice skin and a really pretty smile. You and your sisters are really cute." We resumed walking. For a second time, Mr. Robins placed my hand on the front of his jeans.

"You're not gay, you're not gay," I thought and then said to Mr. Robins as I yanked my hand away before grabbing his elbow again, "What makes you think I'm gay?"

"Oh," he gave an awkward laugh, "I know when I know. Plus, you use to mess with Patric." What? The jerk who used me had told others about what he had done to me? I was aghast. Mr. Robins's compliments on my looks still lingered, but I thought it weird that my sexuality was being tested by someone a lot older than me.

I was barely sixteen years old. I was a boy. I was shocked that Patric had told someone else about what he had done to me. I was full of so many emotions and confusing thoughts when I finally reached the bus and said goodbye to Mr. Robins. Marian chatted with her friends, completely oblivious to the confusion Mr. Robins had just caused for me. I dwelled on the encounter with Mr. Robins during the entire bus ride.

Mr. Robins's sexual violation didn't stop with him forcing me to touch the front of his jeans. In November, he successfully seduced and fellated me in his car in front of the school. Although my body betrayed me, I hated the incident. I froze just like I had during all of the other experiences leading up to that day. As Mr. Robins was my continued key into the popular crowd of BASU, I felt stuck in allowing it to happen. I felt trapped and filthy with the realization that with words, Mr. Robins could make me feel like a beautiful person.

Outside of his sexual violation, I felt honored that an older person found me so interesting and important. However, when Mr. Robins violated me, my religion screamed in my ear, interspersed with my despair that he was breaking the law. A small part of me couldn't escape the feeling that he may have been using me, just like Patric had done. I tried to dismiss my thoughts of the law and religion with statements like: "He cares about me. He thinks I'm beautiful."

At the end of November, Mr. Robins took his exploration to another level. One chilly day before BASU practice after school, Mr. Robins persuaded me to enter his car again, saying he needed to talk to me. He told me how much he cared about me, and how he wanted to be there for me. He took me to what he told me was his mother's apartment. Although I was happy to be with a person who thought me so beautiful, I was weary, hoping he didn't expect more sexual activity. I was wrong.

He guided me back to what he told me was his bedroom, and there too, he violated me in worse ways than before. Again, there came the indescribable freeze. That damn freeze had me frozen in time, a witless witness to what was happening to and around me.

My head screamed with the knowledge that Mr. Robins had done these sorts of things with other BASU male students. How did I get stuck in it too? Now, I was on the long list of students he had violated. I wanted people to like me and think I was worth something, but this wasn't what I imagined. I had no idea what I was talking about or thinking; I had to fit in somewhere. I threw on an actor's hat and tried to pretend as if I enjoyed what was happening with Mr. Robins, but I didn't. I had to pretend I was in ecstasy, listening to Mr. Robins praise my looks. I was just a child, used as a sexual specimen for him.

My heart was heavy as Mr. Robins pulled up in front of Dugson High School nearly thirty minutes later to drop me off. As I used my cane to find my way to the school's doors, my religion and insecurities screamed at me: "You're *gay* Mario. Hell awaits you" Truth is, I didn't want to be, but why did Mr. Robins make me feel so bad, yet so accepted at the same time? I was utterly confused in the head, searching for something. Once in the school, my mind thick with dread, I trudged off to BASU choral practice. When I entered the chorus room, I felt naked, as if everyone in the room were also violating me saying: "It's true. Mr. Robins had him a few minutes ago."

CHAPTER 18— DUGSON GOES ON

Things in the family were starting to heat up yet again. Nancy was very angry with Grandma. She felt that Grandma wasn't offering enough help to take care of us. I knew that Grandma gave her food stamps for us, but Nancy knew that Grandma still received Social Security benefit money for Maria, Marian and me, and she wanted all of it. For some unknown reason, Grandma was unable to give Nancy much. Nancy constantly talked about it at her apartment, and even let slip that she intended to take Grandma to court for guardianship of us. I was stunned and stressed out with this news. Here I was in another family volcano building slowly but definitely close to erupting. Although I hated what we did, my time with Mr. Robins made me temporarily forget my family problems. It was hard to accept that my sister was going to take her own Grandma to court for custody of us simply because she wanted to get her hands on some Social Security checks. What was going on?

Tension continued to build through December, January and into the beginning of spring of 2004. By early April, Nancy's limit had been reached. Over the past few months, she had emerged a bitter person, harboring a huge amount of resentment for Grandma. "Our Mother left us to her for her to take care of us and do real good by us. She ain't done anything but allow her crazy kids to mess up stuff and take advantage." I hated when

Nancy talked like this about Grandma. Although I agreed with Nancy about our aunts and uncles ruining things for us, I knew Grandma had tried to do her best. I didn't always agree with Grandma, but I loved her and I knew she loved us.

On the first day of our spring break, Grandma and Nancy had a terrible argument over the phone. Nancy had made it abundantly clear to Grandma that she was going to take her to court for custody of us.

"You just want them triplets' checks and that ain't much money. You ain't getting custody of nobody, Nancy," I heard Grandma scream.

"I'm staying with Haily. Drop them triplets off over here at Haily's house, Nancy," Grandma said.

"If they want to go, but Grandma, you was supposed to take care of us and them. They were stayin' here and I only got money from you once or twice."

"My money been tied up 'cause of them doctors going in and snatching the money."

"I ain't ever heard any crap like that before Grandma."

"You gonna sit up here and tell me you gonna take your own grandmother to court, Nancy? God knows, something is wrong with you, girl."

When Grandma and Nancy's telephone spat was over, Nancy yelled to us: "Marian and Maria and Mario, are y'all stayin' or y'all goin'? You need to make up your mind now." My throat was tight, and my chest vibrant with the heavy pumping of my emotional heart.

"Y'all taking too long to answer. Either you goin' over there, or you stayin' here." More silence followed.

I was stuck. I did not want to go and live with Haily. She had just put us out nearly six months earlier. At the end of 2003, Grandma and Haily got into a spat with the church which resulted in my grandmother being asked to vacate the church's annex-apartment we had been occupying. Now, Grandma was living with Haily. I didn't want to get stuck in an emotionally abusive atmosphere again.

"I'm stayin here," I said weakly, my voice barely above a whisper.

"And what about y'all two Maria and Marian?" Nancy asked, slamming shut the refrigerator door.

"We gonna go see Grandma." Marian said.

"OK, let's go then, Marian and Maria." Although only Marian had spoken, it was clear that she had spoken for Maria as well. Within minutes, Marian and Maria grabbed their overnight bags we lived out of and left with Nancy. I felt horrible.

In the silence that followed their departure, I sat, rooted to the spot in the living room. I didn't know what I was doing. How would Grandma respond when she realized I had stayed behind? Was I betraying her? Could I stand up to Haily if she got involved? I was confused, wishing for a permanent escape from my family and its ruinous drama.

The cell phone that one of my blind friend's had given me a week earlier rang, and it was Grandma.

"So you think you're grown, Mario?"

"No," I said. "I don't. I'm just staying here."

"We gonna show you how grown you are," came Haily's voice. She was getting involved. "Nancy don't give a damn bout y'all. We gonna show you." The phone died.

I rushed into the one bedroom Nancy had where the new computer that had been purchased for me by the church for which I played the piano was set up. Pastors Clarence and June Dow had agreed to buy me a computer under the agreement that they would take $50 out of my Sunday pay until it was paid off. I was thankful. The computer had been used by everyone in the house for downloading music, browsing the Web and more. But in this moment, I needed it for therapy. I turned it on, activated the JAWS talking software and navigated to the "My Music" folder. Hurriedly, I pressed the letter "E" until I heard JAWS say "Evanescence – My Immortal." I hoped this song could soothe the uncertain feeling I had.

However, as the lead female voice sang the chorus: "When you cried, I'd wipe away all of your tears. When you screamed, I'd fight away all of your fears. And I held your hand through all of these years, and you still have all of me," I was flooded with memories of my grandmother during good and bad times. The time she caught pneumonia. Her taking me to the eye doctor in the snow. Her telling me to stop crying as I fearfully walked to have surgery at five years old. Her crying in the aftermath of something hurtful Haily had done. Her defending my intelligence in front of the school system that had me labeled malfunctioning and a troublemaker. As the bridge of the second verse played: "These wounds won't seem to heal. This pain is just too real. There's just too much that time cannot erase," tears poured from my eyes and a huge despair gripped my heart. I should have gone. I shouldn't have stayed behind. I had to figure out a way to get Nancy to take me to my grandmother, without being angry with me. Even though I would be heading to Haily's house, at least I'd be with Maria, Marian and Grandma again. I was giving up another way out again.

When Nancy returned with Burger King food for me, I gave no indication of my despair. It wasn't until the next day that I seized an opportunity to let her know what I really wanted. As I surfed the Internet, Nancy called the apartment from the Oxmon Social Security Office. "I'm here at Social Security to apply to be your representative payee, Mario, so I can start getting your checks. I need to know, and I'm not playing Mario: are you stayin or what. I need to know so I won't be wasting my time."

Wary of Nancy's rough talk, I froze. "I ... I just want to go see them for the rest of spring break," I said cowardly.

"You know what?" Nancy began in her ghetto drone: "I ain't got time for this. Have your stuff ready 'cause I'm on my way." With that, the phone disconnected. Nancy arrived in ten minutes and I was packed, ready to go. Getting packed was quick and easy as I had been living out of a bag for years anyway. The car ride to Haily's apartment was quiet, tense and uncomfortable. I knew Nancy thought Maria, Marian and me to be stupid and brainwashed but heck, I couldn't turn my back on Grandma. I also knew that Nancy was angry, but again, I couldn't disregard Grandma. Little did I know what would happen four months later that would finally make me do just that. Nevertheless, for now, just like I was when I was pulled from Burgson on the brink of a custody battle, I would be with my grandma, too afraid to hurt her.

Finally at Haily's apartment, I listened for hours as Haily cursed Nancy for hoping to take her own grandmother to court. She cursed Nancy from Maryland to California. All of the family chaos was starting to really take a toll on my mind. I had no venting outlet when my CDS, audio programs and friends couldn't help anymore. The music I performed with BASU was therapeutic, although my BASU involvement was still riddled with Mr. Robins molesting me. Still blocked in, I had no willpower to resist him when he took things to the next level.

One late evening in early May, I was riding home to Haily's apartment with Mr. Robins after BASU practice. I was quiet for much of the ride. Occasionally, he would say something about the practice or about the BASU vocal members, but his talking seemed out of place. I was quiet because I knew something sexual was going to happen, and I was trying to mentally prepare myself. The freeze was already with me. If I allowed it to happen, at least I would feel visible, and somewhat consequential.

"We're pulling in your parking lot," Mr. Robins said. "But hold on." With that, he pulled off to the side of the parking lot. I knew this parking lot well by now and I knew we weren't in front of Haily's building. My heart thudded with the anticipation of the unknown. In no time, Mr. Robins was violating me again. Later, while arrested by the same freeze that paralyzed me in the past, I couldn't move as he undressed and climbed over me, taking his violation to the worst level imaginable. He forced me into a bigger world of guilt, shame and self-hatred. I would get AIDS. I was sure of it, but I couldn't stop him. My head screamed: "This is all you're worth, ya blind, black nothing." My body betraying me, I ended up unwillingly lost in what Mr. Robins was doing. I was too frozen.

"No. I'm gonna get AIDS," I said urgently as Mr. Robins guided me to the stairs leading to Haily's apartment some time later. "I can't do this. I'm not gay. We're gonna get AIDS."

"No we won't," said Mr. Robins.

"Oh my goodness, we're gonna get HIV. Oh my goodness, how many students have you done that with like that? You're making me gay. I've got AIDS."

"No you don't, Mario. I don't have HIV," he said. "You are a very special person. That's why I did that. I don't just let anybody do that. Only someone special that I trust." Ridiculously, foolishly, my insecure mind was touched by Mr. Robins's words. He had called me special, and rather ridiculously, I actually felt special. Here I was, a young boy, the one Mr. Robins wanted? An adult was desperate for me? Despite not wanting these things to continue, I felt invincible and loved. My brain was utterly twisted with this brainwash. Now, how could I let anyone know about Mr. Robins? I didn't want him hurt. He knew everything there was to know about my family, and although I thought them disgusting, I was convinced he did these things because he cared. At the same time, I felt so wronged and confused, but falsely content with the thought that someone loved me.

Although I was blind, he was making me feel visible. For years, my family had called me hurtful names. I was told I was funny looking, ugly, told I had girl-legs, toes that look like thumbs and more by my sisters when they teased me. I had started to believe these things, but there was an adult, telling me something different. My self-esteem was as fluid as water, and Mr. Robins knew it. This made me an easy target. He used this to his advantage, and did so-called affectionate things to me, and in so doing, temporarily solidified my self-esteem. I hated that I couldn't stop what Mr. Robins was doing to me. It was a dizzying, psychological roller coaster of confusion, hurt and wrong that no child should ever have to endure. Mr. Robins never cared for me. I was just a number in a slew of male teenagers he used for his sexual gradification. Given my family's history, I fully accept that I hadn't come from a background of healthy love. As an adult, I understand that this made be more susceptible to persuasive adults like Mr. Robins. My psychological whirlwind continued when I froze again when Mr. Ford, a friend of Mr. Robins, also sexually violated me in his apartment one day after school. As Mr. Ford was a substitute gospel choral instructor for after school choir rehearsal, he invited me to his apartment, located behind Dugson's building, under the pretentious want to review music with me.

The freeze took over again.

"Patric told me about you," he had told me at the end. My brain rolled over, sick with wondering what game my young life had become. Patric had graduated the previous year, but obviously, he had spent some time with both Mr.

Robins and Mr. Ford. This wasn't Mr. Robins doing this to me this time. Why was this happening again? I didn't understand why it was always me being used for amusement. This time also, I had been too frozen to even consider stopping him. My head was telling me that this was all I was worth. My head was telling me that all of the things people were doing to me were reasons for me to feel good about myself. "Another person thinks you are cute, Mario," I told myself. "They like you, they all do. Look, you got adults pressed to get at you. Take it. Let it happen. They like you, man. They think you're cute. You matter to them." Things were changing in my head. When it was over, Mr. Ford walked me to BASU practice. When we walked in the room, he apologized for getting me there late.

"That's OK," I heard Mr. Robins reply. He knew. I knew he knew that Mr. Ford had done something to me.

No matter how much I tried to make myself see these sick adults having sex with me as plusses for my self-esteem, I could never fully escape the idea that I was being used by them. I wanted to start building my self-esteem on the affirmation of people my age. I wanted to be normal. I wanted to be a typical boy that didn't come to school with teachers and substitutes trying to get in his pants. As a result, I quickly decided as I took my place at the piano that I would work for the attention of students my age. As I practiced with BASU, I thought heavily about the afterschool announcements regarding student government officers for the next school year. By now, doubtless because of my involvement with BASU, I was hugely popular in Dugson. Everyone knew me as the blind boy that played the piano for everybody. Moreover, they knew who my protectors were. Much of the school liked me, but my self-esteem was so low that I couldn't receive this. Then, if one hundred people said I was handsome and only one said I wasn't, my world would be crushed. Only the opinion of the singularly opposed person mattered to me. I figured, if I could run for Student Government Association (SGA) vice president, I would keep the respect and favor of all of the students I know from BASU, and I wouldn't have to be Mr. Robins's toy anymore. I wouldn't dare run for the president's post. I didn't think I'd ever when that race, therefore, I was committed to running for number two.

I knew that much of SGA was full of students who also were heavily involved with BASU. I felt that I could impress everyone with my gift of communication, and have my ticket to absolute popularity. At the end of the rehearsal, I was sure of what I was going to do. The following school day, I planned to enter the race for SGA vice president for school year 2004/2005, my senior year.

The next day, after verifying that I met the academic requirements to run for office, I went down to Room 110 where the SGA head Mr. Edmonds' office was housed. I proudly identified myself and my bid to join the SGA race for vice president.

"OK," replied Mr. Edmonds, his voice hoarse and raspy. "We are having speeches next Monday and they will be over the loud speaker. You all are going to do them in the main building, and then we're going to the other building and you will do it again. You need to have someone help you put up posters and stuff for your campaign. The voting will be the following week. I thanked Mr. Edmonds, got his help to the door and then I was off to the library to meet with Ms. Betz-Zachery.

That night, I went home and pulled out my Braille computer device and wrote my speech. I wanted to be well-prepared. I felt like I was ready for politics, especially after my experiences on Capitol Hill in April. In early spring, I had traveled with the Lighthouse for the Blind to Capitol Hill a few times where I had to use superb persuasive language to try to get Congress to provide the Lighthouse with more money for their summer camps for blind kids. After that training, the SGA speech should be a breeze.

When Monday arrived, I found out that the position speeches would be given after first period. This meant I would be a few minutes late for Ms. Pitman's math class. I was elated. However, my voice seemed to disappear as I waited in the front office for other students to finish their speeches for the various offices for which they were running. Erica gave her speech for her bid for secretary, Alex gave his speech for his bid for treasurer, Stacy gave her speech for Class of 2005 president, Ali gave her speech for her bid for SGA president, and then it was my turn. There were two of us running for the VP spot. I loved and hated competition. I wished the other girl running for the same position had given her speech first, but the odds were against that. As Mr. Edmonds held the loud speaker microphone in front of my mouth and said, "OK, go ahead," I took a deep breath and began reciting my speech from memory.

"My name is Mario Bonds," I began, startled by my own voice reverberating through the halls "I am totally blind, but I'll have the naysayers understand that my disability offers no hindrance to my progressing in the position I am seeking. I am running to be your student body vice president. I assure you that I will uphold my election with dignity, pride and the utmost seriousness. I will support the mission of the student body, assuring fairness, equality and a more fun school year. It is my hope that you will take a leap with me and believe in me so that I may become your student body vice president. In advance, thank you for your vote."

"Wow," I heard the girl running for VP as well say under her breath. Although my heart was trying to escape my chest, I felt excited. I had finished the speech without a vocal hiccup or forgetting any words. After my opponent had finished, we candidates left for the other building. Ali guided me, and I enjoyed the moment. If all went well, she and I would be the heads of SGA next school year.

All of the SGA hopefuls campaigned vigorously until Election Day. On Election Day, I spent the whole of lunchtime in the cafeteria, which I'd never visited before now. The voting table had been set up and I helped hand out flyers and sweets to the voters. A fair politician, I would scream out things like: "Vote for Alex for treasurer," and he would return the favor by shouting: "Vote for Mario for SGA vice president." I was having an absolute blast campaigning and loving the political life of high school. I couldn't wait for the end of the school day when the winners would be announced over the loudspeaker. I was a little wary as well. This was the ultimate test for my popularity, and would determine whether students liked me. Sure, many students had praised my speech and said they were going to vote for me, but that wasn't the real test.

As I sat reviewing melodic piano scales with Mr. Allen in my piano theory II course at the end of the day, the election results were given over the loud speaker. Announcements always started five minutes to the end bell at 3:10, and I was anxious to hear them this time. I listened, ignoring Mr. Allen's attempts to get my attention.

"Blah blah blah. Get to the results," I said.

"Son, you know you probably won," said Mr. Allen, giving up his attempts to return my attention to his piano theory lesson. Then, the results came. Boy, was I in for a ride.

CHAPTER 19– TAKING A STAND

"The student body elections are as follows," began a girl's voice. "Class of 2005 president winner is Stacy Heru. SGA president will be Ali Frank. SGA vice president winner is…"—why the hell was she pausing, I wondered—"Mario Bonds."

I heard nothing more after that. I was stunned, in absolute disbelief of what I had just heard. The students of Dugson had voted me into the post I had wanted. I couldn't believe that I, the blind underdog for so long, had bested someone else. I was full of glee. I would be involved in all of the SGA talks, special events and more importantly, I would go higher up in my status of popularity with the students in BASU and the ones who hung out in Room 110. Just then, my cell phone rang. As the bell had now rung, Mr. Allen didn't try to stop me from answering it.

"Hello?"

"Aw, you boosted like," came Marian's voice. Nonplussed, I asked her to repeat herself. I hadn't the foggiest what boosted meant.

"You pressed boy, ya know, excited 'cause you won. That's a good look," Marian said excitedly. After Marian's call, Ms. Betz-Zachery called me to congratulate me.

"Woo, Mario, he did it. Yes, you did it boy."

"Yeah, I'm happy," I said goofily. I was full of such a thrill that I didn't think anything could ever bring me down. My quest to get the affirmation of people my age was winning. My quest continued all the way up to the choral spring concert later that week. It was during this concert where I met prospective student Adam Treadwell, a key person who helped change my life during the years that followed. He was one of the eighth-grade hopefuls that had auditioned for admission to Dugson for the upcoming school year. He was very young, but intriguing. I informed him that I was student government vice president for the upcoming school year, and that I would look out for him. We exchanged numbers and I vowed to keep in contact over the summer break.

I couldn't wait to tell Zoey about the student government association vice president post I had won. By now, things were drastically changing between us. Unbeknownst to her parents, Zoey and I were now boyfriend and girlfriend. After the experience with Mr. Ford, and the epiphany in gospel practice that day, I began to desperately cling to her to shake myself of the gay things that had been occurring. We were truly falling in love, which presented new problems for me in the year that followed. But right now, as the summer approached, I looked forward to my girlfriend, and spending time with her whenever I could.

Things were also changing at home for what one could consider for better *and* worse. After returning home in May after the spring choral concert, Haily revealed that Grandma, Maria,

Marian and me would be moving into our own apartment.

"It's in Steeple Chase," she said excitedly. "It's right across the street from here. All you do is cross Campus Way South."

"Wow," I said, stuffing my face with the Papa John's pizza she had bought. Naturally, I felt indifferent. This was probably a repeat of the situation with the house in Oats, Virginia. I was sure that Haily had secured the apartment some way with the expectation that Grandma would pay the bills with the Social Security checks we all received. I didn't really like living in another home acquired by Haily. Nevertheless, by June 1, we moved into a two-bedroom, two-bath spacious apartment. Grandma had a room, Maria and Marian shared a room, and I was set to occupy the living room, with zero privacy. Things started off quite well. Justin visited quite often, and on some of his visits, seduced and experimentally masturbated me. He was very confused about his sexual identity. Nevertheless, I was sick of being a tool of sexual curiosity and entertainment for people, whether they were my age or otherwise.

Maria, too, found a way to amuse herself. Knowing that I was having a hard time dealing with the cicadas, which were everywhere in the Washington, DC area at this time, Maria did a lot to horrify me with those little beasts. A man though I may be, I am absolutely afraid of anything that crawls with tiny legs, slithers, buzzes or stings.

Although they were harmless, I hated the cicadas, and Maria got a kick out of my fear of them. Each morning, as we walked to the bus stop from the new apartment, Maria would guide me in such a way that I had to step on cicadas that were sitting on the sidewalk. There would be a continued crunch, crunch, interspersed with my yells of disgust and fright as Maria laughed her heartiest laugh of amusement at my expense.

The question whether things were changing for better or worse was quickly answered by June 7th, the day of graduation for Dugson High School that year. Although we were supposed to be focused on being in the choir for graduation, my sisters and I were also dealing with more drama at home. For some unknown reason, Haily was quite upset with Marian and called her to say that she was turning off the service to the cell phone she had given her nearly a month earlier. Maria had a cell phone that had been turned on by Kevin. I knew that the drama would spill over into the weekend. Sure, I knew Haily had the propensity to take back gifts, but turning off the phone meant she was livid about something. I tried to compartmentalize and I played the piano gloriously for the chorus's performance of Josh Groban's "You Raise Me Up," knowing that there would be trouble at home later.

When we returned home, Haily was waiting at the apartment for us.

"Justin told me that y'all be over here making all types of loud noise and stuff."

"What?" said Maria and Marian in unison. I listened as we all sat on the couch.

"Justin lying to you," said Maria, "Anyway, how come Grandma cain't say something to us."

"Right," joined in Marian. The truth is, no one had been terribly loud in the apartment. Nevertheless, I knew that tempers were boiling and something mundane was getting ready to be thrown way out of proportion. My hunch was correct, but things blew up worse than even I could have expected. The next thing you know, Haily was shouting.

"Don't ask me how come my mother cain't speak to y'all about this. I'm grown and I'm speaking to you."

I knew Marian had become quite the fiery teenager, especially when faced with an irate adult. "'Cause Grandma is our guardian and this is *our* house."

"You ain't got no house, you damn orphan." That did it. Haily had said something hurtful for no reason. Here we were, going through it with Haily again. The old Haily was back. "This apartment got my name on it so it ain't yours."

"It doesn't matter," Marian said, her rage unmistakable now.

"Little girl, you need to calm down," screamd Haily. I was growing wary every minute with this exchange. Although physicality hadn't been added, this was far-too reminiscent of the exchange between Asia and Haily back in 1998.

"I said calm down," Haily yelled in Marian's face. Grandma was as silent as I was. Occasionally, she tried to chide Marian for being disrespectful, but it was clear this was Haily's conversation. Haily stepped closer to Marian and gripped her arm.

"Get off of me." Marian screamed. "Why you letting her act like this, Grandma? This ain't even her house."

Obviously resigned to the fact that Haily was in control, Grandma merely said: "Shut your mouth, girl."

"I ain't gonna be disrespected," Haily yelled. "Maria and Mario can stay, but Marian gotta go." My heart leapt into my throat. Did she truly just say that she was putting Marian out? Just because her name was on the lease, she was putting Marian out and Grandma's not saying anything against it?

"I don't give a damn," Marian said defensively and rushed past Haily to the room.

"You stayin Maria, 'cause Marian got to go." I couldn't believe what was happening. I knew it and Grandma and Haily knew it: of course Maria was going with Marian. They were joined at the hip and weren't going to see one another without the other. Maria called Nancy and she happily came to the rescue. In no time, my sisters were leaving out the door. They were leaving me behind to deal with Haily's lies, trouble and inconsistent ways. My sisters were slipping away and I hated Haily for helping to tear us all apart. I knew Grandma was hella heartbroken, but she never tried to put a stop to what was happening. She couldn't, anyway.

I vented to Zoey, upset over what happened with my aunt and sisters. I was ecstatic that I would see Zoey very soon.

It was just Grandma and I who remained in the two-bedroom apartment, and I now had my own room. The only thing that helped me cope with my sisters' leaving was the camp counselor internship I had lined up for the summer. The communications director of the Lighthouse for the Blind had used her pull to get me a paid internship with the organization for summer 2004. I believe she felt compelled to do it as a huge thank you for the Capital Hill poster-child work I had done for the Lighthouse during the school year. On three occasions, I was pulled out of school and taken to Capitol Hill where I was a part of a lobbyist group that was hoping to get Congress to appropriate funds for the camps the Lighthouse held during the summers for blind youths.

Each time, a Lincoln town car with an elegant driver picked me up, offered me food and took me to Capitol Hill where I met senator Steny Hoyer from Maryland, a few other Senators, and I ate at the Capitol Hill Club. It was a joyous experience, especially since it seemed as if they were feeding me every ten minutes in between meetings. In the meetings with each Senator, I would help illustrate what a successful blind student looks like. The pitch was: "If only Congress would help, we'd be able to change the statistics of 75 percent of working-age blind adults being unemployed, and more than 50 percent of blind high-schoolers not graduating." I would listen with intent ears as Dell Otto, the Lighthouse president at the time, who was also blind, would give his bit, and then turn the floor over to me. I don't know whether the Lighthouse ever got appropriated funds, but I had a blast. Now, I was set to be a counselor for the very same camps which needed money from Congress.

During the internship, I was assigned as a blind counselor for three of the Lighthouse's summer camps. The first camp was held for two weeks at the beginning of July. It was a day camp for blind kids where they went on field trips, went swimming, had music activities and vocational training. The camp was held on the campus of Catholic University. Antoine Johnson, the children's program coordinator at the time, had me perform several times for the kids, but most importantly, he had me set-up computers in one of the classroom so that the kids could have time to play video games for the blind. This became my principle duty: to teach blind students how to assemble and manipulate assistive computers.

The second camp was a technology camp, held during the last two weeks of July. At this camp, I provided hands-on instruction, teaching the blind kids how to use JAWS talking software, browse the Internet, write emails and Word documents.

The last camp of the summer was a seven-day overnight camp that was held in Shenandoah, Virginia. I was so excited about this camp that I just had to have my new friend, Adam, come with me. Since meeting Adam at the choral spring concert back in May, he and I stayed in constant contact. He was only fourteen and heading to the ninth grade but we hit it off right away. It didn't matter that I was heading to the twelfth grade. Adam adored my piano playing and I adored his singing. He and Antoine Banks were neck-and-neck as my best friends. Knowing that Adam had a lot of community service hours to cover for high school, I persuaded the Lighthouse to approve him as a volunteer camp counselor so that he could knock out all of his required hours in one go. He was approved and we had a blast at the Lighthouse overnight camp. While there, my social skills and self-esteem around girls were really tested.

Adam spent much of our quiet time, when we weren't looking after the campers, chasing the female counselors around. Although I was with Zoey, I was quite jealous. Zoey was half-blind, and getting the attention of fully-sighted girls was a different world for me. Adam told me that some of the girls hoped I would talk to them, but I was too afraid and uncomfortable to approach. I resented not having Adam's undivided attention at all times. He and I would have singing battles where one of us would sing a difficult vocal riff, and the other would have to imitate. Often times, the vocal battles would end in a loud chorus with both of us trying to outdo the other all at the same time.

A sad testament to my low self-esteem was the night when the camp counselors sat in a clearing on the camp grounds to play truth-or-dare. Of course, there were the silly dares of smooching someone or licking a bug or something else gross, but the truth questions were more interesting. For one truth question, a white girl named Heather was asked which male counselor she would love to go out with. By now, I was half listening, never guessing she would say me. However, she did say in a rather serious voice: "Honestly...it would probably be Mario." A few other female voices joined in: "Yeah."

Astonished and believing them to be making fun of me, I said loudly: "Yeah right." Everyone was surprised by my outburst. I was absolutely sure that they were making fun of me by answering the question in the affirmative. Couldn't they all see that I was really, really dark, blind, and funny looking? Don't they see what my family said about my appearance? I had gotten so used to thinking I was ugly or weird that I typically thought myself beating people to the punch by making jokes about my blindness, color and appearance before they could. Often times, the person thought me strange and would always say: "What are you talking about?" They thought my self-insulting mentality odd.

"We're serious," said the girls. I wanted to disappear. Somehow, I mustered the courage to talk more with Heather that week. We had an instant connection and became friends.

I loved the ghost stories I told during campfire night, the talent show and the incredible ice cream. I had even brought my keyboard from home so that I could perform for the campers and staff. I performed a lot of songs by Billy Gilman from his album *Music Heart Songs*, poems by the late Matty J. Stepanik turned into songs.

After the camps were over, I knew it was time to focus and prepare for the next school year. I had a lot of writing to do for my book report on *Things Fall Apart, a novel I had to read for my advanced placement English class*. Before the camps started, I hadn't been able to do any writing assignments because my computer didn't have a word processor, and my Braille Note PDA device was broken and too old to get fixed. When Haily heard of my problem, she vowed to buy me a new PDA device so I could complete my work. I had already planned to ask the church where I worked to help me, but Haily told me to let her get the machine. Knowing that the device cost at least $5000, I didn't want to believe Haily, but when she came over one day and said "It's on its way," I couldn't help but believe. For the entire month of July, I asked for updates about the device, and

Haily maintained that she had purchased it and it was definitely on its way. I was told to be patient. By the time the overnight camp ended, I was very expectant. I was hopeful that the device had arrived. When I got home, not only was the Braille device not there, but the electricity had been turned off for non-payment. I was thankful that my stipend check for the internship hadn't arrived yet. I didn't want them trying to use my money for the power. Nevertheless, I was absolutely livid to find that not only was the electricity turned off, Haily and Marcus were divorcing, and all of my cousins, including Justin, were also now living in the two-bedroom apartment in Steeple Chase. Boy, was I getting tired of all of this.

I asked Haily about the PDA device she had promised me and was told again that she had purchased it and that it was on its way. Eventually, I got smart and called the manufacturer to inquire about a purchase for a "Mario Bonds" or a "Haily Stevens," and I received some interesting news. After checking three different systems, the attendant informed me that no purchase had been made from the state of Maryland for five months. I was livid and done with the ridiculous lies. She had cost me an entire summer of non-productivity. Now, I would be behind in my class work, and it was too late to ask the church to help.

For over a week, I tried to endure the sweltering temperature and crowded space of the apartment. Each day, Haily lied about when the electricity would get paid, claiming that she had placed the electricity in her eldest son's name, and he was nowhere to be found. Even more frustrating, I didn't have the Braille device she had promised, nor did I have access to the Comcast high-speed Internet I had been paying for with church funds.

When I arrived at Dugson High School for a summer SGA meeting during the second week of August, I was relieved to be in air conditioning and civility again. School was set to start in two weeks and home life was again uncertain. My limit with Haily's lies, dysfunction and control of Grandma was reached. I wanted out of there permanently. I wanted to be with my sisters. I had to do what I knew was a carbon-copy of what Kevin did back in 1998 when he left home in the middle of the night, proclaiming that he needed to be with his siblings. This time, it wouldn't be done under the cover of darkness; I had to tell Grandma straightaway. I couldn't take the abuse, the back-and-forth, and the lies and harm anymore. I hadn't gotten any of my Advanced Placement English work done because of Haily. I had been living somewhere for nearly two weeks with no electricity because of Haily. My siblings in 1998 and this year were ripped from me because of Haily. I was emotionally and psychologically scarred because of Haily. My self-esteem was insubstantial because of Haily. Enough was enough. Finally, I had the strength to do the impossible. I had to break away from Grandma. I didn't want to hurt her, but I couldn't take it any longer. It would hurt me, I was sure of it.

Sitting on the front steps of Dugson after the SGA meeting, I called my brother Adonis. "Adonis, I'm gonna need you to bring Ma's van and pick me up. I'm gonna go to Nancy's house to be with Maria and Marian."

"A'ight, gimme the address and I will come. Actually, if you are still at the school, I can scoop you and we can go, but you need to tell Grandma over the phone now so we don't have any stuff when we get there."

"OK, I will." I said strongly, but I felt as weak as ever. I dialed my cousin Sefra's cell and asked to speak to Grandma.

"Grandma," I began weakly, "I'm gonna go over Nancy's house."

"What you say, boy?"

"I'm gonna be with Maria and Marian."

"God knows. I don't believe this mess. You were the one sayin' you was gonna be OK and you was in here encouraging me. I talk to Haily. She told me you would probably end up doing this mess. Your sisters don't care about you and don't even want to be bothered with you most of the time and you saying you missing them and want to go over there."

"Grandma, I'd rather be with my siblings," I continued in a pitiful voice. She was starting to break my resolve, and I knew I couldn't let that happen. I had to end this phone call and focus. I reminded myself of all of the things Haily had done. The years of abuse, frustrations, lies, uncertainty all permitted by Grandma clouded my mind. Sure, I didn't like the thought of going back to Nancy's place, but it was where Maria and Marian were, and at least I'd be with them again. It would have been weird starting the twelfth grade having to see my triplet sisters only at school due to a ridiculous family break-up.

"Adonis is gonna bring me to get my stuff, Grandma."

"What?" came Grandma's voice. Despite her previous statement, she didn't think I was serious.

"Ma," Haily's voice was in the background, "You did all you can do, Ma. You need to let him, all of them go. Let him go, Ma." A powerful tightness gripped my chest listening to Haily. Who did she think she was?

"You know what Mario, that's what I'm gonna do. We gonna have your stuff ready when you get here." With that, the phone was disconnected. My despair was so heavy that my body hurt under its weight. I wanted to tell Grandma I was sorry, that I loved her and didn't mean to hurt her. I wanted to let her know that the primary reason that I was doing the unthinkable was because of Haily. I couldn't tell her though. I knew that she wouldn't be able to receive it. Most times, it seemed as if Grandma could hear nothing against Haily.

Then somehow, from somewhere, a modicum of peace and resolve came over me. I knew I had to develop a better plan for completely extricating myself from the family. Nancy's place wouldn't be the best for me either, so perhaps I wouldn't stay there long. If things got too difficult, I would leave at a moment's notice and go live with Antoine in Springdale. Who was I kidding? Antoine and his family lived in the hood and their two-bedroom apartment had no room for me and my problems, and money was already tight for them. Nevertheless, I had to have a Plan B in case things with Nancy went bad like last time. From talking to Maria and Marian, I found out Nancy had wasted no time getting the Social Security benefits switched to reference her as the representative payee for them. Maria complained quite often that Nancy treated them like ten-year-olds when it came to giving them money from their checks. I had no idea what would become of me, but for some reason, I felt empowered and hopeful. I was breaking away and telling Haily I had enough.

Nearly ten minutes had passed since the end of my call with Grandma. Adonis pulled up in front of the school and called my name. Within seconds, he was guiding me to the van. I hoped being in his presence would make me feel tougher, strong enough to deal with the weight of what I was doing, but it didn't. My brother's macho aura wouldn't do it this time. I worked hard to make sure he couldn't detect how weak I felt. As we drove, he did however, provide me with valuable encouragement.

"Well, too much been goin' on for too long and Grandma allowed way too much stuff from Haily and her other kids. You doin' the right thing. Now, this means all of us left before we turned 18." I know Adonis was right, but I still felt like putty. I still had to leave, but why did it feel as if I was killing someone now that I was on my way to get my things?

When we arrived at the Steeple Chase apartment, as promised, Grandma and Haily had placed all of my belongings at the front door. There it all was. A computer, clothes, radio, speakers, CDs and cassette tapes. Without speaking a word to our cousins or Haily, Adonis packed up the van with my things. Both of us bid goodbye to Grandma, and with a heavy heart, clouded mind and a burdensome sense of guilt, I left my grandmother, never to live with her as a child again.

I was leaving a life of uncertainty to walk into another life of uncertainty. I loved Grandma and I knew this was hard. It was hard for me as well, but this had to happen. Only God knew what would become of me and my sisters, but this time, even I knew there was no turning back. I was doing something I hadn't been able to do before. I was leaving Grandma.

CHAPTER 20— NEW BEGINNINGS AT DUGSON

I joined my sisters at Nancy's house, spooked by what I had done. I had really left Grandma. How badly would this hurt her? When would we talk again? I missed her very much, but I knew there was no turning back this time. I couldn't.

A week before we started twelfth grade, armed with my stipend check from the Lighthouse for the Blind summer camps, I went school shopping with my sisters. Nancy was excited to help pick out my style for the upcoming school year. I had never shopped for my own clothes before and it was during this trip that I realized I despised shopping. I couldn't stand having to try on dozens of shoes, pants, shirts, and then wait in long lines to purchase. Nothing is more boring to me than shopping.

"So Mario," Nancy began as we left the Old Navy. "You wanna get your ears pierced?"

"Uh, no. I'm afraid of needles?" I said stupidly, instantly remembering that Marian and Maria had obviously told her. Nearly a year earlier, I'd told Marian and Maria that I wanted to get my ears done because it would make me cool. I had been merely boasting.

"They got a piercing stand right here." Nancy said, increasing her pace as I clung to her arm.

Soon I was being led to a chair. "How ya doin', darling?" asked a rather squat white lady as I tried to control my body's attempts to shiver.

"OK, I'm gonna count to three and then I'm gonna hit it."

"Hit what?" I asked, twisting in the chair.

"I'm using something shaped like a gun to do it. Once I hit the trigga, it's gonna pierce ya."

I stalled, and stalled, and stalled, unable to prepare myself. "Wait, wait, and wait." I screamed every time she was half way through her countdown. Finally losing her patience with me, she said: "I'm doing it." and my ear rang with the sound of the trigger being pushed. I screamed like there was no tomorrow.

"It's over. It's over," said the woman, trying to calm me down. Dramatically, I stood up and yelled to my sisters, "What have y'all done." Boy, I hated needles.

Our stay with Nancy ended up being very short. She and Marian got into a very big spat, which resulted in Nancy putting us out. At midnight, two nights before school began, Asia came to pick us up. I was flabbergasted. I was away from Haily with the thought that problems like this had died, but I was wrong. Nancy was putting us out and now we were to be back with Asia, who had put us out nearly a year-and-a-half earlier? I again felt inconsequential and I knew I had to find a place to live, some way, somehow outside the family. The back-and-forth and instability were wearing on me.

"As a reminder, your SGA officers for the 2004-2005 school are as follows." I was sitting in the library of Dugson High School on the first day of school, in disbelief that I was finally in the twelfth grade. I thought I'd never hear the words "2004-2005 school year." Ms. Betz-Zachery and I were going over my class schedule for the first semester, which would end at the end of December. I was excited about Piano Theory 3, Chorus, and Advanced Placement English. I was going to have the same one-on-one math instructors, and the performing arts Program had a new choral instructor whom I couldn't wait to meet.

Ms. Betz-Zachery and I had a long conversation about my grandmother, my living arrangements and how I was doing now that I was no longer around Haily. I realized that if anyone really understood the difficulty in my family, she did. I trusted her, and I felt like her son now. I was glad she cared.

"Now, you know that the SAT and the ACT are coming up soon, and if you want to retake them, you need to be studying now, Mario."

"I know. I'll take the first one of each. I'll do well on them. I'm only going to apply to one college anyway."

"Only one college? Boy, what's wrong with you?"

"I really want to go to George Mason University in Burgson, VA. That's always been my plan since I was in the seventh grade."

"That may very well be true, but you need to apply for more than just one school," She insisted.

I was supposed to be Mr. Big Shot Vice President of the Student Government Association of Dugson, but what a joke. I was wearing a title only. During the second week of school, we held our first meeting to discuss plans for homecoming, the pep rally, prom and graduation. My duty was to stand up, lead everyone in the Pledge of Allegiance, and officially bring our session into order. SGA President Ali Frank and the Chief of Staff, Martin Hark, irritated me. I was intimidated by them. I was afraid to voice my opinions about anything SGA discussed. Ali and Martin had do-all, control-all personalities. I hated feeling like a joke. My quest for peer affirmation long dismissed, I dreaded my post as vice president.

In that first meeting, and in subsequent meetings that followed, I performed my only task: bringing SGA into session and leading the Pledge of Allegiance. It was not at all what I expected. Nevertheless, I needed to focus and use this experience in high school to my advantage. I decided to remain heavily involved with BASU, and with SGA.

Outside of school, things were very strange. By the end of September, Asia, Maria and Marian were constantly arguing over Asia's daughter Erica. Asia thought that since she wasn't getting much from the Social Security checks that came for us, Maria and Marian should be more than willing to baby sit her three-year-old. With this belief, Asia would disappear without a word to Maria or Marian, leaving her daughter for them to watch. Maria and Marian were furious whenever Asia did this.

"I don't care. She needs to at least ask us. I don't feel like being in the house tonight," Maria would scream.

My friendship with Heather, whom I had met at the Lighthouse for the Blind overnight camp the previous summer, was strengthening, and my relationship with Zoey had drastically changed. The last weekend in September, I went to see her. Zoey wanted to celebrate my seventeenth birthday, but since I really missed Grandma, I was rather down. On Saturday morning, on the way to Zoey's in Metro Access, a song came on the radio that changed my life. I found my voice and strength in Kelly Clarkson's "Breakaway: "I'll spread my wings and I'll learn how to fly, though it's not easy to tell you goodbye. I gotta take a risk, take a chance, make a change and break away. Out of the darkness and into the sun, but I won't forget the place I come from. I gotta, take a risk, take a chance, make a change and break away." I was shocked. The song expressed how I felt after leaving Grandma.

"The song is completely me," I told Zoey as we ate ice cream in her dining hall later that afternoon.

"I know," Zoey began, "I've heard the song. It's totally you."

"Zoey." came her mother's voice, "I'm getting ready to leave. I'll be back by 7:00 tonight, and your Dad won't be home until tomorrow."

"OK." Zoey yelled back. Once her mother was gone, I suggested that we go sit on the large sofa in the family room. We were sitting side-by-side, talking, when I decided to lie down on the sofa. Zoey, ecstatic with my being there, continued to chat away about school, her mom, her dog and how much she had missed me.

"Do you wanna lay down too?" I asked innocently, a big yawn overtaking me.

"Sure," She replied. Playfully, I sat up, wrapped my arms around her from behind, and pulled her into a lying position next to me. The sofa was just wide enough to accommodate us. We talked some more as I put my arm around her, peace and contentment in my heart. I began to play with Zoey's hands as she spoke. I noticed for the first time in a long time that they were as soft as silk. As she talked about her mean English teacher, I studied her hands, lost in the beauty of their texture. At times, Zoey would pause, taken by my caressing of her hands. I didn't know what I was doing. I was lost in my fetish for nice hands. Coming to reality, I realized that I had reached full attention during my exploration of Zoey's hands. I let go of her and relaxed my frame, resting my head on her shoulder. She stopped talking.

We lay in silence for a while, until Zoey said in a voice barely above a whisper: "You know? Sometimes, I have dreams that we are finally married and we finally make love for the first time." She had my attention.

"Really? You still want to marry me?"

"Of course I do," she said, shifting, my head falling off her shoulder. We were facing each other now.

"But like I said, we can't ever do anything like that until we are actually married."

"Oy gevalt," I said. "I know that, Zoey."

"But the other stuff is OK," she said, placing her index finger in the middle of my chest. Still at attention, I was having feelings I had never experienced before. A shiver ran through my body and I fought the urge to grab Zoey and bury my face in her hair. For some reason, I got the urge to place my finger in the middle of her chest as well. We lay there, me totally blind, she half-blind, dancing our index fingers in the middle of one another's chests. I became surer of myself and did something I never thought I would do. I placed my whole hand on her chest and without much thought, educationally explored her. I needed to know I wasn't gay. Zoey removed her finger from my chest and lay there, permitting my exploration. I couldn't help thinking that her parents would kill me if they knew. I loved Zoey, and becoming reassured that I wasn't gay made the moment magical. Nothing else existed when I was with her. My family woes, my experiences with gay guys, my stress and depression were all miles away when I was with Zoey.

"Let's undress," Zoey said in a soft voice. The reality of what she was requesting hit me hard, and I was mortified. What if her mom had forgotten something, and decided to come back? How would we get our clothes back on fast enough? Well, I knew I could, but Zoey wouldn't be able to do so.

"Are you sure?" I asked, pulling my hand from her chest.

"Yeah, I want to see you." With that, I completely undressed, and then I helped her do the same. We lay there on the sofa, around the corner from the front door, exploring each other. A male's body was new territory for Zoey, and with all that had happened to me, I was eagerly participative for further confirmation that I wasn't actually gay. She was as lost in her exploration of me as I had been in the exploration of her when we were clothed. Too afraid of her mother returning and seeing me in all my awkward, naked glory, I suggested that we put our clothes back on.

"A few more minutes," Zoey said. Nervous, I lay still, my ears alert for any sound from the front door.

As I rode in MetroAccess on my way home that Sunday evening, I thanked God for Zoey and her family. They had been there for me for over seven years now, and I was very grateful. I was worried though. Zoey's parents trusted me. I felt horrible knowing that Zoey and I were at a level in our relationship that would give her parents a heart attack if they knew. They still thought Zoey and I were childhood best friends, like brother and sister. Somehow, some way, they would need to at least know that we were boyfriend and girlfriend. I planned to persuade Zoey to tell them.

I knew that with the revelation of our puppy love would come the fact that I could no longer spend the night, but I wanted them to know. I was relieved that I wasn't gay. I did, however, feel as if I were being quite irresponsible for lying naked with Zoey while we happily explored one another secrets. At the same time, I thought I had to have been the strangest boy for feeling this way. What teenager would feel ashamed for touching his girlfriend intimately behind her parents' backs? Most boys can't wait for an opportunity like this. I just loved Zoey's innocence and purity. With Zoey, I could be clean, polished, and I too felt pure. I had a real girlfriend.

The new choral instructor had big plans for the choir this year. Mr. Boucher was a long-haired, white, tubby man with a loud, nasal voice. He had an air of wild arrogance that was more comical than unnerving.

"I have a no-nonsense mentality. I'm going to teach *real* Performing Arts program music," he said during choral practice the first Monday in October, "I don't understand what you've been doing, but you should be singing college level choral music and above. I want you doing well at festivals, all your concerts, and I'm planning a trip to San Francisco for a competition." There was a chorus of murmurs that followed the mention of San Francisco.

"The trip is going to cost $700, and it's in March. For those that do not have all of the money right away, we have set up a payment-plan schedule. The forms are in the front of the room. If you are interested, you and your parents need to notify me by next Monday."

"Are you gonna try to go?" I asked Marian, who was seated next to me in the chorus room.

"No. Don't nobody have any money for that. We barely survive. Boy you trippin'." My sister was absolutely right. It was foolish of me to ask, but I so wanted to go to San Francisco. I was now playing for two churches on Sundays. If I could somehow combine the church funds with the Social Security money, I wondered whether I could do the payment plan. I knew it was a shot in the dark, but I had to dream.

Now that I was older, I yearned for a greater sense of independence when traveling.

Metro Access wasn't always reliable, so I needed an alternative. I decided that I would apply to get a dog that was specially trained to guide the blind. I was tired of having to grab my sisters' arms everywhere we went. I knew that riding public transportation could definitely work better with a guide dog.

    The application would be a six-month process. During the second week of October, I submitted an application to Guiding Eyes for the Blind in Yorktown Heights, New York. I heard that they were the best guide dog school in the country. Their application required confirmation of the blindness, which meant I needed to go to the doctor. Grandma usually handled things like this, but as I had left home, I was on my own. I obtained my doctor's number from 411 Directory Assistance, set up an appointment for the following week, and scheduled Metro Access to take me there. I was becoming increasingly independent.

    On the day of the doctor's appointment, I was a little uneasy. I told Asia that I was going to the doctor before going to school. When Metro Access arrived at the appointment, the driver helped me to the door. I thanked him and used my cane to find my way to the counter where I could hear talking.

    "Hello Mr. Bonds," said a Puerto Rican voice.

    "Hi Sandra."

    "Where's your Grandma?" Sandra asked.

"At home." I smiled nervously.

"OK, I'll get you signed in. There's a seat to your left, right next to the counter."

"Thank you," I replied, using my cane to find the chair. A few minutes later, Sandra spoke again.

"Mr. Bonds? Um, I'm not sure, but the insurance company says your insurance card has expired?"

"What?" I replied, my nerves peaking. I knew nothing about insurance cards.

"Yes, you're with Priority Partners, right? It's the Medicaid plan paid for by the state."

"Um, yes," I replied, although I hadn't the foggiest what she was talking about. "One second while I find out what happened," I said, taking out my cell phone to call my grandma. I was thankful that my cousin Sefra still had a cell phone.

"Hello?" came Sefra's voice. "Hey Mario. Why you not in school?" she asked.

"Doctor's. How come you not in school?" I counter-inquired.

"Our school don't start until 9:30. You know that. It's only 8:30."

"Oh yeah, I forgot." I replied, unease in my voice.

"Is Grandma up?"

My cousin replied yes and told me to hold on. There was a pause and then I heard Grandma clearing her throat as she prepared to speak. I was nervous about how I would handle our conversation. This was my first time speaking to Grandma since I left in August.

"What you want?" Grandma asked without a proper greeting.

"Grandma, I'm at the doctor's and they said my insurance don't work."

"What you at the doctor's for?" she asked, clearing her throat again.

"I gotta get a checkup for some forms for a guide dog."

"I know your insurance isn't right. A new card came in the mail for you. If you hadn't left home, you would know that and I could be helping you. Y'all left the nest too soon. That's the doggone truth. Y'all left the nest too soon."

I couldn't and wouldn't get into this right now with Grandma. Did she truly believe we left the nest too soon? Right now, she still could hear nothing against Haily.

"I can give you the new number and see if they will still take you." In the end, Sandra did accept the new number and I was seen, but the conversation with Grandma left me feeling horrible.

Living conditions at Asia's apartment continually worsened. Asia was still disappearing without warning, leaving Marian and Maria to watch her daughter. When Asia returned, the arguments would start. My sisters and I were able to survive off of the little bit of money I made from playing for churches. Asia kept the rent barely paid, and was preoccupied with a new boyfriend. I had to maintain the vision that things would be OK, somehow, some way. I was cold and lonely in our current situation, and I didn't see any escape. Nevertheless, I had to believe that the future would be better.

Marian and Maria were extremely high strung, doubtless finding it hard to deal with our living conditions and the tension between them and Asia. We were living out of overnight bags, and barely eating. My sisters' frustration with life became quite evident in the act they soon committed to protect me from bullying.

Thomas Mineral was an openly gay eleventh-grade boy who had recently joined the concert choir after schools on Mondays and Wednesdays. He and I developed what I thought was a friendship. We would chitchat on the phone sometimes, and quite often, I sat next to him in chorus. After school one day, Maria was full of rage.

"That boy Thomas told Shania my best friend you was gay." she yelled as I turned on the television, loading Tyler Perry's play *Diary of a Mad Black Woman* into the DVD player.

"What?" I said, dread filling me.

"Yup," joined in Marian, "riding home on the bus yesterday, Shania said Thomas told her. They ride the same bus."

"I don't even care." yelled Maria. "Dude's gonna get dealt with tomorrow."

"What do you mean?" I asked, sitting down on the floor. My heart was thudding a million beats per second.

"He said you told him you were gay," said Marian.

"I never said anything like that to anybody," I said, my panic unmistakable. How could this be happening? I had confided in Thomas about Patric and Mr. Robins, but how could he have betrayed me?

"Well, me and Maria gonna handle the dude tomorrow."

"What do you mean?" I said urgently.

"Don't worry about it. Boy wants to go around telling lies on a blind person? That's alright."

Now I couldn't enjoy the play on the TV. I was afraid of what this could turn into. My sisters couldn't be controlled when it came to protecting me, not even by me. My sisters could do me wrong, but when anyone else did, they became relentless protectors. I was also confused as to why Thomas betrayed me like that. I had mentioned things about Patric and Mr. Robins because I thought I could trust him. I needed someone to hear my pain, but Thomas betrayed me.

CHAPTER 21— THE DUPREE FAMILY RESCUES

The next day, as Marian walked with me to my first class, I pleaded with her to leave Thomas alone.

"He was probably just joking, Marian."

"It don't matter." she said sharply, silencing me, "You should just stop talking. Me and Maria are gonna be suspended and that's that." With that, our conversation ended. Marian and Maria felt suspension was inconsequential if it meant teaching someone a lesson about saying bad things about their blind brother. I wasn't gay, but I still couldn't tell my sisters about Mr. Ford, Patric and Mr. Robins. I was so mixed up and scared.

Later that morning as the chorus practiced for our school's Christmas concert in the auditorium, my worry increased. I sat in the audience area as some of the students helped assemble the risers we were to sing on. I heard Thomas' voice and I knew he was seated behind me. He got up, said hello to me and my throat tightened. Where were Maria and Marian? Just then, I heard the exterior door to the auditorium open and Maria's voice.

"You told my best friend my brother was gay." Maria's voice was deep, angry and menacing. Her words came out like a statement rather than a question.

"Oh my God. No I didn't." said Thomas in his feminine voice.

"Yes you did." Maria screamed as her hand struck Thomas' face. She pummeled Thomas with punches.

"Gay self. My brother ain't gay," came Marian's voice. She leaped into the combat, two females against one male. Thomas was tall, but thin and lanky. He stood no chance. The other students watching were yelling "Oh my God. They effed him up." I wanted to disappear. Was this my fault? The shame of Patric, Mr. Robins, and now telling Thomas? Gay, gay, gay, boys with boys. I couldn't stand the mental torment which grew with the sound of every blow that landed on Thomas' face. Eventually, my sisters dispersed as the choral teacher came running towards them screaming: "Stop. Get out."

Later that day I went to after school choral practice, sad and afraid for my sisters. This particular afternoon, the chorus class was uncommonly subdued as Mr. Boucher went over our new music. My sisters were skipping practice, aware of the fact that the school administrators were looking for them. Twenty minutes into practice, the chorus room door creaked open. Mr. Boucher fell silent, as did the few other students who were talking. After nearly a two-minute scan of the room, the bulbous security guard Mr. Barns said:

"I'm looking for the Meryo sistas."

Several students started laughing, unable to stop themselves. I wanted to laugh too, but I couldn't.

"They aren't here," said Mr. Boucher.

When the door closed again, reality returned. Students would probably be afraid to be my friend now. My life was upside down at school and at home. I quickly turned to my first love: writing music. I wrote three songs that Adam and I recorded at Cue studios, a well-known facility in Burgson, Virginia that Kevin had told me about. Still a valuable drug and my saving grace, music helped me cope during this tough period. My home life drove me to focus on my secret relationship with Zoey. Her family invited me to spend Thanksgiving with them, and I quickly accepted. It was during the Thanksgiving break when Zoey's and my relationship changed dramatically, ending up in a place of no return.

After a wonderful Thanksgiving dinner of turkey, sweet potato and marshmallows, green bean casserole and chocolate pie, I retired to the Jacobs' guest bedroom. Zoey was sad that her dad was on a trip, but she said I made the Thanksgiving dinner still worth a lot. We spent time talking and listening to music, grateful to be together again. One of our favorite pastimes was to record our conversations. I was no longer calling my recordings "Life at Zoey's House," but I still had to have them as memories. At about 12:00 a.m., Mrs. Jacobs came into the guest room.

"Zoey, I have to work tomorrow so you guys will be on your own for all of Friday."

"OK," said Zoey, yawning. I was ecstatic that we would be alone together all day.

"There's food to heat up so you guys should be fine."

The next day, Mrs. Jacobs stayed long enough to have breakfast with us, and then she was off.

"Mario, can you hold me please?" asked Zoey urgently, as soon as her mother had gone.

"What do you mean?" I asked.

"With no clothes on. Please, hold me like you did last time."

"Zoey, what if your mom comes back home for something?"

"She won't. Mario, please." she was speaking quickly and quietly as if she were afraid of being overheard.

"OK," I said, giving in. We trudged up to Zoey's room. With speed, Zoey undressed. I took my time, scared that her Mom would return, we wouldn't hear her, and then she would barge into Zoey's room and lose control when she saw a naked black boy with her daughter. Still, I lay down with Zoey, but my mind wasn't in it. Absentmindedly, I explored her with my hands. Every few seconds, I stopped, listening hard, my paranoia heavy. The fifth time I stopped, I heard the jingle of the bell that hung on the front door. With lightning speed, I jumped from Zoey's bed, frantic to get my clothes back on. Zoey did the same. I tripped up as my left foot got stuck in the fold of the pants leg. I could hear her mom ascending the stairs. Throwing caution to the wind, I yanked up my pants, my underwear only on one leg. Knowing I didn't have time to adjust my belt, I pulled it off all together and threw it under Zoey's bed, at which point Zoey's bedroom door opened.

"I forgot my notebook. Are you guys OK?" asked Mrs. Jacobs. She didn't seem at all bothered by the fact that the door had been closed. It struck me hard how much she trusted us. I was arrested by a huge feeling of guilt. "I'll see you guys tonight. Love you." And with that, she left. I sat there in silence.

"Come on, Mario," began Zoey, "She's gone and she's not coming back."

"No Zoey. I'm scared. Your mom and dad are trusting us."

"Don't you love me?"

"Of course I do," I said, listening hard to be sure I heard the roar of Mrs. Jacobs' departing SUV.

"We're gonna be married in a few years. Please Mario. Just Touch me. Please?" We undressed again, but although I was sure Mrs. Jacobs wouldn't return again, I was still weary of breaking her trust, and of what Zoey and I were doing. Zoey and I lay down together, clumsily rubbing one another's bodies. I attempted to kiss her, but I was taken aback when she unskillfully

flopped her tongue around my face, trying to
French kiss.

"It's OK. We can do it," she said.

"What?" I asked.

"We said we were gonna wait for marriage,
but I trust you. I trust you. We just can't get
pregnant."

"Zoey." I said. Was she hinting at us having
sex? Was this the moment of ultimate confirmation
that I wasn't gay? I was struck. Her parents trusted
us. Lying naked was one thing, but that would be a
whole new world of weird and wrong.

"Please Mario. Make love to me." It took
nearly thirty minutes of Zoey's begging before I
caved.

"Zoey, I don't know."

"Don't you want me?" she said, pleading.
She was still whispering and talking fast, as if time
was running away from us. I knew my brothers
would think I was crazy if they knew I was having
reservations while a girl was offering herself to me.
Despite all the times I thought I would never
experience it, there I was, poised to be with a girl
for the first time, and I was frozen with fear.

"Please?" she said, grabbing my arm.

As it happened, disbelief filled me. We had
no idea what we were getting ourselves into.
Nothing and no one else existed anymore. Her
parents no longer mattered. Life no longer
mattered. But briefly, I wondered whether we
should stop. It was a glimpse of the ounce of

reason I had before we even started, but I couldn't bring myself to stop. I needed to know I wasn't gay. I had to know I wasn't gay. I would know I wasn't gay.

"We can't get pregnant." Zoey yelled, "We can't get pregnant." Her words, though loud, seemed far away. Suddenly, both of our bodies convulsed, and that frightened me. I quickly moved away from her. When reality returned, I was dazed with shock. I had committed the ultimate betrayal against the Jacobs, who had done so much for me.

"Get up." I demanded. "Go clean." I screamed.

"What?" Zoey said, alarmed.

"Just go clean. Go clean." Zoey took her things and left to shower as I hurriedly redressed.

"What have I done?" I said aloud. "What have I done?" I ran my fingers across the surface of the bed, the feel of the wet sheets increasing my horror and guilt. "I violated Zoey," I said, smacking my own face. Was I now like Mr. Robins?

When Zoey finished her shower, she came back into her room to dry and dress.

"That can't happen again," I screamed, my voice thick with regret.

"What do you mean? As long as we don't get pregnant, we're fine."

"Zoey," I began, and then I decided against talking for a moment. "You got to tell your parents about us," I said once I had found my voice again.

"I can't tell them we made love."

"I know. That's not what I'm talking about. You got to tell them that we're boyfriend and girlfriend."

"Um. I will," Zoey said, uncertain.

"Zoey, you *have* to." I said, grabbing her shoulders and pulling her towards me. She needed to tell them. I had to know what they thought about the idea of us together as a couple. The poor black boy and their daughter.

During the weeks that followed, the telephone conversations between Zoey and me were quite strained. I was a little detached because I still couldn't believe we had gone all the way. According to society, I should have been celebrating the fact that I had scored, but I couldn't. I was confused. Zoey and I decided that she would tell her parents during the first week in December, but their response was more than I could handle.

"What did you say?" I anxiously asked Zoey over the phone.

"I told them that you and I are boyfriend and girlfriend."

"That's how you worded it?" I asked.

"Yeah, but it's not good." She sighed.

"What happened?" I was panicked. I needed her parents' stamp of approval for our relationship. Little did they know Zoey and I had already inexpertly done what they would try to prevent by refusing to allow me to spend the night anymore.

Zoey began to cry.

"What did they say, Zoey?"

"They said that they don't like...they don't like it, Mario. My mom said we need to realize that it'd be hard for us since...since you're black and I'm white and we both have a visual impairment." My heart sank to my knees. I knew her parents loved me, but I never expected them to say something like this. This wasn't the 1960s and I thought her parents knew that. They were afraid of Zoey having a black boyfriend, or was I not understanding them? They were OK with me, as long as I didn't want to be their dauhter's boyfriend? But no one else understood Zoey like I did.

I sat in silence. Then, "This is not good Zoey," I said. "We can't continue this." I was angry—no, furious—now. "We can't continue this. I can't believe your parents. Why would they say that?" I didn't understand and my fury was in control now. "I can't be with you like that. We can't go together anymore. Your parents just hurt me. That hurts. We can't be together. We got to be friends. Your parents don't think I'm good enough" With that, I hung up on Zoey. I was embarrassed, hurt and angry all at once. How could I visit Zoey's house again without thinking of her mother and father's disapproval of our relationship? How could I ever face them again? It was hard knowing that they didn't want a blind, black boy dating their daughter. I felt betrayed. I was going to insure that sex never happened again, but now, I was absolutely convinced that I couldn't be in a relationship with Zoey at all. I didn't want anything to do with a romance between us anymore. I wanted her to tell her parents that we were just going to be friends, and that we hadn't been serious. I loved Zoey, but I was too hurt by the basis of her parents' disapproval.

Zoey was passionately and irrevocably in love with me, but I had to find some way to turn her off. Everything had to be reframed. We needed to just be friends. "Operation: Make Zoey Fall out of Love" had to happen, and soon.

My mind was taken off my problems with Zoey when abruptly, my living arrangement changed again. In mid-December, Asia, Maria, and Marian had the biggest argument yet over Asia's daughter. In the end, Asia said, "Well, if y'all can't babysit my daughter whenever I say you need to, y'all don't need to be living here."

"What?" said Maria, "you sayin if we don't agree to watch her whenever you want us to, we can't live here? That's not right."

"Oh well. Guess ya'll gotta go." With that, Asia put the three of us out on the street. I was so exhausted with having to go through this again. Kevin came that night to drive us to Aunt Diane's house in Alexandria, Virginia. Nancy was now living there, and since she was expecting to get a new apartment soon, she persuaded Diane to let us stay there with her until she moved into her own apartment the following month. Back-and-forth from sister to sister we went. As we left, Asia said "Poor Mario. Cuz y'all don't wanna do right, he don't have anywhere to live again."

I was furious. Once again, I was bouncing around again. I was wrong to think this sort of life would have ceased after leaving Grandma. Now, we were to indefinitely stay all the way in Alexandria, Virginia?

My sisters were permitted to ride with me on MetroAccess so we could get to school from Alexandria, Virginia and back. The continued uncertainty of our forever changing living arrangements made this a very stressful period. However, I couldn't ignore the persistent vision that I would have a better life if only I could find a way to extricate myself from the family, permanently. Here I was, no longer living with Grandma, and no longer at the mercy of Aunt Haily's drama, yet things felt the same. My older siblings had me in the same cycle of drama, dysfunction and moving around. The prospect of living with Nancy, or anyone else in the family again horrified me, but what else was there for me to do? Since I could remember, we had been on the same cycle of moving back-and-forth, and my older sisters seem to be unable to break themselves from the Bonds family curse of dysfunction. Every memory of being displaced attacked my mind. I needed to leave my family. As fate would have it, venting to one particular friend changed my life.

"And, there's no telling where we are going to live or what will happen with us." I said to Keenan during one of our evening phone conversations.

"Hold on," he replied one night, "I'm gonna talk to my Mom. I'll call you back." When Keenan did call me back, I heard a different, but familiar voice I remembered hearing at school concerts.

"Hello." Said the voice. It was the voice of a woman, whose voice was quite dramatic.

"Yes." I replied.

"My name is Ms. Dupree. I'm Keenan's mother. Keenan told me what was going on with you and your family. He's been telling me for years little things he knew and I just want you to know that you and your sisters have a place to come."

"Huh?" I said, perplexed.

"Y'all welcome to stay here with me and Keenan. We live in Bowie, Maryland. We'll be in this together." Needless to say, I was full of many emotions by now. Was I grateful? You bet, but what was God really doing? I was a little surprised that someone was offering their home to me so abruptly, but here was an escape. Was this the door to my vision of a better life? My mind revisited the time I refused to ask Social Services for a way out, and my aborted escape with the Smiths in the eighth-grade.

"I understand y'all been bouncing around for a while?" asked Ms. Dupree.

"Yeah," I began, "my family is a little messed up." I spent two hours on the phone with Keenan's mother, talking about everything. We went through all of my family's history, and it felt good to talk to an adult who seemed to really care. Then, something inside me clicked. I realized I was being handed survival tools, and that I'd better grab on to them if I was going to have any kind of life. For college, I would need stability and support. I was sick of moving around and being homeless. I was sick of the fighting. I couldn't do the Bonds' way of life anymore. I decided that without fail, whether my sisters came along or not, this time, I was going to leave the family. I was determined to rise above the 16 years of horrors that lay behind me. I had to rise above my adversity, and with my acceptance of Ms. Dupree's invitation came the biggest reward for my choice to overcome.

Already, I trusted Ms. Dupree with every fiber of my being. I needed to trust her.

"It's amazing none of you are on drugs after what ya'll been through." Said Ms. Dupree.

"Well, like I said. My home is open to you if you want it. Right now, we're in Kentucky for Christmas, but if y'all wanna move in, we can come back early." I was so thankful for Ms. Dupree. If I moved in with her, there was still no way of knowing what would become of me, but I had to maintain hope that a master vision for my life was somehow, finally in play.

After getting off the phone with Ms. Dupree, I explained her offer of help to my sisters, and it was no surprise that they flatly refused it. Still, nothing would keep me from the stability Ms. Dupree was promising.

I ran the offer past Kevin, and he approved. Nancy, on the other hand, was completely against the idea, and it was she who successfully persuaded Marian and Maria to disregard the offer. I didn't care. Marian and Maria could stay in the chaos if they wanted to, but nothing, and I meant nothing was going to thwart my escape. A time would come when Nancy would be putting them out again, and I was relieved that I wouldn't be around for it. I knew that I was making the best decision I would ever make.

The day after Christmas, I was picked up by Metro Access, and driven to my new home in Bowie, Maryland. I was taking a chance, confident that God was in control.

CHAPTER 22— VISION BECOMES REALITY

I rang the doorbell at the Dupree house and nervously waited for someone to answer it. When the door did open, the smell of fried food hit me in the face.

"Welcome. Welcome to your new home. My home is now your home." Said Ms. Dupree, her voice polite and as-a-matter-of-fact as it had been over the phone. As she offered me her arm, I stepped into the house. She hugged me and assured me that we were in this together.

"Thank you so much." I replied, excited and nervous all at the same time.

"Hi Mario." Came Keenan's voice from upstairs.

"You gonna show him the house Keenan?" asked Ms. Dupree.

"Oh, yeah." He replied, descending the stairs. I took Keenan's elbow as Ms. Dupree closed the front door.

"Right in front of the front door is the hallway that leads directly into the kitchen. In front of, but to the right of the front door are the stairs to go upstairs. We can start there I guess." With that, Keenan led me to the right and up the stairs. Ms. Dupree followed us around as if she too were getting a tour for the first time.

"Now that we are at the top of the stairs, if you go left, your bedroom is straight ahead. My bedroom is next to yours and the guest room is next to mine. The bathroom is to the right of your bedroom door. Let's walk it. Oh yeah, directly to the right of the stairs is Mommy's room. Com'on." I was a fast learner. After we walked the top level, I let go of Keenan's elbow and headed for the stairs alone. Keenan and Ms. Dupree followed behind me.

"Wait a minute." screamed Ms. Dupree when I had reached the top of the stairs. I knew what I was doing. Without warning, I ran down the stairs.

"Oh my God, wait." Ms. Dupree shrieked her panic rising. She stood there, stunned that a blind person had run down a flight of stairs, without holding the rail. Amused by his mother's expression, Keenan laughed hysterically.

"I didn't know a blind ... what?" Ms. Dupree couldn't even finish her statement.

After a tour of the living room, the family room, basement and my favorite place the kitchen, I showered and prepared for the next day. It was going to be extremely weird seeing my sisters at school only, but this was my new life, and already, I felt like I had struck gold. From my perspective, I could anticipate a life devoid of dangerous arguments, abuse, physical fights, drama and constant moving. I didn't know all of what would become of me, but I was going to cherish this moment. Ms. Dupree had done an invaluable, selfless thing in taking me in so abruptly. She was so ecstatic and supportive that she ordered tons of literature from her local library, and set about learning all things about the blind. For my first two weeks there, enthusiastically, she would inform me of something she had read.

"This is amazing," she would say, "It says when you enter a room where a blind person is, you should announce yourself so you don't startle them. Then, it says you should always identify yourself, even if you think the blind person already knows your voice." I would always reply with things like: "Yeah, that's right." Or, "Man, they touched on everything." I was just as amazed that someone had taken the time to pen information on how to live with the blind, although I wasn't your typical blind person.

Discovering that I had a super thirst for independence, Ms. Dupree set out on a mission to give me a higher level of self-sufficiency.

"You should cook just like the rest of us." She told me one day after school in late January 2005, nearly one month into my stay.

"Huh?" I replied quizzically.

"Yeah, I read in them books that blind people cook so you should cook too." Silently, I gulped. I hadn't cooked anything since my brief time at The Maryland School for The Blind during the summer of 2002.

"Com'on Mario so we can start. The first thing you're gonna cook is cooked carets."

"Cooked carrots." I squealed in disgust. I hated cooked carrots.

"Yeah, we're gonna make them like sweet potato." She pulled out a circular bowl, and instructed me to wash my hands at the kitchen sink.

"I got a bowl and a pan. You're gonna take the caret, scrape it down on all sides like this." She picked up a caret and holding it in one hand, placed a knife in my right hand and guided my hand as the knife slid down the caret. She rotated the caret and helped me repeat the knife sliding action. Then, she told me to put down the knife and feel what had been done to the caret. The caret no longer had its horizontal impressions anymore. Instead, the knife had created vertical lines down the sides.

"Make sure you knife the caret over the bowl that's in front of you on the counter, and then put the caret that is ready in the pan to your right. Yeah. That's right. Like that."

When I had finished knifing the enormous pile of carets and had placed them in the pan, she had me pour cinnamon, butter and a dash of sugar on them. Then, she explained the baking process to me as she loaded them into the oven.

Later, as she, Keenan and I ate, my face gave me away.

"What's wrong with you Mario?" asked Ms. Dupree. I wasn't enjoying the carets.

"These don't taste like sweet potato." I said, smiling.

"Yes they do." Ms. Dupree said defiantly, her mouth full of food, "If I had cooked them without you and I had never told you what they were, you would have never known the difference." But boy was she wrong. I would have known sure and simple that they were gross, cooked carets. No. Try repugnant.

Declaring the clothes I owned unfit to wear, Ms. Dupree completely reestablished my wardrobe. She bought new clothes, and recycled some of Keenan's clothes for me to wear. She told me that eventually, she wanted my wardrobe to be so organized that no matter what I pulled out to wear, I could be sure 100% that it would match. But for my first few months there, either she or Keenan would pick out my clothes for school. Interestingly, I started receiving a greater amount of compliments on my appearance at school. It was a major boost to my fragile self-esteem to have boys and girls filling my head with the thought that I was gorgeous. They praised me for having such good-looking clothes. Still insecure, I didn't really know how to handle the increased attention. I even became buddy-buddy friends with one of the most sought after boys in Dugson, James Allen.

Now that I was living outside the family, and experiencing stability, the clock seem to speed up. I could solely focus on school, and I was no longer worried whether I would have anywhere to lay my head at the end of the day. Ms. Dupree constantly reminded me: "This is your home. We're in this together."

Making new friends, coupled with all of the attention I was getting because of my appearance, I was on cloud nine. I was SGA Vice President, had a new happy home, was dressed to kill and I was becoming friends with the popular people.

"You put way too much snow in the shovel." Screamed Ms. Dupree from across the front yard. The first real snow of 2005 was upon us and Ms. Dupree said everyone had to do their part. Yes, that included the blind kid. I am thankful to her that she treated me just like Keenan. Feeling a little mischievous, I decided to play around with my new mom. I listened intently to hear where she was standing. I filled my shovel with snow again, and then I intentionally flung the snow in the area where I thought she had been shoveling.

"Nooooo." she screamed, "dump it the other way. Dern. I just cleared this path." She said as Keenan and I roared with laughter. My hope that she would think the task too difficult for me failed. She was aware that I knew what I was doing. Ms. Dupree thought me to be no different from the next person.

"If he could run down the stairs like hell, he can shovel snow. He ain't crippled. Hell." I heard her telling her best friend Marianne one day.

Ms. Dupree turned out to be an absolute riot. A straight talker, and a woman with frugality as a best friend, one would always know what she was thinking. As a joke, I used to ask her: "Are you one of those people, who are so cheap, they keep from looking out of their eyeglass lens for fear of wearing them out?" She would laugh. She only purchased things on sale, and was famous for taking things that cost less than a dollar back to a store if she detected even the slightest imperfection. I joked about these things, but in truth, she taught me vital principles of money management and survival that I always carry with me.

For the first time, I could really breathe and live out the vision for my future. With the stability afforded me by Ms. Dupree, it was time to focus. My vision of a better life included getting a Guide Dog, graduating High School, going to college, and working while desperately chasing my dream to become a performer. It was up to me to make all of these things happen. As her parents told her that an interracial, blind couple wasn't possible, as far as I was concerned, it was impossible for a romance with Zoey to be a part of my vision.

"It seems you don't call me as much now that you have a place of stability now." Zoey said one Saturday night in early March.

"What do you mean?" I quizzed.

"You don't call me back, or you don't call at all." Zoey was surmising that the cause of my lack of communication was my new life with the Dupree's. I felt terrible for hurting her, but I couldn't tell her how I felt about her parents' thoughts on our relationship.

"I dunno Zoey." I said, "I've been preparing for the San Francisco trip and I have to be focused."

"San Francisco trip. What about that? You never told..."

"I just forgot. I've been paying a few dollars a month out of the money I get from the churches I play for to pay for a trip to San Francisco. Dugson is competing in some tournament and I have to go."

"Is James going?"

"James?" I responded, laying back on the bed and opening a pack of star bursts, "No. James is in the band, not the chorus." I said. James was one of the most popular boys in Dugson who had befriended me shortly after I moved in with the Duprees.

"Oh. Can we talk about him Mario?"

"Uh ... I guess." I replied, becoming nervous.

"Whenever we do talk, you spend all of the time talking about James. You talk about him with the enthusiasm with which you use to talk about me and last week, you called him your only friend. I feel like you're ... uhh... you're putting me on the back burner." My heart was thumping by now.

"Zoey, James is the coolest person in the world. I've never been close to anyone like this and it's nice to have a male friend to be close to here," I began defensively, "I can't see you often, but we're good friends always."

"Friends ... you just called me your friend."

"You know what I meant Zoey. We're OK. I got to run. Ms. Dupree wants me for something." I lied, unnerved by the turn of events.

I climbed into bed, troubled by the conversation with Zoey. There was a lot of truth in what she said to me. Being friends with the most popular and sought after boy in Dugson had me feeling like royalty. James had energized my self-esteem in a way no one had ever done. Even becoming SGA Vice President hadn't increased my self-esteem like James had.

My 12th grade school year moved along quickly. In late March, Dugson won the choral competition in San Francisco. The first Saturday in April, Ms. Dupree drove me to George Mason University's campus in Burgson, Virginia, to audition for the music school.

"Just do your best." She said, backing in to a parking spot in one of the University's garages. Beep.

"Shut the hell up." She yelled out the window to another driver.

"That lady thought I was going to hit her." Ms. Dupree's way of talking always cracked me up. She was a riot.

Although so nervous I thought I would faint, I auditioned two Italian pieces for my vocal audition. The professor had a number of questions about Braille music, and I answered them excitedly. I was working my application to George Mason from every angle possible. Although I wasn't enthused with the idea of studying music academically anymore, I knew that a recommendation for admission from the music department would be a valuable boost for my application.

CHAPTER 23— THRIVING

As planned, I left in mid-April for York Town Heights New York where Guiding Eyes for the Blind was located. This school specializes in training and placing guide dogs with visually impaired handlers. I was excited and scared at the same time. I was told that the biggest part is letting go, trusting the dog, and allowing the dog to guide you. Initially, the idea of putting my safety in a dog's paws was scary, but I trained hard and did it. I knew the dog would mean a higher level of independence for me.

Although the training schedule for first timers was 26 days, I trained with a German Shepherd named Dave for 19 days before we were sent home as a pair, in time for me to attend my prom with Heather from the Lighthouse summer camps. Dave was fast, strong and very smart.

By mid-May, high school was pretty much over. I was eagerly awaiting graduation day, and the start of my internship with Federal Financial Analytics, the consultancy owned by Karen and Basil Petrou. I spent most of the rest of May getting acclimated to life with a guide dog. My schedule now revolved around my dog.

On June 5, graduation day, I dressed Dave in a red shirt I had gotten from Ms. Dupree, so that he could match the black and red school colors I had to wear. I proudly draped my SGA emblem over my shoulder, and when it was time, Dave and I walked across the stage to receive my high school diploma. The stadium erupted in a tumultuous applause.

On June 13, I started an internship at Federal Financial Analytics, a consultancy in Washington, D.C., managed by Karen and Basil Petrou. They act as watch dogs for a number of large-scale banks and mortgage companies. I met the Petrous through a contact with the Lighthouse for the blind, back when I was a technology counselor for its camps. They instantly promised me an internship that would start right after my high school graduation. As they were clearly making good on their promise, there I was, ready to learn from them. Karen Petrou's federal financial sector opinion is frequently sought after by the media. Also a guide dog user who was slowly going blind, she made sure I had my work cut out for me. I had tough administrative responsibilities. During my summer internship with the Petrous, I edited documents written by Karen, preparing them for client distribution. Several times, she sent me off to cover Congressional hearings alone. I was then responsible for providing a substantive summary of what occurred at the hearing. As I was only 17-years-old, this was a horrifying experience.

Karen Petrou was a tough boss. I would worry whether my summaries would be substantive enough. What if I missed something? Several times, when I had sent a document back to her for her review and signature, I was hit with a storm of complaints and requests.

Mario, I'm listening to JAWS just like you. If I can hear these mistakes, you can to. We're not paying you for me to correct your mistakes." Sometimes, I thought my mistakes, lady, you wrote this stuff.

Before my experience working at Federal Financial Analytics, I thought I was a skilled writer. However, Karen Petrou showed me what it really meant to be a skilled writer. Editing her writing introduced me to a whole new world of vocabulary I had no idea existed. She is the best proof reader, and this forced me to get better.

"I know how hard it is for blind people in the workforce. I'm hard on you because I have to be. It's the only way you'd be ready for the world of no mercy out there."

Karen was right, and I am immensely grateful to have her in my life. It is because of her why I am now a superb writer and editor. Basil and Karen Petrou are still closely involved in my life now. They are like parents, and I love them very much.

June quickly faded into July, and July into August. Before I knew it, my first day of college arrived. I continued to work for Karen and Basil two days a week. Scared, anxious, hopeful, but charged with a vision for my life, I was ready. I remembered that back at Hamax, Mrs. Smith told me that I would be

the master of my own destiny. With that
knowledge, I clung to a strong vision for my life. I
had every excuse to be an alcoholic, drug addict or
otherwise, but I was going to choose the path to
overcoming. I developed a plan A and B for my life.
My plan A was to become a motivational,
Hollywood entertainer to demonstrate to others
that choosing to overcome bad circumstance and
adversity is just that, a choice. Music and art is the
language I speak, and I feel most alive when I am
performing. Only when I perform do I experience
the fullest sense of my purpose, to help others and
to be an example. This made me desperate for Plan
A to become a reality. I vowed that I would leave
no stone unturned in my journey to make plan A
reality before I turned 25. That was an ambitious
vow, but I had determination on my side. Naturally,
while working towards Plan A, I was going to need
a good fallback. My plan B was to get an adequate
college education from George Mason University,
score gainful employment with the federal
government, and obviously, be able to support
myself. I was on a mission, and now that I had a
stable home, and was surrounded by healthy loving
people, nothing would stop my vision for success in
either plan A or B.

I chose Communications with a concentration in
Journalism as my major. I plunged into college.
Although I was deeply grieving the end of my
friendships with both Zoey and James, I thrived
academically during my freshman year. Michele

Weil officially became another Mother figure for me during my college days. I often tell others: "She's my Sandra Bullock, but this is officially from the blindside."

After what had already seemed like a lifetime of adversity, and being abused, I was still finding it hard to trust people. At the beginning of my college days, my issues with trust were paramount. Being in somewhat of the real world and the new environment of college spooked me, so I began to live as if only the dog and I existed. I avoided opportunities to make new friends, and whenever others offered to help me, I refused it. The dog and I took public transportation to travel to another state to the CVS store because that was the one CVS I knew how to get to independently, without needing help. There were dozens of CVSs closer but I was a creature of habit, and I refused to allow myself to need anyone.

Each weekend, I went home to Bowie, Maryland to be with the Dupree family, but on campus, for my first two years at George Mason, I lived as if only Dave and I were existing. I got a huge wake up call to stop doing this when one day in the spring of my second year of college, I awoke from an evening nap at 10:00 to find a horror in my dormitory.

"Dave." I called out, scratching my eyes. I had been sleep for hours, dwelling in depression over losing James' friendship. To my astonishment, the dog hadn't come to me. I noticed that the room was eerily quiet. I couldn't hear Dave's signature, German Shepherd breathing. I wondered whether someone had come into my dormitory and had taken him.

I quickly got up and rushed to the foot of the bed where Dave slept. When I reached it, I kneeled down and felt for the dog. I found him. The state of Dave's body made my world stop. I had never touched anything deceased before, but I had enough sense to know what I had touched. Dave's body was stiff with death, and his eyes were frozen open, and dry as a rough paper towel. I jumped back, letting out a humorless laugh.

"That is not what I just touched!" I screamed in disbelief. I moved forward to touch Dave again. I stood up, grabbed my cell phone from the bed and called the Dupree home. Keenan answered on the second ring.

"Where's your mother." I said, my voice direct and impatient.

"She sleep. What's wrong?" Keenan asked.

"Put her on the phone." I yelled, emotion flooding my voice. I needed to talk to my new mother. Seconds later, I heard Keenan waking his mother up.

"It's Mario. Something's wrong with him."

After being told what had happen, Ms. Dupree, Keenan and her eldest son, OC were at George Mason to get me. It was after midnight. I cried bitterly over Dave. Ms. Dupree, not an easy handler of emotion, tried her best to cheer me up when she saw me in the lobby of the dormitory. Her first gesture came in the form of one single question: "You want a soda!"

With my guide dog's sudden death, the new world of independence, and stubborn self-sufficiency at any cost that I had built disappeared at once. By choice, I didn't have any friends on campus, and I was now in a struggle because of that choice. With no dog, and having to depend on using a cane again, I would need help from people who could see. I needed people, and I was now in a position where I would have to ask for assistance, whether I liked it or not. I had returned to having to use a cane again. I mourned Dave bitterly.

I urge you to never be afraid to ask for help, to reach out to others, and to allow others into your circle, especially those who can contribute positively to you. This is essential.

Nearly a year later, in my third year, I trained with a new guide dog named Sidney. He is an English Labrador with more energy than a new born puppy. With the new dog, my level of independence had increased, but this time, I had friends to call on who adored Sidney and me.

In truth, my college years were thick with unthinkable challenges as well, but every challenge resulted in greater growth, and my vision to succeed became a stronger reality each day. I ended up in romantic relationships that seem to mirror the drama and abuse I experienced in my childhood. I sunk into massive depression over being a fatherless son. My biological family would call to add drama, and at first, I didn't have the ability to shut them out. My older sister stole my identity, and ruined my picture perfect credit. Depression caused me to balloon from 185 to 240 pounds. With all of this, coupled with trying to reach educational and professional success, and unresolved pain from the adverse experiences in my childhood discussed in this memoir finally causing a breakdown, I sought counseling to become a better me.

I also turn to my faith in God. I learned that I wasn't "Super Mario," and that I could finally let go. A good counselor will help you have the best conversation with yourself. I don't want others to be afraid of counseling to sort out the distraction of unresolved issues.

At the start of my senior year of college, I scored employment with the federal government in August 2009. Plan B was then in full operation. Throughout my college years, I auditioned for several music competition TV shows, and came close to my plan A several times. I was never going to give up, especially sense my good plan B was a reality. I graduated from George Mason on May 14, 2010, and my faithful lab, Sidney, was right by my side. The Washington Post highlighted my graduation in an article titled: Blind GMU Graduate Achieves His Dream." The article, coupled with the massive graduation barbecue celebration Ms. Dupree gave me made this an amazing time. My determination had made me beat the odds of more than 50% of blind high school students not graduating, let alone going to college. Three months after graduation, I moved into my own place with Vinson Young, a good friend who had been helping me chase my plan A Dreams for many years. Originally a friend of Keenan's, Vinson, in need of a place to stay, had moved in with us nearly three years earlier. As for me, after six years of a stable home with Ms. Dupree, and with frugality my best friend as well, I thought she had done well in preparing me to attempt living on my own. At that point, Plan B was officially signed, sealed and delivered.

After graduation, I further dug into my work in the federal government. I was gainfully employed as a Program Assistant, but I was discontented with not living in my plan A. I needed a deeper purpose. I wanted to perform. I wanted to be visible to the world, although the world was invisible to me. I was discontent until the year 2011 brought an opportunity to me in which my determination and grit to succeed made me a winner. Karen and David Blass, parental figures I met through Michele Weil, coached me through an experience that took me from plan B to plan A.

With Karen and Michele's push, I auditioned for a show that changed my life.

"Mario, I watched the first season of this show, and I said to myself, Mario could easily be on this show." said Karen over the phone during one of our "you should audition" talks. Only time could tell, but this experience became the ultimate proof that even a bad deck of cards can make you a winner.

CHAPTER 24— DREAMS DO COME TRUE

The Glee Project was a competition show on the Oxygen network, in which the winner would win a spot on Fox-TV's award winning series, Glee. The Glee Project had posted that online auditions would be accepted for 2 months between August and November of 2011. It took me some time to muster up the nerve to submit a tape. At the last minute, with Vinson, my close friend and roommate twisting my arm, I submitted an online audition. Vinson had been helping me chase my dreams for nearly four years. Sometimes, at his own expense, we would fly, drive or bus ourselves across the country, reaching for my plan A.

I didn't think many guys would be singing Broadway songs, so I took a calculated risk and learned "Out Here on My Own" from the musical Fame, a song I had never heard before. The Glee Project was also holding in-person auditions in New York. Initially, I had decided not to attend because I didn't think I could face the disappointment of being told "no" in person, but at the very last minute I decided that, yes, I wanted two bites of the apple. Well, to wake me up, it took Vinson telling me: "I don't think you'll be told no this time. It's a shame I believe in your talent more than you do." I went to New York with my sister Marian, and Vinson to audition in person.

The auditions started at 10 in the morning on November 12th, but by noon, we were still on the bus to New York. I didn't care. My determination that this was my shot was real. When we finally arrived in the city, with sonic speed, we headed to the audition site where we got in a very, very, very long line of Glee Project hopefuls. The fact that we were two hours late, and in the back of a line of over 6,000 people still hadn't deflated my determination. After a short amount of time, to our surprise, a producer came to the back of the line and asked the three of us to skip the line and come inside. Vinson was the only one who wasn't auditioning. He was there as my right hand, and I was thankful for that.

Once inside, we were ushered into a room where there were 8 people being seen at a time. I was glad they let Vinson stay in the room. This meant he would see both of us audition. The eight hopefuls were told we each had 20 seconds to sing something that would be memorable. We were reminded that they were looking for adults who could convincingly pull off a teenage look. When it was my turn, with a determined, unbreakable smile, I stepped forward and said: "My name is Mario. Uh … I'm 24 but I look 15, or at least, that's the lie people tell me. I'm blind." That made the producers in the room laugh. Then I belted a few bars of my audition song.

After the 8 of us, including my sister, auditioned, they said "Mario will you please step

forward. The rest of you, thank you for coming."
Besides being shocked that my name had been
called, I was more shocked that my sister hadn't
been chosen as well. She was phenomenal.

I was taken to another room for a second
round of auditions. This time, they wouldn't allow
anyone I knew personally to accompany me, so a
producer guided me to the next audition. I had to
swallow my emotions over my sister and grab onto
my determination again.

"How's it going beautiful people?" I
screamed in a cartoon voice akin to Alan Reid's
version of Fred Flintstone as we entered the room.

"Hi Mario Arnauz Bonds. What a smile."
Said a female's voice.

"What's your name?" I asked, my voice
sounding teenage.

"I'm Alana Balding."

"No middle name?" I asked.

"No. My Mom and Dad didn't give me one."

"Your parents should be fined for not giving
you a middle name." I said, laughing. Alana thought
that was hilarious. After I sang, Alana ecstatically
told me that she was placing me in consideration
for the third round of auditions.

"Thank you for coming. So far 55,000
people have auditioned. We've been narrowing it
down until we come to the top 80, and we'll let you
know in three weeks. Keep that gorgeous smile
Mario."

Meanwhile I had a church performance in Maryland the next day, so we caught an early bus back. Early the next morning, my cellphone rang, and the voice on the other end, said, "Hi Mario. I'm Ashley from The Glee Project. Have you left New York yet?"

"Oh no," I began, "I left my phone down there didn't I. My cell. Shoot." Then it dawned on me that I was talking to her on my cell. I felt like an idiot.

"No. Robert Ulrich, the casting director for The Glee Project is here today, and he wants to meet you in person. Can you get here by 6 pm?"

"Sure." I screamed, jumping up and down. After ending the call, I ran in circles, knocking over a lamp, and screaming.

"Vinson, they want me to come back. They want me to come back. You gotta drive me to New York. Can you do it?"

"Stop yelling." yelled a sleepy Vinson who had been abruptly brought to consciousness by my noise.

Right after my performance in Baltimore, we headed back to New York. Karen coached me over the phone during the long ride. As luck would have it, we got stuck in traffic on the New Jersey Turnpike. Of course, I panicked, thinking I was going to miss my chance. We knew there was no way we were going to make it by 6 o'clock. I ended my telephonic coach session with Karen to call and tell a producer our predicament, and was simply told to get there as soon as I could. We pulled into the city at 6:45, parked and ran through the streets of Manhattan, running towards my plan A. To my utter surprise, Robert Ulrich was still there waiting for me. For me. I thanked him profusely, and he asked me to sing.

Despite my nerves, somehow I was able to belt out my original audition song, and follow it with "How am I Supposed to Live without you" by Michael Bolton. There is something to be said for being blind. I couldn't see his reaction as I performed and I could completely focus on the words and emotion of the song. He thanked me for coming and said he'd be in touch.

I left there floating, in disbelief and exhausted by all that had happened that day. It was time to return to the real world, plan B, and wait with bated breath to find out whether I would be getting a taste of plan A.

The days dragged on during the eternity that was the waiting game until I heard back from The Glee Project. Each day felt like a week. My determination had faded. I started questioning my purpose again. I wanted to live my purpose, not postpone it. I had something to prove, that a blind person could be of value. I wanted to share my message.

The day before Thanksgiving, I was feeling really down after a long day at my federal government job. I really needed some good news. I fell asleep in the middle of the afternoon, and awoke six hours later. To my utter amazement, I had received the email of the year. It read: "Mario, congratulations, you're among our 80 finalists for The Glee Project. We want you to come to Los Angeles."

I thought I was dreaming. When I realized this was the real deal, I started crying. I rushed to my cellphone and desperately tried to call Vinson to tell him the good news. I was going to Hollywood.

Though I'm a positive person by nature, I couldn't help but think, there's no way they're going to pick me. Only 14 people out of 80 were going to make it to the actual televised show. What was I thinking? A blind black guy? Yeah, right. But Karen, Michele and Ms. Dupree kept telling me: "Mario you're the whole package. Just go do your best and fate will handle the rest." So I headed off to Los Angeles. As I was going to need assistance, the network paid for Vinson to accompany me. Upon arriving at the hotel, the first thing Vinson told me was: "There's another blind person here who is going to audition."

The other blind guy was Mac Potts, a WHITE 19-year-old from Washington State. He had been blind since birth. Two blind guys at the same audition, amongst the top 80? I feared that the one thing that set me apart from the crowd was gone. I would be competing with myself.

"He can play the piano really well." I said to Ms. Dupree. I was undressing after a day of audition rehearsals. All of the hopefuls had rehearsed in front of each other in an auditorium earlier that day. Mac chose "Let's Stay Together" as his audition song, and he accompanied himself on the piano. Oh man, did he play the piano.

"I know they're gonna pick him. I don't have a chance."

"Y'all ain't the same person Mario. You can act, and sing and dance. Do they know you can dance yet?"

"No." I said, feeling like I should just request to go home.

"Well, you got the full package. They ain't just lookin' for a piano player, and because he play the hell out of the piano, you wanna give up." I knew Ms. Dupree was right. Vinson, Karen, and Michele felt the same way she did. They thought the other blind guy wasn't a threat to their blind guy, me. I was thankful to have them.

For the final audition for Ryan Murphy, creator of Glee, and a number of other TV success shows, not only would we have to sing, we also had to dance in a group number. Zack Woodlee, celebrity choreographer from Glee showed the blind guys the moves first, and then showed them to the rest of the sighted hopefuls. To learn dance routines, I touch a choreographer's feet, legs, and arms so I can get a mental picture in my head of what my body is supposed to be doing, then I do it. During a private moment, Vinson gave me consequential news.

"He only showed you like 5% of the dance. All he showed you was simple stuff like raising your hand and turning around. The other people are spinning and doing all sorts of stuff."

"Oh really," I replied, "Watch this." I was determined to learn the whole dance.

Later, I sought out another Glee Project finalist, Savion Wright, who knew the whole routine and asked him if he would teach me the rest of it, which he did.

Savion taught me the entire dance routine, including the difficult spins. When it was time to perform the group number the next day, I performed the whole dance, difficult spins included. I blew the choreographer's mind, and left the producers surprised as well. It was up to me to show them I had much more to offer than they thought. I was not going to let my disability or anyone else's expectations of me hold me back, especially when I was so close to plan A. I had taken that chance and showed them that what they thought was impossible was possible. I was able to perform just like everybody else. I also showed them that I was unrelenting. After the first day of auditions, they cut the group of us from 80 to 40, and then to 30. I was still in. This taught me not to underestimate what I'm capable of.

For my top 30 audition, I had been asked to sing Celine Dion's "All by Myself," a huge, classic ballad. This audition was in front of Ryan Murphy, Robert Ulrich, Zack Woodlee and Nikki Anders, lead music producer for Glee. I knew I had to leave everything I had on the stage. With my talents in singing, changing my voice, impersonations, and comic abilities, I planned to leave Ryan Murphy with no choice but to select me for the show. This was the deciding moment.

"Hi. What's your name?" asked Ryan, his voice fatherly.

"I'm Mario Arnauz Bonds."

"I hear you do an impersonation of me."

"Yeah I do." I replied, my trademark smile on full display.

"Let's hear it." I took a deep breath, and to his face, I impersonated Ryan Murphy. The small theater we were in exploded with laughter. Even the camera crew had forgotten themselves, and were laughing loudly. I was then asked to impersonate Robert Ulrich, and again, the room exploded. When Ryan asked me to impersonate Zack, I declined with: "That would require a lot of cursing." I then sang for my life.

After the final audition I had to wait two and a half weeks to find out if I had made the Final 14. They were going to choose seven boys and seven girls. December 22, 2011 was one of the happiest days of my life, when I received the ultimate Christmas present. I was sitting in Karen' and David's kitchen in Rockville, Maryland awaiting a scheduled Skype video call from the producers with the answer. It was about 2 o'clock, and we were nervously eating chocolate. The incoming Skype call ringer sounded, and it was Robert Ulrich.

"How are you?" Mario.

"Fine. How are you?" I replied, my mouth still full of chocolate.

"I'm doing alright. Well, it's been a difficult day, because I've had to give more no's than yes's, but you're a YES." That's all I heard from Robert before jumping up, screaming with such a high voice, I could have replaced Mariah Carey.

"Oh my Goooooooooooood. Yeeeeeeeessss. Oh my Goooooooooooooooooood."

Each time I tried to compose myself to see if Robert had more to say, another fit of excitement would overcome me and again, I would be giving Mariah a run for her money. Plan A was going to become a reality. The last words Robert spoke before ending the call were:

"Filming starts in January. We'll send you the details."

I felt like I had won the lottery. From 55,000 people, I was chosen as one of the 7 guys. Those are huge odds for anyone WITH sight, no less without it, and I had made it. I was immensely grateful. I left plan B, resigning from my job to film The Glee Project between January and March of 2012. My episodes started airing on Oxygen in June of 2012, and this caused my life to change dramatically. Since then, I have been blessed to live my dream to entertain, and I have been further blessed to become a sought after motivator. Competing on The Glee Project for six weeks in front of millions, I showed Hollywood and the world that a person with a disability can rise to meet any challenge. Now that Plan A is officially signed, sealed and delivered, I see syndicated TV shows, speech and performance tours, music awards and more waiting for me in the future. I'm only just getting started.

Chapter 25– OVERCOMING ADVERSITY

Throughout my life, with every victory – from the smallest to the largest – came the increasing desire to become more self-sufficient, and to live a better tomorrow. It was a process, and it took some climbing to get here. Just how does one overcome adversity? I offer a three-part process that I identified after reassessing my own journey of overcoming. I call it the "Recognition Action and Preservation" or "RAP" Formula.

Recognition: to overcome, you must first recognize what it is you must overcome. What is your adversity? What was your adversity that still has you trapped? Then, you must want more than your current situation, no matter how adverse. With your recognition could come a vision, a dream, a hope or a thought. In time, with recognition comes the realization that another world exists outside your situation. Are you without money? Have you been abused? Every time you look around, you don't have a place to stay? You want to be a writer? You want to sing? Know that a world of endless positive possibilities exist for you, away from your current struggle. I was blind, black, abused and more, but once I recognized and accepted my setbacks, I decided I wasn't going to let adverse circumstances define who I am. Here, I implore you to do the same.

My experiences of moving from setback-to-success are symbols that anything is possible.

The important thing is striving to make the journey to get there, no matter the curveball. What happens after recognition? This takes us to the second part of the formula.

Action: When you finally want to play the cards life has dealt you, you must make the decision to take action, and to create an action plan. It is not enough to recognize an issue. At some point, one must "take action" to resolve the issue. Such is the case with not allowing your adversity to own you. I adopted a plan A and B philosophy that I followed until success came. First, I had to define what "success" would mean for me in either plan A or B, and I continually worked to reach both plans. You must do this also. You want to go to college? Apply for a school and seek mentors. You want to stop suffering from your childhood or other pains in the past? You must stop waiting and make an appointment for your first counseling session. A good counselor will help you have a much needed conversation with yourself. You must take action.

Cease bottling things up inside. Discontinue or minimize your connection with people who only contribute negativity. Surround yourself with positive people who have been there, done that. Find individuals with values who can be a support network.

Trust me, taking action is a process, but every journey begins with a single step. Don't expect taking action to be a quick process, but be headstrong in your resolve to start it, and more importantly, to finish it, or die trying to finish it. I was afraid of failing, but I woke up one day and decided that I would rather fail trying than fail having not tried at all. I applied this to both my road to healing, and to reaching my dreams. I conquered unthinkable odds, so beloved; I know what I'm talking about. The truth that "possibilities are endless," is all I have to offer you. Know that barriers only exist when you acknowledge them. I chose not to acknowledge them, and now, I am living on the other side of adversity in success. I am helping others recognize and take action to get to the other side of adversity as well.

Are you trapped by the inability to forgive someone who hurt you? This too requires recognition and taking action. Sure, I was abandoned by my father, and this hurt for years. However, reuniting with him in 2013, long enough for the broken-hearted little boy in me to finally grow up set me free. I've forgiven my father, and I now know that it's my choice whether he is heavily involved in my adult life.

With my recognition came what Oprah Winfrey taught me about forgiveness being the "giving up of the hope that the past could have been any different." Counseling helped me do that with all of the pain in my childhood.

Bestselling author and world renowned motivator, Iyana Vanzant, inspired me to break free from the regrets, pain and bitterness that enslaved me for so long. She has said: "an absent father enslaves his son's soul to sorrow, and suffering, and questions that he never gets to ask." That's exactly how I felt. Nevertheless, I made the decision that my adulthood would look nothing like my childhood. I made the decision that despite my deck of cards, I wouldn't sit still and let adversity describe me. I would become more than what I had been introduced to. I decided to go from victim-to-survivor.

Being molested, homeless, abandoned, abused and not even blindness could hold me back. Now, I sit amongst the clouds. I had a right to overcome. You have the right to overcome. We owe it to ourselves to take action. No matter the obstacle, it doesn't have to define you, nor does it have to destroy you. My own journey considered, I am an authority on this, and I will defend the following statement until I die. WE HAVE THE RIGHT TO SUCCEED. Once you've began your process of taking action, for whatever it is you wish to do, you must embrace the third and final part of the formula.

Preservation: Your progress must be preserved so that it can't be undone. This involves taking care of your mental, emotional, physical and spiritual health on a daily Basis. For your "mental health," make counseling, journaling or meditation your best friend during your process to "take action." For your "emotional health," be careful who you let into your circle. Again, surround yourself with positive people. Emotionally healthy people will compliment your road to success, recovery and improvement. Your "physical health" speaks to adequate exercising, and healthy eating habits. Eating correctly will make you feel better. Exercising is a vital stress reducer, and it can make you feel better about yourself. You needn't become a runner or body builder, but employing 30 minutes of physical activity a few times a week would be invaluable for your health.

Lastly, let your "spiritual health" be fully nourished by whatever your choice of worship. My Christian faith helped me in the aftermath of my breakdown during my college days. I sought counseling, but coupling this with my faith made a difference. Become one with whatever your faith is, and live in the peace your faith offers. Your mental, emotional, physical and spiritual health must all be addressed on a daily basis if success is your ultimate goal. Notice how they all affect one another. Your preservation will be a delicate balance between all four.

I've come so far from extraordinary odds. From being blind and being abandoned to proving to myself that I could do it, whatever IT is. In this world you always have a choice, and just because you're dealt a bad hand doesn't mean you have to play those cards. As I finished this memoir at age 27, I had already experienced a lifetime of difficulties in adversity. But now that I've accepted and grown from what's behind me, I know the forthcoming years will be rich with rewards. Determination, grit and surrounding myself with positive people who have been there, done that is what helped me survive. Now, I am living in my truth and experiencing the fullness of my life's purpose, and my dreams come true. Plan A and B were realized because I worked hard to get to them, and now, performing and motivating the world is my life. I offer this to you, yes, you beloved. From here, go build a bridge from opportunity to success, and also be a leader of overcomers. Despite all of the things stacked against me, I did it, and trust me, you can too.

GO GET YOUR DREAMS!

Made in the USA
Monee, IL
04 September 2024